If this book, should chance to roam
Wrap it up, & send it home

Robt Nelson
21723 - 24 Ave
Langley

W9-ALY-508

Con′
tre·pre·
neurs

* *n. pl.* 1. Perpetrators of stock market fraud. 2. Money launderers. 3. White-collar criminals (esp. in Canada).

Macmillan of Canada
A Division of Canada Publishing Corporation
Toronto, Ontario, Canada

This book is dedicated to police and prosecutors and to good men like Adrian du Plessis who try to make the world a better place

Copyright © 1988 Scorpio Publishing Ltd.

All rights reserved. The use of any part of this publication reproduced, transmitted in any form or by any means, electronic, mechanical, photocopying, recording, or otherwise, or stored in a retrieval system, without the prior consent of the publisher is an infringement of the copyright law.

Canadian Cataloguing in Publication Data
Francis, Diane, date.
Contrepreneurs
Includes index.
ISBN 0-7715-9915-3
1. White collar crime – Canada. 2. Commercial crimes – Canada. 3. Money laundering – Canada. 4. Securities fraud – Canada. 5. Telemarketing – Canada. I. Title.
HV6771.C3F73 1988 364.1′68′0971 C88-094124-3

Designed by Don Fernley
Printed in Canada

Macmillan of Canada
A Division of Canada Publishing Corporation
Toronto, Ontario, Canada

CONTENTS

ACKNOWLEDGEMENTS

This book would not have been possible without the help of the Royal Canadian Mounted Police and securities commissions in Ontario, Quebec, British Columbia, and Alberta. And there are also many individuals to whom I owe a great deal. Among them are RCMP assistant commissioners Rod Stamler and George Allen, as well as Jake Mol, Douglas Ormsby, John Beer, Murray Wood, Butch Bouchard, Derek Hatfield, Alistair Dow, Rick Bowlby, Ron Harvey, Robert Preston, Greg Pattison, Jean Gunn, Len Doust, Henry Knowles, Vern Macmillan, Bill Rivers, and John Leybourne. I also owe a great deal to a number of fellow journalists who have covered some of the situations or persons I profile in this book over the years, providing me with information and insights. Among them, are Jim Dubro, Tom Naylor, Peter Moon, Peter O'Neill, David Baines, Der Hoi Yin, Allan Robinson, William Marsden, Tino Bakker, and Tony Hetherington.

I am also indebted to my associate, Nancy Thomson, my editor, Philippa Campsie, my researcher Tim Howes, and my agent, Beverley Slopen, for holding my hand during this ambitious project. Once again, I must thank my children Eric and Julie and my husband, Frank, for putting up with someone so obsessed.

Most of all I would like to thank Jan Koers, Jan van Apeldoorn, and Rodreck Casander whose dogged efforts to mete out justice are admirable and above and beyond the call of duty. Last, but far from least, I want to thank Adrian du Plessis, a rare person with the courage to have made enormous professional and personal sacrifices because of what he believes in.

INTRODUCTION

Contrepreneurs are entrepreneurs who swindle; white-collar con-artists of the first order. They can steal more money in minutes through stock market manipulations and money laundering than bank robbers can in a year of living dangerously. The name of their game is stock-market fraud and money laundering. Their weapons are computers, telephones, and fax machines. Their unwitting accomplices are Canadian stock markets, brokerage firms, and banks. Their victims are investors, shareholders, taxpayers, governments, and business people who want to raise money for their enterprises.

What is most remarkable and threatening about the contrepreneurs is the multinational scope of their schemes, which makes them all but immune from detection or prosecution. Brilliant enough to make it legitimately, they are driven by excessive greed and may never be caught. Every day their tentacles reach more deeply into Canadian, and American, society.

For a number of reasons Canada has become a mecca for contrepreneurs. Its proximity to the United States, its role as one of the biggest transshipment countries for narcotics, and the continuing naivete of its lawmakers have encouraged widespread stock-market fraud and money laundering. Although most Canadians may never be affected directly by such crimes unless they buy shares, the indirect costs to society are enormous. White-collar crime spreads. The Vancouver and Alberta stock exchanges are especially strong attractions for white-collar con-artists. After years of regulatory and legal neglect, these exchanges are often nothing more than gigantic money-laundering vehicles. Stock-market frauds divert much-needed investment capital from worthy projects to outright scams, costing the country business opportunities and jobs. Most difficult to quantify is the cost of such crimes to Canada's reputation as a safe, fair place to invest and the toll they take on the time and efforts of our courts, police forces, and regulatory agencies. *Contrepreneurs* begins with "The Boiler Room Boys," a case involving a handful of Canadians who pulled off one of the world's biggest scams, a $6-billion money laundering and stock fraud operation perpetrated between 1983 and 1987. This was a highly sophisticated crime based in Amsterdam using companies listed on Canadian and American exchanges as bait.

Part II, "The Stock Jockeys," illustrates some of the more sensational, as well as relatively unpublicized cases of stock fraud that have taken place here in Canada, often involving the same Amsterdam boiler-room contrepreneurs, or their colleagues. Canada has always been one of the capitals of stock-market frauds, and the cases profiled here reveal links between this kind of scam and organized crime, drug smuggling, and murders. They also show how several generations of impotent, corrupt, or ignorant regulators and police have allowed criminals to operate in our stock-market business.

Part III, "The Money Launderers," describes two types of illegal operations. The largest involves the hiding of money derived from political or business kickbacks and drug trafficking. The other type involves the laundering of flight capital, money made honestly by people who want to hide it from tax officials, central banks, or ex-wives. By far, the biggest need for money laundering is among drug traffickers, because more money is spent on narcotics around the world than is spent on food. Organized crime pays launderers (known as smurfs in the trade) handsomely to deposit hundreds of billions of dollars into the banking system. The money can then be spent or invested without suspicion. Canadian banks, particularly those operating in the Caribbean, have been the dupes of drug dealers for years, and many still are. Even as the Americans crack down on the kingpins of the drug business, dirty money streams into Canada in suitcases, destined for Canadian banks. Canada lacks the sort of anti-money-laundering laws that have been enacted in the U.S., which means that any Canadian can launder funds for American criminals with complete immunity from American prosecution. Anomalies in the laws between the two countries, added to the lax way in which the Vancouver and Alberta stock exchanges are regulated, have inspired increasing numbers of foreign crooks to move their operations to Canada.

The stories told here represent only a fraction of the hundreds of stock fraud and money-laundering scams occurring every day in Canada. After completing the manuscript, I became aware of many more swindles — enough to fill a dozen books of this size. As these cases reveal, the free enterprise system itself could be imperiled as the contrepreneurs grow in number. After leaving Amsterdam, many have set up shop in other locations, such as Eire, Cyprus, Monaco, Spain, Belgium, Costa Rica, Mexico, and Switzerland. They continue to prosper because their pursuers are virtually unarmed. Police forces worldwide mostly direct their limited resources toward the pursuit of violent criminals. Stock-market swindles are little understood, are hard to prove in court, and are often regarded as a victimless crime. Also, police operate in a vacuum. Like bank robbers who used to escape justice by getting across the border with their booty, swindlers who are able to place a number of borders between themselves and their crimes are virtually home free. Meaningful international cooperation is non-existent when it comes to white-collar crimes of any sort, a problem underscored at the 1988 economic summit in a communiqué on the need to suppress drug traffickers and money launderers, signed by the leaders of the world's seven largest free-enterprise economies. For example, Canada's extradition treaty with the United States is the only one that includes white-collar crimes, and it is full of loopholes.

This book is a plea for Canadians, and policymakers, to look at what is happening. There is evidence that contrepreneurs control hundreds of companies in Vancouver and Alberta and have started to spread their holdings to Canada's prestigious exchanges in Toronto and Montreal. Because the country lacks anti-money-laundering laws that carry force, dirty money continues to pour in to our banks, directly and indirectly through businesses, currency exchanges, and brokerage firms, and continues to be reinvested in legitimate businesses.

Canada must declare war on these crimes. A Royal Commission to investigate the links between our stock exchanges and organized crime is badly needed to determine the depth of the problem. The federal government and brokerage community must conduct a thorough audit of the operations of the Vancouver and Alberta stock exchanges, with a view to moving in as regulators in the light of so many scandals in the past and expected in future. Canada should also increase the powers of its white-collar police, whether they are members of the Royal Canadian Mounted Police or investigators working for the provincial securities commissions. Money must be allotted to the RCMP and other regulatory bodies for training, investigations, and prosecutions. Laws must be changed and diplomatic initiatives must be undertaken to secure international agreements so that criminals can be brought to justice more easily. Without these changes, the contrepreneurs will continue to flourish, to spread a cancer that threatens to become an underground force of overwhelming power.

Note: The cases presented in this book have been chosen from among dozens of interesting instances. Unfortunately, because court proceedings will be under way at the time of publication, certain cases that may be proved to contain elements of contrepreneurial activity cannot be discussed. The reader may, however, find it interesting to compare newspaper coverage of these trials with the activities discussed in this book.

I

The Boiler-Room Boys

1/The Crime

Jan Koers hunts Canadians out of an office in Amsterdam's low-rent district. In May 1986 Koers, a Dutch crown prosecutor, orchestrated a series of raids on a handful of Canadian brokerage houses, known as boiler rooms. These were high-pressure telephone-sales operations that employed hundreds of people to peddle phony Canadian and American stocks, or real ones at phony prices. Koers had driven all of them out of business by the end of 1987. The boiler-room owners got away, unfortunately, along with most of the loot. Theirs was a crime that may ultimately rank as one of the biggest swindles in history. Koers estimates that twenty or so boiler rooms bilked thousands of investors all over the world out of a staggering $6 billion in just two or three years.

I interviewed Koers in May 1987, a year after the raids, in his sunny but sterile government office. He spoke softly in accented English, measuring his words deliberately, as though he were dictating the terms and conditions of a complex contract. His government wants him to bring the biggest players, all of them Canadians, to justice. For hours he described the elusive quarry he hunts, a handful of men who he feels rank among the world's foremost white-collar criminals. Together they managed to turn Amsterdam into a financial slum. Although hundreds of people were involved in many different capacities, Koers's investigation has focused on four men: Irving Kott, David Winchell, Barney Altwerger, and the late Guy La Marche.

"All the big players were Canadians, and the best boiler rooms were too," says Koers. "They began coming here in 1980. First Commerce [Securities] BV, opened up in 1983, and by 1986 it was the Amsterdam telephone company's biggest customer. Its monthly bill was $400,000. It had two shifts of forty salesmen each who were calling long distance all over the world selling stocks every day of the week, every week of the year."

Koers, born in 1950, put himself through law school by working full time as an office clerk. He looks like a determined and tenacious man. He needs to be. His resources, like his physique, are slim. He is one of only six crown prosecutors for the entire city of Amsterdam and the only one working full time on this gigantic international case. "This is a very great tragedy. These people must be made to pay," he says.

But bringing the criminals to justice may prove to be impossible. Perhaps this will turn out to be the perfect crime, so international that it will forever frustrate prosecutors and police. A boiler room might be owned by a numbered company on one Caribbean island, which might in turn be owned by another company on a different island or by a Liechtenstein *anstalt*, a company whose ownership is hidden. Salaries were routinely transferred to Swiss numbered bank accounts or to banks in secrecy havens, such as the Isle of Man or the Bahamas, where owners' names cannot be divulged without a special court order.

Amsterdam was uniquely suited for the boiler-room sting. The city had a good reputation, an efficient phone system, no securities laws, and no extradition treaty with Canada. By tacit agreement, Amsterdam's boiler-room boys were careful not to foul the nest, and none solicited Dutch investors. They also avoided soliciting in Canada and the United States, where regulators could take action against them. Complaints and cases are scattered through dozens of countries, such as Australia, New Zealand, Sweden, Norway, and Britain. This has complicated matters for Jan Koers. Without Dutch complaints, the cases are not a Dutch priority.

Boiler rooms are, in effect, unregulated securities firms. An unregulated firm does not have a seat on any stock exchange and is therefore not subject to the rules and regulations that protect investors from fly-by-night operators. Many brokers operate in North America without exchange seats, but they are subject to securities laws that allow governments to impose similar rules. It is illegal, for instance, for Canadian brokers to solicit stock-market orders from the United States, and vice versa. The Netherlands had no securities laws of any kind until July 1, 1986, one month after the boiler rooms were raided and shut down. Until then brokers were governed by the laws of the land, such as the criminal code or income tax act, but these regulations do not cover the activities of securities firms.

Armed with a securities law, regulators in Canada or the U.S. have an arsenal of weapons to use against boiler rooms. All brokers and firms must be licensed, which allows authorities to keep out undesirables or incompetents. Once a firm is licensed, complaints about its selling practices or about the prices it charges for stocks can trigger surprise audits, investigations, interrogations (officials have no right to silence and must answer all questions under oath), costly and embarrassing public hearings, shutdowns, or the removal of sales staff or the firm's license.

Because the Dutch had no such controls, complaints about boiler rooms went to the Amsterdam police, who had little expertise in these matters and could not get involved unless they were convinced that a criminal offense had been committed, such as fraud or theft or income tax evasion. They had to prove that a telephone call made in the Netherlands to a victim outside the country constituted a Dutch crime. In some countries, courts have ruled that the victim's place of residence is where the crime occurs; in others, courts have said that it occurs where the perpetrator resides. These swindles were cleverly designed to be crimes without a country.

The boiler rooms rarely filed income tax returns, much less deducted taxes from paychecks. But the Dutch have no tax treaty with Canada, and few countries recognize tax evasion in another nation as an extraditable offense. Although it may be relatively easy to prove that most of the boiler-room boys were tax evaders, Jan Koers and his colleagues in the police department know that pursuing this course leads up a blind alley.

Koers is concentrating his efforts on a few cases of possible fraud and working away at an investigation involving David Winchell. Officials in Switzerland are also investigating a boiler-room operation allegedly linked to David Winchell in Geneva. And the RCMP has charged Winchell with defrauding the public by manipulating the price of a stock listed on the Alberta Stock Exchange, a stock that was allegedly about to be peddled in Amsterdam. Koers also has pursued Barney Altwerger to an out-of-court settlement, but his investigation of Guy La Marche ended abruptly when La Marche was murdered in Toronto in March 1987, almost a year after the boiler-room raids.

The Amsterdam police have focused their attention on Irving Kott, although Kott has denied through his Montreal lawyer any involvement in the Amsterdam boiler rooms. The police believe that Kott was the controlling mind behind First Commerce.

The Dutch are dogged, but they are running out of time and money. Statutes of limitations preclude charges from being laid years after the fact. About $600,000 has been spent by Koers alone, not including the cost of police and court efforts. Without one Dutch victim at hand, continuing the investigation will be a tough sell, politically speaking.

Prosecutions involving international frauds are exceedingly expensive and difficult propositions. The guilty parties usually hide behind several layers of nominees who act as fronts for corporations registered in countries like Luxembourg or Panama, where true ownership need never be disclosed. Even if investigations trace the perpetrators' role, prosecutors like Koers face the enormous obstacle of extradition. Canadian diplomats were about to negotiate an extradition treaty with Holland in the early 1980s, but their efforts were directed to several South American countries instead. The result is that even if Kott or one of the others were to be convicted in absentia, it is doubtful whether Koers could ever extradite them to serve a jail sentence. In 1987 the Dutch government gave up after ten years of trying to extradite a convicted swindler who bilked Dutch victims, then immigrated to Canada.

But giving up is not a notion Jan Koers entertains. "I want to get Kott. It is tricky. I have my doubts, but I have time for him," he says.

2/THE RAIDS

The party came to an end for the Canadians on May 1, 8, and 9, 1986, when Koers, accompanied by a Dutch judge and twenty plainclothes policemen, marched into the offices of seven boiler rooms: First Commerce Securities; Financial Planning Services; Tower Securities; BA Investor Advisory Services; Capital Venture Consultants; United Consultants; and Consulting Brokerage Corp., which the Canadians nicknamed CBC. All but United Consultants and CBC were Canadian owned or operated.

In Holland, as is the case under English common law, judges issue search warrants to prosecutors and police, who must ensure that civil rights are respected and that only evidence related to specific allegations is seized. Unlike our judicial system, the Dutch judges who sign the warrants must be present as the searches begin, to supervise police activities. Every time a raid was staged, Koers and the judge led the procession, personally delivering the judge's warrant. The judge oversaw initial arrangements for the search and then left. The police, on the other hand, stayed for hours, particularly at First Commerce Securities, the largest firm, with more than 100 employees.

Koers organized his raids carefully. Although the layout of each boiler room was uncharted, all the firms operated in virtually the same way. Each had a large, open-concept sales floor where brokers sat behind shoulder-high room dividers, a back office where accounting records and other vital pieces of information were kept, and a suite of executive offices, where important correspondence and the vaults were located.

Once inside a boiler room, Koers and Amsterdam fraud squad chief Arnold Peters cased the place, then sent policemen in various directions. The police had preassigned tasks. Some rummaged through the drawers and shelves of sales staff, looking for suspicious or revealing documents. Others rifled through filing cabinets or pored over computer printouts and invoices. Still more hunted for evidence in the wire room where trading records were stored and where telex and wire-service machines clattered away, spewing out stock quotes and news stories. (Such machines are vital in any brokerage business. Information is the lifeblood of the stock market; fortunes can be made, or lost, from earthquakes or elections as well as from economic policies.) Here Koers and the others often hit paydirt, finding telexes about specific trades or transfers of cash out of the country.

On May 1 two more raids were also under way in Geneva. One zeroed in on a boiler room with connections to Amsterdam's Financial Planning Services, allegedly linked to David Winchell; the other, on an operation linked to Tower Securities, which was connected to three other Canadians. The plan had been to pull off the Swiss and Dutch raids simultaneously, at ten o'clock in the morning. The two police forces failed to synchronize their watches, however, and Geneva officials ended up raiding their boiler rooms minutes ahead of Koers and his entourage. By the time Koers burst into the offices of Financial Planning Services in Amsterdam, many of its employees had already fled out the back door, taking with them some documents and files. In the wire room the Dutch investigators discovered a terse telex sent by a Swiss boiler-room worker: "We are being invaded. Get everyone out of the country."

The Dutch saved their biggest and best raid for last. On May 9 they stormed into First Commerce Securities. They arrived at 8:30 in the morning and did not leave for nine hours. This was a particularly time-consuming operation because the Dutch did not have the authority to shut down the boiler rooms during the raids. The proof Koers needed for a cease-and-desist order could only be obtained after the raid had been conducted, the evidence catalogued, and the evaluations completed. This slowed things down because it meant that boiler-room managers were allowed to photocopy any document they needed to continue operations before it was seized as evidence. Virtually everything, from clients' trading records to payroll ledgers and phone bills, was copied. At the end of their long day at First Commerce, the police had seized enough paper to fill a large truck.

At the time of the 1986 raids, there were at least twenty separate boiler rooms in Amsterdam alone. Many had the same owners, but each operated independently of the others. Competitors poached staff from one another's payrolls and sometimes swapped sucker lists (boiler-room jargon for lists of existing or prospective clients). Despite such a large number of stock shops, the Dutch strategy was to make the raids staggered and selective. Only seven boiler rooms were raided, and four of the biggest were Canadian controlled. These raids were a message to the other thirteen or so to get out of the country.

Most of the boiler-room boys fled with documents and money. Many left behind unpaid payrolls and massive bills to tradesmen, landlords, hotels, and other suppliers. The Amsterdam telephone company was eventually stuck with an unpaid bill for $750,000 from First Commerce Securities.

The seven boiler rooms that were chosen were picked because they were the likeliest to result in convictions of fraud or tax evasion. Raids were also staged over the course of a week to maximize publicity, to tell the world that the Dutch were finally cracking down on boiler-room operators once and for all. At the same time, the Dutch government was about to enact its first securities legislation designed to license and control stockbrokers, the ultimate measure needed to clean things up. (A handful of similar raids in December 1985 had shut down a firm or two but had failed to stem the growth of this sleazy industry.)

Koers had planned the raids in his fifth-floor office with the help of two RCMP officers on loan from Canada. One was Corporal Derek Hatfield, an intelligence specialist attached to the RCMP's commercial-crime division in Toronto. Now an investigator with the Toronto Stock Exchange, Hatfield had worked for more than two years gathering intelligence and monitoring the operations of convicted white-collar criminals such as Irving Kott, David Winchell, Barney Altwerger, Guy La Marche, and others. The other RCMP officer was Sergeant Jean Gunn, a French Canadian from the force's Montreal commercial-crime division. Gunn is an expert on Irving Kott and has tried to prosecute him several times.

Two months before the raids, Koers and Amsterdam fraud squad chief Arnold Peters had traveled to Canada to do some groundwork. In Montreal, they gathered information from Gunn, and then moved on to Toronto where Hatfield provided them with more information and introduced them to new sources. Koers also met with Toronto Stock Exchange and securities regulators, and in Ottawa, with justice officials to explore how Kott or the others could be extradited, if at all and for what crimes. After several days of helpful and friendly meetings, Koers and Peters returned to Holland and, through formal police channels, asked the RCMP to lend Hatfield and Gunn to assist with strategy planning.

The two RCMP officers flew over separately in late April, one week before the raids. They spent a total of two weeks in Amsterdam, but they did not arrest any of the Canadians. The Canadians were safe, even though their activities in Amsterdam would have been illegal back home. Gunn and Hatfield were there to provide the Dutch with information about players and companies and previous convictions and to offer advice on what might or might not constitute evidence in stock-fraud cases. The Dutch knew they had a massive securities scam on their hands, but they had little practical knowledge of such crimes.

In Canada, and elsewhere, the associations, investments, and movements of previously convicted criminals are closely monitored by domestic intelligence experts, like Hatfield and Gunn. Details about the police records, lifestyles, and friends of these criminals fill police intelligence files, and this information is shared by police departments worldwide. Many white-collar criminals start off as street criminals. For example, Barney Altwerger had been convicted for offenses such as break and entry, possession of burglar tools, and keeping a common gaming house and he eventually graduated into big-time frauds and lucrative stock market schemes, which earned him more money in minutes than a dozen bank robberies could have in a year.

Canadian police forces have developed a unique expertise in securities crimes because Montreal and Toronto were the Amsterdams of the 1930s, 1940s, and 1950s, preying on Canadian and American investors. "The lights of Bay Street burned brightly in Toronto all throughout the depression," recalls senior *Toronto Star* police reporter Jocko Thomas. "It was these guys, we called them stockateers, selling the world a bunch of junk from Canada." After several celebrated scandals in Ontario and Quebec, the police eventually cracked down, and provincial governments enacted securities laws for the first time to curb abuses.

The criminals and their crimes did not disappear, however, they simply went elsewhere. Some went west to the virtually unregulated Vancouver or Alberta stock exchanges, or south to Florida and California. The most successful ones graduated into the multinational big leagues, running deals through dozens of countries to frustrate investigation and prosecution. Armed with years of experience acquired at home in the bad old days, these criminals have protected themselves from legal actions and play one country or police force or set of laws off against another. Their crime is the financial equivalent of murder, a scam that represents one of Canada's most expensive exports to the world.

3/THE CROOKS

THE BIGGEST BOILER ROOM OF ALL

When the police arrived on May 9, 1986, First Commerce Securities occupied an entire floor (75,000 square feet) in Amsterdam's flashiest and newest office complex, the World Trade Center. It paid Manhattan-sized rent and was remarkable for its elegance, given that many boiler rooms operate out of basements. Its attractive Dutch receptionist reigned from behind a large, carved French provincial desk; behind her the company name and logo were emblazoned on the wall in huge gold letters. Visitors sat on plush seats beneath oil paintings and were served coffee in china cups. The company library, boardroom, and executive offices were paneled in mahogany and carpeted in beige wool. Beyond the reception area's double doors was First Commerce's sales floor.

At first glance, the huge, open sales space looked like a big-city newsroom, with its sea of desks and banks of clocks, labeled with the names of cities in a dozen time zones, such as New York, London, Beirut, Singapore, Tokyo, Sydney, Los Angeles, and Toronto. Salespeople looked like reporters, telephones glued to their ears, surrounded by clutter, and separated by low-slung dividers designed to soak up sound.

Each salesperson was encircled by plenty of drawer space, shelves, and a place to pin notes, messages and even typewritten sales scripts. Attached to most phones were tape recorders; supervisors encouraged the staff to tape and replay their sales spiels to themselves in order to improve their techniques. Most of the boiler-room sales men and women were in their early twenties. At any time in that room, there were a dozen nationalities manning the phones and dozens of languages being spoken. The supervisors were older and Canadian. Despite their differences, all of the people in the sales room had one thing in common. They were ruthless and greedy. And oh, how the money rolled in. It rolled straight out again to offshore tax and secrecy havens.

Top-notch salespeople could make up to $400,000 a year, tax free. First Commerce threw lavish parties for its staff and racked up enormous bar bills at the posh Hotel de l'Europe, where Kott used to stay, as well as at other night spots. First Commerce had the largest switchboard and the largest telephone bill in Amsterdam in 1984 and 1985 ($300,000 to $400,000 a month). Every day of the week, the forty salespeople in each of the two shifts were constantly using the long-distance lines. "They would make cold calls to Saudi Arabia or Australia and talk to guys for an hour or more. Can you imagine that?" says Derek Hatfield.

The day the Dutch police arrived and began to sift through the firm's documents, the forty sales personnel and another forty from the back-office employees began to gather in the coffee room, exchanging opinions about what was up. After being reassured by the management, a few continued to work, but the disruption caused many to abandon that day's efforts. Many of them merely lolled around, chatting to one another. They were allowed to leave if they checked out with police, giving their names and addresses and answering a few questions about the place. Midway through the day, there was a shift change; forty new salespeople arrived and put in their time unaffected by the presence of the police. First Commerce had no intention of ceasing operations and, indeed, continued to do business for many more months. It was raided a second time in November 1986 and was eventually bankrupted by court order in January 1987.

Unfortunately for Jan Koers, during both First Commerce raids in May and November 1986, police believed that potential evidence had been destroyed. "When we got in there in November the shredder was actually working away, and there was a five-foot pile of paper. Important files were missing," says First Commerce's bankruptcy trustee, Jan van Apeldoorn. "This has really hurt our case."

Koers and his crew did not know exactly what to expect on May 9, 1986, when they handed over the six-page search warrant to First Commerce's managing director, Dutch-born Walter Bonn. He cracked a slight smile, even though the raids signaled a lot of trouble for him personally. As chief executive officer and managing director, he is legally on the hook for the many millions of dollars the firm owed to investors, employees, and Dutch tax officials. Bonn said nothing, took the warrant from Koers, read it slowly, then called a lawyer.

Bonn has been charged, and is out on bail, for running a criminal organization. If convicted, he faces a lengthy sentence. He insisted that there was no connection between First Commerce and Irving Kott, and that his only connection to Kott was the $70,000 he borrowed from Kott to buy an Amsterdam home. He also said that Kott brought First Commerce a high-tech stock, DeVoe-Holbein International BV, to underwrite and resell to the public. Bonn told Koers that he had no idea who owned First Commerce Securities. Technically, a Luxembourg holding company called Alya Holdings BV is the registered owner. But Alya's ownership is difficult to trace. The boiler room has also been owned by, among others, a Bahamian holding company.

Although Kott denies any connection with First Commerce, his twenty-eight-year-old son Michael was present during the raid. He approached several policemen and chatted briefly to one officer. He held up a copy of *The Sunday Times* of London, which had printed the dates of the raids before they occurred, and said, "We were expecting you a few days ago. What took you so long?" Michael Kott is vaguely connected to the firm. His name was not found anywhere on the company payroll, and Bonn says he was a consultant whose fees were paid by Alya Holdings.

Missing on May 9 was Bahir Uddin Hussain, another well-known Kott associate. Originally from the Middle East but now a naturalized Canadian citizen, Hussain lived virtually full time in Amsterdam for two years while he set things up as First Commerce's controller. Ruthless and bright, Hussain has worked for Irving Kott for many years. He was controller for his main holding company in Montreal until 1988. Hussain was not present during the raid, but the Dutch authorities found him a year later in Panama, where he spent twenty-four hours in a filthy Panamanian jail as the Dutch probe escalated. He is still being investigated.

One year after the raids, Koers issued "warrants for the arrest" of Kott around the world, except for Canada, in connection with fraud and tax evasion "charges." "We have asked several countries (all the European countries, the U.S., and about one dozen others) to arrest Irving Kott except in Canada because your system is very difficult for us to obtain extradition," Koers told me in a *Financial Post* interview on April 13, 1987. Kott is "charged" with fraud involving the activities of First Commerce; manipulation of DeVoe-Holbein stock; and tax evasion in Holland. "Kott is the person behind First Commerce and we have charged him with fraud and stock manipulation. He gave orders to make false papers so his company would not pay enough taxes."

Kott is not connected in any way with First Commerce, his lawyer and spokesman Michel Proulx told me in 1987. "He [Koers] has one witness who says that [Kott is involved with First Commerce] and all the other witnesses are to the contrary," said Proulx. "He [Kott] never owned First Commerce and he denies being the operator."

The "warrant" means that if Kott travels to the U.S. or Europe or elsewhere he will be detained and will have to await an extradition hearing. It is the equivalent of a subpoena. As Proulx pointed out, "In Canada, when you are charged it means the investigation is completed and you will stand trial. In Holland, charges mean it is under investigation. This means they are at the stage of investigation and of course they want Mr. Kott and of course they want his skin."

Koers also issued warrants worldwide for Hussain. Many countries, including the U.S., honor the Dutch warrants, which means that Kott and Hussain are subject to arrest, detention, and extradition if they go where the warrants are accepted. This greatly restricts their travel to the handful of countries that do not honor the warrants, unless they use disguise and aliases.

THE BOILER-ROOM BOYS

The boiler-room salespeople were fixtures in Amsterdam's more fashionable restaurants and hotels. For short visits, most preferred to stay at the fancy Sonesta or Marriott hotels, at a cost of US$250 per night. For longer stints, they shared lavish canal-side apartments costing up to $1,500 a month, paid for by the boiler rooms. Barney Altwerger even rented an entire twenty-room hotel for his twelve Canadian salesmen, around the corner from his boiler-room offices. He filled it with furniture from IKEA and gave his guests a full-time cook and a maid and cars and drivers. They were flown home at company expense every six weeks or so. Some salesmen brought their wives and children over. Seventy-year-old Altwerger was occasionally accompanied by his wife, daughter, and a grandchild, who spent their days shopping in the city.

Irving Kott spent a minimum of 181 days a year in Holland, meticulously checking in with Dutch immigration officials for tax purposes each time he arrived and departed. (Canadians who live 181 days outside the country during a year are not considered Canadian residents and do not have to declare any income from outside Canada for Canadian tax purposes.) While in Amsterdam, Kott preferred the elegant Hotel de l'Europe near the city's red-light district. Most nights, groups of Canadians hung out in l'Europe's piano bar where a Canadian beer costs $7.50. They also liked to dance at glitzy Juliana's disco in the Amsterdam Hilton. "They were the best tippers we ever had," a Hilton bartender recalls. "They were friendly and always wanted to party. We miss them."

Mr. X has been a stockie all his life. A beer-bellied boiler-room boy, he has bilked with the best and never been caught. He starts drinking neat Scotch by 10 a.m. most days and calls what he does for a living "redistribution of wealth." Others would call it fraud. "Most of my mates were 'tin men,' you know, guys who sold aluminum siding and shit."

Mr. X agreed to talk to me about life in the boiler room. We met at nine in the morning in a Toronto office walk-up near the site of the old Savarin hotel, a 1950s cocktail lounge done in red leather and studs, where for decades the stockies drank to celebrate big paydays from fleecing Yanks. I arrived with a mickey of Cutty Sark for our morning meeting. Breakfast. Mr. X had drunk most of it by noon out of the bottle or a paper cup.

"Whaddya want me to be? Valachi?" he said when I asked if I could publish his name. (Joseph Valachi squealed on the Mafia and died years later without ever being able to leave protective custody.) "These guys aren't necessarily violent, but they can buy muscle and, besides, I'd be ruined in this town if I ever blabbed."

Being ruined means an end to a gravy train that can net as much as $20,000 to $30,000 a month, tax free, in boiler-room commissions abroad. And Mr. X says Amsterdam was a good gig. "All day you sell stocks, and every night most of the guys would go to the red-light district to get laid or just get a blow job. The boiler rooms were all Canadian, but we never mixed, for competitive reasons. But we'd bump into one another in hotels and bars and stuff. Every Friday people would be paid in cash and then everyone would go nuts over the weekend."

Even after the Dutch raids in 1986, there was plenty of work for old hands like Mr. X. In the spring of 1987, he was among a dozen or so boiler-room boys enlisted to sell stock from a company based in sunny St. Kitts in the Caribbean. The operation, which was scuttled when a series of *Globe and Mail* articles by Peter Moon exposed the fraud and embarrassed the local government, was to be run by Marty Resnick and the late Billy Ginsberg. "Every week, Ginsberg would come from Miami with a suitcase full of twenties in U.S. currency to pay us. Ginsberg was an old tin man."

The salesmen were put up in a fancy stucco hotel, all expenses paid. Sometimes their expenses included a small credit line at the local Jack Tar Village casino. They played by day and worked by night. "They would send cabs to the hotel at 11 p.m. and we worked until 6 a.m. selling to the U.K., Saudi Arabia, France, Spain. Checks were sent c/o Lloyds of London. They sent them in like pigeons."

Being a stockie means working the graveyard shift, catching clerks or mechanics or widows after supper to hawk stock. To be a stockie, conversation, and immorality, must flow easily. Sometimes, confesses Mr. X over swigs, the suckers get to you. "People buying and buying and there is no selling. It all turns out to be dreck. I don't like to admit it. Only once I felt badly. I refused the sale.

"This guy and I went to this guy's house somewhere around Niagara Falls, I think, and the guy opened up the door. He agreed to buy 5,000 shares at twenty-five cents each. Just $125. But I happened to have a little bit of heart. He wanted another $150 worth. The shares were really worth nothing. I took a look at the piano in his parlor and he had lost two sons, killed in action during the war. I said to the guy I was with when he left the room, 'We can't put this guy on. He shouldn't have been sold in the first place.' The guy said, 'C'mon, he's in the palm of our hands.' But I walked out the door."

Sometimes, Mr. X says, the suckers scare you. "When you're talking on the telephone you know nothing about him. I got this guy in Michigan, and he kept phoning me about wanting to sell. We don't want to hear from these guys. But this particular guy decided to come to Toronto," he recalls. "I didn't know he was a six-foot, four-inch colored guy. He wanted his money back, and the boss hands me his credit card and says, 'Take him out to lunch and cool him out. Or dinner.' I said, 'Bullshit, I won't take that nigger out to lunch. Give him his goddamned money back. He's going to kill me. Shove your credit card.' The boss was just kidding me and we gave him his money back."

In the world of the boiler room, the sales force is divided into openers and closers (or loaders). Openers make cold calls and are paid to accumulate a list of potential clients, who think they are giving their addresses and phone numbers for a free subscription to an investment newsletter. Openers place names and addresses on index cards, ideally twenty per eight-hour shift. In one Amsterdam boiler room, two U.S. army deserters were paid about $300 a week to call hundreds of American servicemen stationed at bases around the world. Names were placed on index cards, which supervisors could simply file away and then hand out to new shifts or to different salespeople on a rotating basis.

Another way of attracting clients was through advertisements in magazines and newspapers. As police combed through the boiler rooms, they found invoices paid to some of the world's most prestigious publications, international periodicals like *The Economist, The Times,* the *Financial Times* of London and the *International Herald Tribune*. These advertisements offered free newsletters as a means of accumulating sucker lists. When people responded to the ads, they received newsletters, called tout sheets or tip sheets. Initially, these publications would analyze trends and advise readers to buy legitimate, blue-ribbon stocks such as IBM or General Motors. After lulling marks into a false sense of security and conservatism, the tip sheets would start recommending highly speculative or even fraudulent stock. In a few cases, stock-price forecasts for companies listed on the Vancouver or Alberta stock exchanges would come true, possibly because of illegal stock market manipulations back home. And finally, the closers or loaders would call, moving in for the kill.

The Canadians had multicultural sales forces to tailor the loaders' approaches to specific clients. Training programs, manuals, and other paraphernalia alerted salespeople to nuances and differences in pronunciation, statutory holidays, and attitudes. Police found memos at First Commerce which carefully explained local religious, business, and social customs in various target countries. For instance, Friday is a religious holiday in Muslim countries, but it is okay to call until an hour before sundown if the marks are Jewish.

The techniques of tailoring pitches to investors were perfected by First Commerce. Sometimes the company hired and trained specific ethnic groups. In 1985 it brought in twenty Swedes, Finns, and Norwegians to blitz Scandinavia. In another case, First Commerce hired the entire cast of a bankrupted theater troupe in Britain to call the United Kingdom. Not surprisingly, most of them stayed on because the successful ones made a fortune.

Stockies' skills, like those of snake-oil salesmen, are mainly self-taught, and the tricks of the trade are designed to give the wrong impression without outright lying, says Mr. X. "You never tell a guy he can sell his stock because you know he can't. You just tell him he can liquidate. Sell means you need a buyer, but what the hell does liquidate mean? Liquefy it or what?" Salespeople talk in terms of "companies in Toronto which are listed," he says, as opposed to "Toronto Stock Exchange listed companies." "If the companies are on the Alberta or Vancouver exchanges, they might as well be listed in Oshkosh. Those exchanges are jokes and anything gets listed on there and then it's never watched by anybody. Better yet, it doesn't trade anywhere, so you can make up the prices."

Mr. X learned from experienced loaders how to handle skeptics. "I was a new guy and got rebuffed, so Henry [another loader] got involved. He knew how to handle every rebuff that ever was. The mark wanted to know if we'd done any drilling on a mining property the company owned and what the drilling results were. Henry says, 'Let me talk to that jerk.' Then he says, 'What do you think we are in Canada? Drilling all over the place like Swiss cheese? We do magnetometers and scintillometers before we drill. Do you think we're stupid up here? You ought to be ashamed of yourself. What do you think we are? A bunch of beavers?' The guy bought 20,000 shares and Henry said to me, 'Whenever they give you that drill crap, give them the Swiss cheese story.' "

But more often than not, the Swiss cheese story and others simply didn't sell. That's when stockies gave prospects the "TOL" or "taken off the list." Sometimes they would call an eager buyer, but the guy was broke. "I had one friend who would write 'yiskidol' over an index card. It was a Yiddish word usually spoken in a cemetery at a funeral. It means the guy's got nothing left. It's over." Not surprisingly the turnover of stockies and clients was constant.

The Canadians in Amsterdam not only were legendary for their sales skills, but were also admired for their brilliant money-laundering schemes. Their techniques were designed to tap so-called flight capital from wealthy professionals and businessmen who wanted to smuggle cash out of their countries to circumvent local tax or foreign-currency restrictions, or both. Boiler-room boys would also help criminals smuggle out their drug-trafficking profits. Sometimes they actually laundered the money, but sometimes they double-crossed their clients.

Double-crossing involved targeting countries where capital restrictions or high taxes existed and making cold calls to entice the wealthy. Sweden was one of the first on the hit list. The favorite sales line was that each client was told he could kill three birds with one stone: get around currency restrictions, beat the tax man, and have a shot at making capital gains.

A courier would appear once a week at a certain hotel in Stockholm. Investors would go to his room and swap their krona for stock certificates or simply sales slips. The cash would then be smuggled back to the Amsterdam boiler rooms. Sometimes the share certificates were never sent to the investors, which meant that, after the boiler rooms were bankrupted, buyers technically didn't own any stock. After several weeks of plundering one country, sales efforts would then shift to another.

This was an almost undetectable way to steal. Even if investors discovered that their stocks were worthless or had been sold to them at fraudulently high prices, they could not alert authorities without exposing their own crimes. The boiler rooms were often accessories to their crime of money laundering or tax evasion. One consortium of twenty Austrians invested $1.2 million in one of First Commerce's favorite stocks, DeVoe-Holbein International BV, using money that was smuggled out of the country illegally through a Swiss bank account. Although the stock's price collapsed and some of the would-be investors never received their share certificates despite payments, First Commerce was never sued by these customers nor were the police contacted.

Boiler rooms may steal funds with impunity from legitimate businessmen who are trying to evade taxes or currency restrictions, but they don't dare steal from criminals who use their services to launder illegally gotten gains. Bilking button-down bankers or professionals is one thing; cheating a drug dealer can get you killed. Dutch officials think they cheated clients selectively, laundering for some and not for others.

"Boiler rooms are ideal ways to launder money by constructing share dealings through several jurisdictions which are untraceable," says Koers. "You could use forty bogus stocks and thousands of fabricated transactions, then construct the scheme so that profits end up in tax sheltered havens."

Police believe that some of the boiler rooms were laundering money for U.S. mobsters.

Stockies must be immoral, cynical, or both. What they do for a living makes them rich but gives them little status. So they joke about it among themselves. It may have been the only psychic relief from what is essentially a boring, and unjustifiable, existence. Clear evidence of the disdain felt by some stockies for their jobs appears in an anonymous poem scooped in Montreal during the 1973 raid on Kott's L.J. Forget brokerage firm. Forget's license was eventually revoked. (While Kott never owned the brokerage firm shares, the Quebec Securities Commission said he controlled its operations and masterminded its strategies.) Here are a few stanzas.

> I listened to Kott
> I foolishly bought
> I listened to Arthur
> I must be a martyr
> I listened to Rickeys
> Now I'm drinking mickeys
> I'm making "Whoopee".
>
> The key man is Harry
> Whose father is Ben
> They take a stock at fifty

And push it to ten
They tell you it's profit-taking
For me it's headache-making
I'm making "Whoopee".

The profits you're showing
Appear to be fine
But it's all on paper
You never see a dime
If you should ever want to sell
They'll tell you to go to hell
I'm making "Whoopee".

4/PICKING UP THE PIECES

The boiler rooms would still be going strong in Amsterdam if it hadn't been for John Leybourne, a craggy-faced and somewhat cranky former Metro Toronto cop. Until 1987, he headed investigations at the Ontario Securities Commission. A veteran of many boiler-room battles, Leybourne is an expert on Kott and many of his colleagues. "Most of them started off as old tin men in Toronto," he says. "You know — those guys who would sell you aluminum siding you didn't need at prices you couldn't afford."

In July every year, for a number of years now, Leybourne and several dozen securities regulators and commercial crime police personnel from around the world attend a three-day conference at Cambridge University sponsored in part by the Commercial Crime Unit, a small, poorly funded investigative and intelligence arm of the Commonwealth Secretariat. Its chief fraud officer is Dr. Barry Rider, a British barrister who works as a Cambridge professor and as an investigator.

The conference, which offers seminars on all types of economic crime, is hosted by Rider and a Canadian-born lawyer named Saul Froomkin. Originally from Winnipeg, Froomkin was a Department of Justice prosecutor in Ottawa until 1975, when he became the attorney general of Bermuda. Leybourne and Froomkin had worked together over the years on various fraud and securities prosecutions.

In July 1985 Leybourne spoke at the Cambridge conference about Ontario's boiler-room cleanup in the 1950s and

1960s. Amsterdam fraud squad chief Arnold Peters happened to be in the audience at the time and collared Leybourne for more information. After their chat in a local pub, Peters realized that his government had a serious problem on its hands because most of the same Canadian scoundrels were up to their old tricks in Amsterdam.

Leybourne agreed to speak at another Commonwealth crime conference in the fall of 1985 in Australia. "I brought up the subject of how we were helping the Dutch to keep tabs on their boiler rooms. I dropped a couple of names, and suddenly one of the Australian regulators in my class stood up and said he had received a bunch of complaints from investors about high-pressure telephone salesmen calling from Amsterdam to peddle Canadian and American stocks. Sure enough, it was the same bunch."

Local papers picked up Leybourne's remarks and by the time he left Australia two weeks later, the boiler-room operations were front-page news. Headlines shouted, "Don't Go Dutch" or "Going Dutch Means Going Broke." Papers from around the world picked up the scandal. A Singapore paper published stories about victims there and criticized the Netherlands: "Very few countries have weaker regulations for the protection of the private investor against this sort of practice." As publicity spread, thousands more victims came forward. Within weeks, Dutch embassies in the Far and Middle East were deluged with complaints. Fleet Street jumped on the bandwagon, and diplomats from Australia and elsewhere sent stern notes to The Hague. As a result, in November 1985, the Dutch parliament rushed through a new emergency securities act which would take force on July 1, 1986.

The Netherlands' brand new securities act required all unregulated brokers and their salespeople to apply for a license. To qualify, salespeople needed two years of experience. Brokerage houses were required to provide a list of their qualified sales personnel, to describe the stocks they were going to sell, and to prove they had $107,000 in capital on hand, held in trust and guaranteed by a bona fide bank. Some 100 individuals and firms came forward, including First Commerce. None was approved.

By the fall of 1986, Koers had enough evidence from the raids to convince Dutch courts to place the seven raided boiler rooms in bankruptcy. (Dutch prosecutors can ask that companies be bankrupted if there is more than one complaint and if it is an issue of public interest.) Two bankruptcy trustees were appointed to find and seize assets so that victims could be paid off. Jan van Apeldoorn, of the law firm Hauta van Haersolte, handled four boiler rooms, including First Commerce, believed to be controlled by Irving Kott; Rodreck Casander, of Casander & Co., went after Barney Altwerger and two boiler rooms linked to David Winchell. Their efforts were important in the months that followed, when the number of people assigned to chasing boiler-room assets, owners, and salespeople virtually tripled.

5/The Good Trustee

Dutch lawyer Jan van Apeldoorn greets visitors and clients in the courtyard of a seventeenth-century Amsterdam complex. Tall and thin and earnest, he led me up five flights of narrow stairs to his tiny attic office. Every square inch of Amsterdam is utilized, and van Apeldoorn's compact cubbyhole is as much a function of the price of office space along this fashionable canal street as it is a measure of the efficiency of the Dutch. We talked about Irving David Kott, a near-obsession with van Apeldoorn, as he is with Jan Koers, the crown prosecutor. Both believe Kott is behind First Commerce. An entire room, larger than van Apeldoorn's office, is stacked with letters and claims from 10,000 victims of First Commerce plus thousands more from three other small boiler rooms. The piles of correspondence are a constant reminder of unfinished business. The professional lives of both van Apeldoorn and Koers are wrapped up full time in the pursuit of Kott.

Van Apeldoorn's job is different from that of Koers, who is conducting a criminal investigation. Van Apeldoorn is a lawyer in private practice who was appointed by a Dutch court in January 1987 as the boiler rooms' bankruptcy trustee. Trustees must find, freeze, and seize assets to pay off creditors. Most of the boiler rooms left behind staggering bills to suppliers, and they owe money to investors and tax collectors. There are few assets left to pay off creditors. First Commerce had only $400,000 in cash and other valuables. The money owed to investors is believed to be in the millions, maybe even the tens of millions. Without access to many important documents, no one knows for sure what the final figure might be.

In January 1987 Dutch police sent letters to victims worldwide, asking them to complain formally. Thousands of replies streamed in, especially after newspapers around the world published the request for complaints. "In the beginning [after the bankruptcy], I was getting 100 calls a day," says van Apeldoorn. "It was jamming the telephone exchange out of order in Amsterdam. Every newspaper in the world printed my phone number and address. There were at least 25,000 investors in four companies. Sometimes my secretary spent the whole day just opening letters from investors. But I'm sure most investors who have never gotten share certificates they paid for have decided not to come forward."

During our interview, van Apeldoorn produced a copy of a letter which, he feels, links Kott to the boiler-room operations, particularly the peddling of a stock called DeVoe-Holbein International. The original is locked away in a vault somewhere, away from the room full of letters and telexes and trading records. Though it is only a copy of the letter, he holds it as though it were a piece of delft pottery.

The letter is on First Commerce stationery and is addressed to Lowy & Chernis on Madison Avenue in New York. It is dated October 8, 1985. "Dear Sir," it reads, "Please find enclosed the prospectus of DeVoe-Holbein International B.V. that was done for the Dutch Parallel Market, as discussed per our telephone conversation. If you need any further information, do not hesitate to call me. Yours truly, Irving Kott."

Van Apeldoorn says that the letter is proof that Kott was operating out of the boiler room in some official capacity. Of course, on its own it proves little. But the Dutchmen soldier on.

6/VICTIMS

Most people assume that boiler-room victims are gullible or greedy. But Rick Ellis is neither. Well-educated and a savvy investor, he remembers getting a phone call one summer day in 1985 from Guy La Marche. Ellis is a computer expert who was hired by Bell Canada, along with another 1,200 Canadians, to work on its multibillion-dollar contract for a new phone system in Saudi Arabia. The Canadians lived in a closed compound with recreational facilities and planned activities. Life was boring and lonely at times, but many of the Canadians took the job to get ahead. Their entire income was tax free because they were living outside Canada for more than 181 days in a year, and oil-rich Saudi Arabia has no income tax.

These expatriates were natural targets for the boiler rooms. They were a little homesick and easy prey for smooth-talking sales types like La Marche, who worked hard at establishing a rapport. Ellis admits he was seduced. But he thought he was dealing with a bona fide brokerage house which looked after its clients. In reality, Ellis was just another name on an index card. His mistaken judgment cost him $42,500.

La Marche called Ellis and dropped the name of other Bell employees. Ellis checked and discovered that La Marche was indeed also dealing with them. "Guy La Marche handled my account for a year or so, then it began to be rotated, but I didn't think that was unusual for an expatriate organization," recalls Ellis. "I remember several salespeople, Sharon was one.

We'd have long drawn-out conversations during the course of a year. Most of the time she would bitch about how she wanted to get back to Canada. She couldn't stand European weather or the stock market. She also put me into some legitimate stocks, IBM and stuff. But I bought a bunch of dogs too."

The first several tout sheets the boiler room sent out boosted legitimate stocks like IBM and talked astutely about economic trends. Boiler rooms could buy and sell legitimate stocks; they would accept orders and "jitney" them (hire a broker with a seat on an exchange to do the trading). Though they made little or no commission on these transactions, they would jitney trades to establish credibility with educated buyers like Ellis.

Later, the tout sheets would start to mention more speculative stocks and make specific price forecasts, particularly for companies on the Vancouver or Alberta stock exchanges. When the next newsletter came through these forecasts were astonishingly accurate, which further enhanced the boiler room's credibility.

When Ellis checked around, he found that a lot of his colleagues were quite satisfied with their dealings with the boiler room. At the time, La Marche was working at one of two boiler rooms allegedly linked to David Winchell. After a few months, Ellis felt confident enough to buy one speculative stock in Vancouver's Orrwell Energy Corp. and Night Hawk Resources. Both companies were later investigated by police for their violent price swings. (In Orrwell's case, the RCMP has charged Winchell and others with manipulating its prices in order to unload it at artificially high prices to investors like Ellis.)

Ellis says he did business with the boiler rooms over the course of many months but never received his stock certificates. This is normal practice in the brokerage business and is called "leaving it in street name." Brokers hold onto the certificates so they can be traded at a moment's notice. "It was a reasonably good way to operate from the Middle East. North America was too far away time-wise. Guys I talked to said they operated normally, without any problem paying people out and the brokerage firm held the certificates for you."

Ellis also bought shares in Portinax, renamed Federal Ventures in 1985, a stock which traded nowhere and sold a variety of products such as Yesterday's News (kitty litter made out of old newspapers) and a liquid coffee concentrate. "Orrwell and Night Hawk aren't too bad and are still trading, but Portinax you can decorate your bathroom with," says Ellis.

The same shenanigans were happening elsewhere around the world. The British were among the biggest victims of these boiler rooms, easy prey for the mostly Anglophone Canadian stockies. According to estimates, stockies bilked as much as £1 billion from residents of the United Kingdom or from Britons living abroad. Ken Wight, who worked in Kuwait as a British electronics engineer, eventually lost $25,000 in savings, after he was sent an unsolicited investment letter in the summer of 1984. While on holiday in England, the boiler-room stockies tracked him down at his hotel and got an order. Wight telexed the boiler room months later with a request to sell his shares. But they were never sold. The company claimed the telex never arrived. Perhaps the shares were never even bought in the first place.

Though Ellis had been solicited by Amsterdam salespeople, he received a letter in early 1987 from the Swiss police where his trading records had been kept. The police notified him of the bankruptcies and asked him to fill in a claim form. "I wrote to the boiler-room address where the bankruptcy trustee was, then I wrote to the trustee giving him details of my holdings as requested and I got no satisfaction. I sent a follow-up letter this spring, but it was returned to me and says 'Return to Sender,' the party is no longer here any more. The trail is totally cold."

Similarly, Ellis received no satisfaction from officials at

Portinax or the other companies he bought shares in. They told him that it was not their problem. Legally speaking, it was not.

It wasn't just investors who suffered. Two Canadian professors are desperately trying to get out from under Irving Kott's influence. Their reputations and nerves have been shattered, their savings are gone, and they feel that their life's work has been endangered. The story of DeVoe-Holbein International BV is a bizarre tale which links the professors to Irving Kott and to McGill University, one of Canada's foremost institutions of higher learning. First Commerce peddled dozens of different stocks, but Koers had been concentrating on what happened to DeVoe-Holbein. He estimates that at least $200 million has been invested worldwide in buying the shares of the Canadian high-tech company. Those shares are worthless, but the technology may not be. It is a frightening example of how the boiler-room boys can ruin even potentially viable, respectable companies.

It is January 1988 in Montreal. The city is depressing and gray. Bruce Holbein and his new partner, Denis Kidby, pick me up at Dorval Airport. Holbein is a thirty-nine-year-old microbiologist from Arnprior, Ontario. He met forty-nine-year-old Kidby at the University of Guelph when he was a doctoral student and Kidby was teaching chemistry. Holbein later became a professor at McGill University where he met Irving DeVoe.

In the early 1970s, Holbein and DeVoe were conducting research into gonorrhea and spinal meningitis and found that the body stores iron to protect itself from disease. They decided that if they could isolate the organism that extracted iron from the rest of the blood and stored it, it could also be adapted to extract other metals such as gold from seawater or the cyanide-laced sludge formed after gold-bearing rocks are crushed.

To test their theory and develop a salable technology, Holbein and DeVoe needed millions of dollars for research. One of the governors of McGill's board introduced them to Irving Kott in the early 1970s. At that time, Kott was the city's biggest financier, whose trading and stocks represented as much as half of all trading on the Montreal Stock Exchange. Kott agreed to underwrite the company, to buy shares to provide the company with research funds. He could keep the shares or turn around and resell them to the public.

Two companies were formed and named after the two professors. DeVoe-Holbein International was set up in the Netherlands Antilles and DeVoe-Holbein Technologies in Amsterdam. Like most junior high-tech companies, its only assets were some ideas and the patents protecting them.

Holbein, Kidby, and I drive to DeVoe-Holbein's low-rise plant in suburban Pointe Claire. The company is running out of money. Two of the six workers have not been paid salaries for a year. Holbein and Kidby have drawn no salaries themselves since 1985. Nevertheless, the 6000-square-foot plant is comfortable, if spartan. Files and computer printouts are piled high, and a white-coated technician straddles a stool in front of a bank of impressive-looking scientific equipment.

The heat is on today, but it wasn't on in December, nor was it on for most of last winter. The phones are intermittently cut off when unpaid bills get too high. Local bailiffs must know the address by heart; they routinely repossess equipment until payments can be brought up to date. Holbein lives off his savings and the money raised by selling his home. "When the heat was off we worked with two sweaters on under our coats. We've been lucky this year," says Holbein.

This is all that is left of DeVoe-Holbein, a company that was once touted as a shining example of a spinoff from a university-based research company. It was felt to be on the leading edge, showing how universities could pay their own way and research could turn a profit. But now it is an example of how a technology that deserves a chance may not survive, thanks to its association with a boiler room. "DeVoe and

Holbein were a pair of foolish professors. They are not crooks," maintains Koers.

DeVoe got out in 1987 and now lives in California. "His nerves were shot over this Kott thing. He just couldn't take it any more, chasing Kott every day for money to stay alive," says Holbein. Kidby has replaced him. Speaking in a monotonous, Australian drawl, he says the technology is potentially worth "hundreds of millions of dollars." The professors believe their technology can replace a considerably more expensive process of gold extraction. Money could be made by licensing the process and selling the extraction compound in the form of granules. But there are no takers and the professors blame Kott for that.

Trouble began in 1983. By that time, Kott had been convicted once for fraud. McGill became embarrassed because of the bad publicity and tried to distance itself from the professors and their company. McGill had been a shareholder since the beginning. It was a unique arrangement that recognized the right of universities to a portion of the proceeds from research conducted by their professors. In this case, McGill accepted DeVoe-Holbein shares in lieu of a royalty. The arrangement was innovative at the time and became the toast of the scientific community.

In 1983 the university commissioned a Montreal lawyer to study the situation. He concluded that DeVoe and Holbein were involved in a conflict of interest because at the university they were in a position to commission further research while they had a vested interest in a public company doing similar research. The two left McGill and the university put its shares into a blind trust.

In 1984 Holbein talked to Kidby in an attempt to sell the process. Tests were conducted and Kidby agreed to get involved in 1985. He was backed financially by two Australian partners from his native city of Perth. The Australians put $500,000 into DeVoe-Holbein in return for the right to distribute its technology.

"I knew all about the trouble with Kott, but he's a convincing guy," recalls Kidby. "I'm not easy to fool, but I must say after meeting Kott the third time, in October 1985, and speaking to him at length to determine whether he was really what he said he was, I guess I was fooled. It was not too long before I realized he wasn't what he purported to be. He's persuasive when he talks but it's only when you see the performance and the non-performance in various areas you realize the guy's words are inconsistent with his actions."

Kidby and Kott met frequently in First Commerce's Amsterdam offices. It was apparent to Kidby, Holbein, and DeVoe that Kott was the boiler room's boss. "I am convinced that Irving Kott was the owner of Amsterdam stock broker First Commerce. He may maintain he was a consultant to the brokerage firm, but he gave orders to all employees and had the kind of power that only a proprietor would have. I don't know this as merely an observer but as a participant in business arrangements with Kott," says Kidby. "For instance, in order to garner interest in 1985 in what I was proposing to do with DeVoe-Holbein — First Commerce lending it money through debenture loans — I had to convince Kott personally. I met with Kott about this issue at First Commerce's offices in Amsterdam in Kott's office there and also at Janus Financial Consultants in Montreal.

"At no time was Walter Bonn around when I was there and at all times I was present Kott was giving orders. In October 1985 he stopped the entire sales floor at First Commerce to announce that I was going to become DeVoe's managing director. I also saw Kott instruct Roger Croft and other writers as to how to phrase the copy about companies being sold by First Commerce. I also saw Kott giving directions to the head sales persons at First Commerce," says Kidby.

Kott talked to Kidby in Montreal in 1988 about First Commerce. "Kott said to me that he was going to go after Dutch bankruptcy trustee Jan van Apeldoorn over the conversion [into common shares of DeVoe-Holbein] of the debentures, and the only person who could have an interest in doing that is someone who had a beneficial interest in First Commerce which owned the debentures."

Bruce Holbein also says Kott owned and ran the boiler room operations, despite Kott's denials. "He said to me, 'This is mine and I run it.' He said this statement several times in Amsterdam and Montreal. Given that and plenty of other persons who could corroborate his role in the running of First Commerce, I do not know the extent to which he can hide from admitting he owned it. There was no question he ran the place."

Holbein recalls an incident in the winter of 1985 when his father wanted to sell $40,000 worth of his DeVoe-Holbein shares to pay off a loan. First Commerce was always reluctant, or even refused, to buy back shares from investors and there was not a real market for them, so his father was rebuffed by the Amsterdam salesmen at First Commerce and was told, "It must be cleared by Irving Kott." Holbein's father called him and Bruce called Kott to get clearance for the share sale. "Kott said, 'I'll take care of it.' The cheque came shortly after for the shares for my father and the cheque came from First Commerce. There is no question in my mind that First Commerce was Irving Kott's boiler room."

Kidby recalled details from his meetings in Amsterdam. "When I was first introduced by Kott to the sales floor at First Commerce, there were forty-odd salespeople running around with phones on either sides of their heads. It operated twenty-four hours a day. Irving was running things. There was an eight-hour time difference between Amsterdam and eastern Australia, and yet they were making cold calls there. Thousands of them," says Kidby.

One day Kidby went to a partner's office in Perth, Australia, and the partner was on the phone to a First Commerce salesman. "It was about 3 a.m. in Amsterdam at the time. This guy never bought because he knew better, but he was called at least six times before they took no for an answer."

During 1985 and early 1986, Kidby got upset because Kott was making promises to raise more money and wasn't coming through. Meanwhile Holbein moved his family permanently to Europe to organize a pilot project to test the process at Salsigne in southern France, where the world's largest arsenic mine produces gold as a byproduct. Oddly enough, the pilot project had been arranged by Western Allenbee Oil and Gas, a Vancouver company linked to Kott, in return for 50 percent of the gold produced. Salsigne got the other 50 percent and Western Allenbee would pay DeVoe-Holbein's costs.

Western Allenbee arranged the whole deal first and told Holbein about it later. It issued a press release without consulting the scientists, even though Holbein and DeVoe were officers of the company that owned the technology. But, Holbein says, "We went along with it anyway, in the hopes that at last we could prove our process worked profitably."

Western Allenbee and its shareholders made money and Holbein says that the stock went from forty cents to nine dollars on the strength of the project. Unfortunately, DeVoe-Holbein didn't do very well out of the deal. The French were not sufficiently impressed with the technology to turn the pilot project into full production. Holbein moved back to Canada in March 1987.

Kott and the professors were barely talking to one another by the time the 1986 boiler-room raids occurred. Shortly afterward, the Dutch bankrupted DeVoe-Holbein Technologies, which owned the rights to the process. In 1986 Western Allenbee attempted to take over DeVoe-Holbein. The deal was announced, then dropped months later without explanation to the investing public. Bahir Hussain and the late stock promoter Alan Abernathy, both associates of Kott's, were Western Allenbee directors. The professors had to divorce themselves from Kott and First Commerce or shut down.

Kott had raised $5 million for the company and probably helped orchestrate the pilot project. Kott paid twelve cents a share for his first lot of stock, which he eventually sold and resold for as much as fifteen dollars each. By the time the Dutch took over the company, hundreds of shareholders' claims came forward for 60 percent of the company's 21.4 million shares held by First Commerce. (DeVoe and Holbein own 12 percent each and McGill University, 6 percent.)

One way of getting out from under the problem was to find a new financier to pay for more research, marketing, and patent fees. The professors decided to stay in Montreal and make their problems public just to spite Kott, who avoids publicity of any kind. They formed a Canadian corporation called DeVoe-Holbein Canada Inc. and convinced First Commerce's bankruptcy trustee, Jan van Apeldoorn, to sell DeVoe-Holbein Technologies' patents back to the Canadian entity. In return, DeVoe-Holbein Technologies' estate got shares in the new company and a 33 percent royalty on any revenues derived from selling the technology.

Kott was furious. "Kott called about one month ago [in December 1987] and wanted us to sell the technology back into the international company so Michael [Kott] can do an underwriting," says Kidby. "He sicced some Chicago lawyer named J.J. Bellows onto me in person, and they played a good guy-bad guy routine. I met them for hours in his Montreal office, and he said, 'I can get you into court and you can't do anything about it.' Kott is strung around our necks like a millstone and nobody will touch us because Kott has shares.

"Nobody can work with Kott. We are trying to operate a company with inherent profitability. Kott just wants to promote stocks. We nearly got a Quebec Department of Trade grant, but they backed out at the last minute. They said they could help us only if we could break from Kott."

7/Two Key Players

IRVING KOTT

The object of Holbein and Kidby's rancor, Irving Kott, was born on October 12, 1930, in Montreal, one of three children in a tightly knit family in Montreal's east end. Like many in that neighborhood, he and his brother Cecil went into the "shmatta" business (Yiddish for rag trade). Cecil stayed in that game. But brother Irving went into the stock market. Kott certainly has had a hectic business life dogged with controversy and court cases.

By most accounts, Kott is an extremely generous employer who inspires a great deal of loyalty. His receptionist, Electra, has been with him for years, as have his associates Dominique Schittecatte, Bahir Uddin Hussain (First Commerce's controller in Amsterdam), and an elderly French-Canadian bookkeeper named Yvonne Tremblay. Legend has it that Tremblay was charmed by Kott into lending him $200 when he worked part time at the Montreal Stock Exchange. He bought his first stock with her money and made a handsome profit.

"She treats him like a son. And he acts like one. He also contributes towards an orphanage on her behalf," says Bruce Holbein, who has met them all many times. "He is very generous with her. Once I went to his Laurentian place for a weekend meeting and there were a bunch of nuns running around with Yvonne. We said a meeting was scheduled, but

Yvonne said Irving had loaned his estate as a retreat for the nuns to use for a week or more."

Denis Kidby describes Kott as a brilliant actor. The two once argued bitterly when they were discussing company affairs in First Commerce's office in Amsterdam. Kidby told Kott that Holbein and he were becoming increasingly disgusted with the complaints and letters they were getting from shareholders who had been sold DeVoe-Holbein stock at outrageous prices. "He cried. He actually started to cry because I stuck it to him," says Kidby. "On another occasion, in front of me, he was brought a letter from some woman with kids who had lost her shirt buying junky stock. Irving read it and said to an employee, 'Take care of this, please. This is tragic.' Then he wiped his eyes and paused for awhile before he resumed our conversation. He's good. There's no doubt about it. I think he even believes himself."

"The man is a genius. He's absolutely brilliant, but he's so greedy he cannot help himself," says Bruce Holbein. "That's his problem."

Janus Financial Consultants Ltd. is listed in the Montreal telephone directory on fashionable Sherbrooke Street. Janus Corp. is a part of the Kott family empire, according to evidence produced at an Ontario Securities Commission hearing in 1985. Janus is named after the ancient Roman god of doorways and beginnings, whose two faces look in opposite directions and who guarded heaven. Technically, Kott is a Janus consultant, but he goes in most days, working the phones every bit as feverishly as if he were a full-time, commissioned stockie. The result of decades of wheeling and dealing by Kott is that Janus has indeed guarded the doorway to financial paradise for Kott.

His youngest son, Ian Kott, is president of Janus Corp., a fact which came out at an Ontario Securities Commission hearing in December 1985. Kott and his wife Rhoda were fined $6,700 by Revenue Canada for failing to file income tax returns for two of their companies between 1972 and 1979. Kott's children have never been in trouble with the law.

Kott and his wife commute between their Montreal penthouse and their $3-million Laurentian retreat, complete with servants, tennis courts, hot tub, indoor pool, and a small indoor basketball court. Kott, who stands over six feet, was a high-school basketball star in Montreal and works out by the hour shooting baskets.

Kott's two sons Michael and Ian run various family businesses. Michael left Amsterdam after the 1986 raids and runs a Florida broker-dealership, Greentree Securities, with offices in Boca Raton and New York. He also runs Greentree International in Frankfurt and London. Ian is currently president of Tricor Holdings Company Inc., a highly speculative stock which does not trade on any exchange. (Kott also has a daughter who is a physician. She is married and lives in Florida.)

Greentree Securities is a "wholesale market maker," through which investors can buy and sell 1,200 tiny U.S. and Canadian stocks not listed on any stock exchange. It functions essentially as an informal stock exchange. Like an exchange, it is the repository of information about bids and prices; it also records and publishes bids as they occur. Unlike an exchange, it can dabble in the stocks themselves, a built-in conflict of interest, particularly since most stocks are highly speculative and volatile. But it is all strictly legal and is known as an over-the-counter market.

Kott observers say that Michael may be the nominal head of Greentree, but his father is probably its puppeteer, with help from Dominique Schittecatte, Yvonne Tremblay, and Bahir Uddin Hussain. (Hussain is no longer Janus's controller, and left that position in 1988.) "Everyone, including his sons, know just a bit. But no one except Kott himself knows everything about operations or the empire," says a policeman who watches Kott closely.

The Dutch warrants pinning him down are making Kott angry, particularly since they apply in the U.S. This makes it difficult, and dangerous, for him to visit his children or his businesses south of the border.

In November 1987 Kott met secretly with two Canadian policemen in Montreal. He wanted to set the record straight to someone in authority and also to bitch about the RCMP and the Dutch police. He said they were harassing him and blowing his role in Amsterdam out of all proportion. Kott told the policemen that he had "done two deals" there worth a "mere" $14 million. He added that anyone who knew the business would know that commissions on that amount were substantially less. "Big friggin' deal" was his message.

"He said that if his lawyer knew he was talking to us, he [the lawyer] would quit, that he had to be careful what he said," reads a confidential police memo written after the meeting. "We assured him what he said was not for prosecution. Kott was very nervous, continually checking the rest of the room. When Kott opened his jacket to get out a business card, he leaned forward obviously checking for tape recorders. After a few more reassurances he appeared to relax again."

Kott stayed with the two cops for an hour or so, talking in general about his associates and about how he wants to retire, clear his family name, and leave the running of his businesses to his two sons. It was all very strange. Why had Kott called to arrange the meeting?

His principal concern seemed to be that the Dutch had estimated the entire boiler-room swindle, by all players, to be in the order of $6 billion. Police believe Kott's anxiety had something to do with the mob. They knew that Kott had been leaned on by mobsters as far back as the 1960s and early 1970s.

"We found out by accident in a way," recalls RCMP Sergeant John Beer. "I was investigating Somed Mines which was a Kott and Syd Rosen deal. In the course of that I talked to

Stan Bader, who was working with Rosen out of Bay Street. Bader wanted to make a deal and plead guilty to the stock fraud and in the course of those negotiations he told us about an extortion payoff by Rosen to Hamilton godfather Johnny 'Pops' Papalia."

Bader testified as a witness at extortion and fraud trials involving Rosen, Kott, and Papalia. He was murdered years later, in March 1982. Most people believe this was a mob assassination because of his cooperation with the police. His murder certainly was a professional job, said a Florida policeman. "Down here a life is worth $500, maybe $700, tops."

At the 1974 trial in which Bader was a witness, Kott was charged with conspiracy to defraud the public by manipulating Somed Mines' stock. Rosen and others were also found guilty. At the same time, L.J. Forget's license was revoked. In 1976 Kott pleaded guilty to fraud and netted the largest personal fine in Canadian history up to that point, $500,000. He was also put on probation for one year. Nearly three years later, in 1979, Kott was convicted and sentenced to four years in jail for conspiring to issue false information in a business prospectus involving the 1972 promotion of another L.J. Forget stock, Fallinger Mining Corp. At that time, he was described by the presiding judge as the "principal actor" in a wide-ranging fraud that deprived small investors of their savings. (That conviction was overturned, and Kott was acquitted in 1981 by an appeals court. Its judges ruled that, despite attempts by the original judge to clarify the complex evidence, the jurors had not understood the case.)

In 1975, the RCMP charged Kott and eighteen other individuals with 52 counts of conspiracy, 24 counts of fraud, 22 counts of credit under false pretence, and one count of paying secret commissions with regard to Continental Financial Corp. and its subsequent loans to Fallinger Corp. and Cinevision, on whose board Irving Kott sat. (Charges were dropped in October 1986 after a preliminary hearing because a witness had disappeared.) But in December 1978 Kott and his wife were ordered to make restitution payments totalling $270,779 and interest to a man regarding a loan to Continental Financial.

Even before Bader was killed, Kott had been threatened by the mob. In the spring of 1978, Toronto mobsters Remo and Cosimo Commisso hired a hit man, Cecil Kirby, to assassinate Kott. Kirby claims that he was told by the Commisso brothers that they wanted a man in Montreal killed on behalf of someone who would realize a profit at Kott's death. Others speculated that the murder was ordered because Kott refused to pay an extortion demand.

"In late July, Kirby flew to Montreal and met with Cosimo at the Bonaventure Hotel," wrote author James Dubro in *Mob Rule*. "The two then did some surveillance of the intended victim's home and business addresses. At this point, Kirby found out that the target was none other than Irving Kott, the famous stock promoter and manipulator, who was also a well-known associate of the Cotroni family in Montreal."

Dubro described how Kirby bought a .22-caliber handgun in Toronto and also constructed a bomb. At one point, he nearly shot Kott through his front picture window but was frightened away by a passerby. "On August 28, 1978, he called Kott's office at eight in the morning and found that Kott was there. He then went to the underground parking lot at 5425 rue Casgrain and found Kott's car. He placed a bomb with a trigger mechanism beside the muffler pipe and right under the driver's seat. A little after five that evening, two men associated with Kott were walking through and noticed the two wires hanging from the car. They stopped to check it and the bomb went off, hurling both men into the air. The car was a total write-off but the two were not seriously injured, except one man had his hearing permanently impaired." Kirby gave up after that.

A second unsuccessful attempt was made on Kott's life in 1985. Not surprisingly, he is now extremely cautious. When he goes to Europe, for instance, he routinely buys two airplane tickets, one to Paris and another to Amsterdam. Both tickets are made out in his name, and he decides which to use at the last minute. He does not cancel the other flight ahead of time. Police also believe he uses aliases, such as Dr. or Mr. Sanchez or, as he was known in Amsterdam, Irving David, his first and middle names.

Kott's business involvements are spread through many countries. Just days after Koers completed his First Commerce raid on May 9, 1986, Bermuda Attorney General Saul Froomkin read about the crackdown in British newspapers. He called John Leybourne at the Ontario Securities Commission to get more details, then he called the head of Amsterdam's fraud squad, Arnold Peters, to talk about the First Commerce link to his tiny island. Dominique Schittecatte was a director of several Bermuda companies, along with George Ross McPhee, another expatriate Canadian living there. McPhee was a former president of the L. J. Forget brokerage firm in Montreal which was financially controlled by Kott. (Ironically, McPhee's office is a floor above Froomkin's in the same office building. For several years, the two Canadians often shared the elevator and chatted to one another without knowing that their paths would cross.)

Froomkin called McPhee and arranged a meeting with Dutch and Bermuda police in the fall of 1986. The Dutch police also met with a man called Dawson Roberts in the Bahamas in the fall of 1987. Both men had acted as nominees for Irving Kott in the two secrecy and tax havens, and both named Kott as the actual owner of the Dutch boiler room.

McPhee was involved from September 1983 to January 1984 while Roberts was involved from 1983 until after the Amsterdam boiler-room raids in May 1986. McPhee, who ran the Kott-linked L. J. Forget brokerage in Montreal years before, said he was first approached to act as the nominee-owner of the Amsterdam boiler room's parent company,

Euro Placement Securities, by Eric Smith. (Harry Eric Smith ran H.E. Smith, a Toronto brokerage firm which was shut down by Ontario Securities Commission authorities in the 1970s.) "In September 1983, I visited Amsterdam and met with Eric Smith at the offices of First Commerce Securities BV. To the best of my understanding, Eric Smith was the managing director of First Commerce Securities. Arrangements were also made that a company in Bermuda be formed under the name First Commerce Securities Limited.

"I arranged the opening of a bank account in Amsterdam for First Commerce (Bermuda) to facilitate the delivery of securities and the transfer of monies. A 'Mr. Dolphin' appeared to be the driving force behind the sales personnel of First Commerce BV and was in communication frequently by telephone with Mr. Kott. I was to be the managing director of First Commerce and was told that it would be reasonable if I also stated to the Bahamas attorney that I was also the beneficial owner of Euro Placement Securities. In both of these matters I acted exclusively as a nominee and held both positions as nominee for Irving Kott. It was understood by me that both of these matters were very temporary."

The relationship soured and McPhee told Kott and his associates he wanted out. "After a confrontation with 'Dolphin' in December 1983, I had grave reservations about continuing any association with First Commerce Amsterdam. It seemed to me that the entire operation of the company was completely out of control. I had grave fears of the consequences of continuing any association with that company with 'Dolphin' and Irving Kott. I resigned as managing director officially early in 1984 and advised the attorneys in the Bahamas that I would not continue to be held to be the beneficial owner of Euro Placement. Arrangements were made that Yvonne Tremblay and Michael Kott would attend in the Bahamas to designate a new beneficial owner."

The police asked McPhee, "When did you realize that the actions of those that you were associating with was resulting in the defrauding of investors in DeVoe-Holbein stock?" McPhee replied: "I would prefer you to have said 'alleged' defrauding. As [I] previously stated, I became disenchanted with all of the people and the operations being conducted in December 1983. Any activity on my part subsequent to that date was quite simply formalizing all details of disassociation."

Like McPhee, Dawson Roberts spoke with Dutch police in the presence of local police. His Nassau offices were the subject of a search by police. (His firm operates a chartered accounting and trust business.) "I supply nominees as shareholders, officers, and directors; provide the beneficial owner with declarations of trust from the nominee shareholders; I have nominee shareholders endorse the share certificates in blank; I have the officers and directors execute undated resignations; I give these documents to the client or hold them in the file here. In this way, a client can acquire a very high degree of anonymity. In this way I am the only one who knows who owns the company," said Roberts.

In late 1982, he incorporated Euro Placement whose original owners were noted on official Bahamian documents as Eric Smith, a Mr. Funt, and a Mr. Alter. Funt and Alter dropped out and on November 3, 1983, Roberts said he obtained permission from the Bahamian central bank to transfer beneficial ownership to George Ross McPhee on the instructions of Eric Smith. The company did not operate but was only a holding company which owned the shares of the Amsterdam boiler room, First Commerce Securities. "As far as I'm aware, the only function of Euro Placement was as shareholder of First Commerce Securities," Roberts said. "Its only function was to act as a channel through which the instructions of the beneficial owner were transmitted to First Commerce. The construction prevents [anyone from] tracing who the beneficial owner is.

"At that point I was not aware of any interest of Irving Kott, although several years later Smith indicated to me that

Kott was involved with him in the company [Euro Placement] and that he [Smith] could not live with him. From McPhee the beneficial owner changed again [in June 1984]. Yesterday I told you that the next beneficial owner was Irving Kott. After reflecting and checking my files I am not sure. Michael Kott and Yvonne Tremblay visited me in connection with the change around June 1984. As far as I remember I was told that we, i.e., the Kott family, would become the new beneficial owner. Although I was never explicitly told whether Michael or Irving Kott was the new beneficial owner, there is no doubt in my mind that Irving Kott was my client and as such the final authority in all matters. Through an oversight, no permission was asked or obtained from the central bank for this change in ownership," said Roberts.

Roberts kept Euro Placement shares in his possession when Smith and McPhee were owners, but these were handed over to Michael Kott and Yvonne Tremblay and the receipt was signed by Michael, he said. "Subsequently, I was informed that the company had been transferred to Irving Kott. Some time later I was asked by Kott to come to Amsterdam and in Amsterdam Kott informed me that because of his past record on the Montreal Exchange he found it difficult to appear as the owner of any company. He said he had no need to make any further money and that he was in First Commerce only to provide a future business for his children. I was taken around to two buildings in downtown Amsterdam where First Commerce carried on its business operation and I was introduced to various employees as the owner of the company."

After the Amsterdam raids, Roberts was summoned to Luxembourg for changes. "The next main event is the meeting in Luxembourg in June 1986. Irving Kott instructed me to come to Luxembourg. Kott paid the travel and the expenses. [Altaf] Nazerali didn't ever pay anything. This meeting took place in the Intercontinental Hotel," said Roberts.

In October 1984 Euro Placement was "sold" to Altaf Nazerali for $4 million. "The money is to be transferred from 'my' account 56892 to Garland Holding. This instruction was signed by me at the request of Kott, or Kott and Nazerali. I cannot tell you anything about either account. I certainly received no money for the sale of Euro Placement. The only thing I know about the whole transaction is the instruction I signed on request. I must have signed the instruction inside the bank in Geneva. I think I must have opened an account there, otherwise they would not have accepted an instruction by me. I do remember signing some papers in a bank in the presence of Michael Kott. The instructions must have come from Irving Kott, since they always came from Kott."

After the raids in June 1986, Nazerali got out of the ownership of Euro Placement, says Roberts. There was an agreement between "Alya and myself dated June 19, 1986. The agreement is signed both by Nazerali and myself and effectively cancels the earlier agreement. The reason for this was that Nazerali wanted out of the earlier agreement and Irving Kott gave me permission for this.

"At the same time I signed a letter to Walter Bonn in which I confirmed that I was the beneficial owner [of Euro Placement]. That was not really true since the beneficial owner was Irving Kott. I signed the letter on the instructions of Nazerali and with the permission of Irving Kott. It might have been the other way around. The letter was drafted and signed in Luxembourg. At that meeting and another in Amsterdam it was discussed how to go on. The decision was not to liquidate the company [First Commerce, the boiler room] but to apply for a license. The license was refused. There I heard the possibility [discussed] to transfer First Commerce Securities' activities into an American company, Greentree Securities."

He said that he knew nothing about the share certificates being transferred to Metropolitan Securities in Panama and stated that "I have never given permission for this." He also said he was unaware that the boiler room was bankrupted by the Dutch in January 1987. "Your exhibit 19 mentions that Irving Kott had no direct or indirect interest in First Commerce Securities. As I have already told you, Kott did of course have at least a direct interest in Euro Placement and Euro Placement is the owner of First Commerce Securities."

Roberts also talked about the roles played by other Kott associates. Dominique Schittecatte had sweeping authority over some bank accounts and other important duties. "Later I realized that she had a close personal relationship with Irving Kott. Moreover, Kott once told me that she protected the money. I was told by Kott that Nazerali was being brought in to put things in order in First Commerce Securities. Arthur Dalfen told me he was a Canadian and ran the office of First Commerce Securities in Amsterdam together with Irving Kott."

Meanwhile back in Canada, investigators with the Ontario Securities Commission continued to try to shut Kott out from any stock market activities in the province. It was once again to be a test as to whether Kott, who never appears to come forward as a shareholder in various companies, was the so-called controlling mind behind a company. The company involved was Tricor Holdings Company Inc. (formerly Fallinger Mines). Its president, Ian Kott, asked Ontario to lift its ban on trading in Tricor shares imposed in the late 1970s. During two days of hearings in 1987, one in November and another in December, investigator Bill Rivers testified before the Commission. In June 1988, the Commission refused to lift the trading ban after a staff recommendation to that effect because of the failure to prove ownership and the possible involvement of Irving Kott.

Rivers said Tricor was still linked to Irving Kott because Nazerali, Schittecatte, Hussain, and others were involved in trading Tricor shares. Rivers linked Nazerali to Kott when he told the Commission that Altaf Nazerali had opened an account at the Toronto brokerage firm of Merit Investments for Luxembourg's Asset Investment Management (AIM). This company is related to Alya, which held some First Commerce stock. "The call was initiated by Irving Kott who introduced Nazerali to Merit, made the proper introductions, and then passed the phone to Mr. Nazerali who in turn opened the account," Rivers testified. "AIM has a number of directors and officers. It was also determined that certain instructions in the trading came from known Irving Kott associates. These particular people were Bahir Hussain and Dominique Schittecatte. These people have been closely associated with Mr. Irving Kott for a number of years.

"Mr. Hussain has also been named to the board of directors of a number of other companies as well as working from First Commerce Securities in Amsterdam which was subject to investigation by the Amsterdam authorities, and it is believed that Mr. Hussain was acting as an accountant in that capacity. Another AIM director, Albert Wildgen, has now been named to the board of directors of Western Allenbee Oil and Gas which again we indicate may be subject to Irving Kott's influence."

The issue in the Tricor case involved the ownership of a block of shares which Ian Kott said he did not know much about. Rivers said Irving Kott's involvement in Switzerland and Luxembourg, where companies or banks held Tricor shares, "gives the shadow of opinion that Irving Kott has control of those shares."

Rivers also commented on Kott's operating techniques. "Mr. Kott does not show up as either a director or officer of any companies which he has been associated with, nor does he indicate share positions which he may be affiliated with. He has proven in the past that he prefers to be more or less a silent partner or a silent associate of various firms and individuals in which he still influences control."

Rivers said Kott controls the people who own the shares of companies. Rivers cited "confidential sources" as his evidence of this. But at the same hearing, Ian Kott denied his father's involvement. "Is your father directly or indirectly involved in any way with Tricor's business?" he was asked. "No, he is not," said Ian Kott.

When asked if he knew who Tricor's shareholders were, he said he did not.

"It doesn't concern me [who owns shares]. I do my job to fill my mandate as president of the company with the other directors and if I wasn't doing the right job then I guess my mandate wouldn't be renewed."

The commission lawyer asked Ian Kott why his father simply did not swear an affidavit that he neither directly nor indirectly controlled Tricor so that Ian Kott could get permission to trade the shares in Ontario. The Commission formally requested the affidavit in a letter sent to Kott's lawyer. "You could have said, 'Dad, I'm having trouble with the Securities Commission. Could you help me out?'" said the lawyer. "Your father could have said, 'I will swear an affidavit.' You don't know of any reason why he couldn't do that?"

"No," said Ian.

GUY LA MARCHE

The king of Canada's stockies was the flamboyant Guy Joseph Maurice La Marche, who was murdered by a former business partner on March 9, 1987, in Toronto. La Marche, a French-Canadian dandy from Cochrane, Ontario, was heavily involved in boiler rooms in Amsterdam and elsewhere around the world. He also owned sizable pieces of two Canadian companies, Hawk Resources and Beaufield Resources Ltd., both listed in Vancouver.

Although he was fabulously wealthy when he died at the age of fifty-three, La Marche was down and out in the early 1970s when Metro Toronto fraud officer Sergeant Jake Mol first came across him. "He was just scratching to get by. He had a rental unit, but no furniture. However, he always loved clothes and would wear a great outfit, even if it was the only one he owned. He liked boutonnieres, and used to wear a black cloth coat with a black velvet collar and a white silk scarf. He was also partial to fur hats and a fur coat and patent leather shoes."

La Marche's criminal record dates back to April 1, 1955, in Fruitvale, British Columbia, where he was found guilty of false pretenses (a form of fraud) and fined $15 plus $6.50 in court costs. From there he graduated to more serious offenses. He started in the brokerage business as an errand boy at Richardson Securities (now Richardson/Greenshields), a Toronto brokerage firm. Around 1970 he was convicted of fraud and wash trading, which is the disguised buying and selling of shares to yourself in order to fool the public that there is interest in the stock. In 1981 he was convicted of defrauding a bank of $152,000 and fined $200,000.

But La Marche's forte was salesmanship. He peddled his services worldwide, in part because his record rendered him ineffective at home as as legitimate stock-market promoter. In Amsterdam, La Marche linked all the boiler-room boys from Canada. He capitalized on his boiler-room expertise and ran a temporary employment agency for openers and loaders and back-office personnel, called Tête de Tête Consultants, an Office Overload for criminals.

"They would call up Guy and say, 'We would like a few dozen loaders and a few dozen openers for two months in Amsterdam, can you help us?' Then they would call again and ask for six guys to go to Hong Kong or something for three weeks," says Koers. La Marche would round up the salespeople and collect a handsome fee. Sometimes he even did a little selling and supervision himself.

In 1987 La Marche returned to Toronto after making a fortune in Amsterdam and elsewhere. Recently separated from his wife Jacinda, he lived in grand style in Toronto's Harbor Castle Westin, in a $2,500-a-month suite.

La Marche never missed the annual Prospectors' and Developers' Convention, a mining confab always held in Toronto's large and slightly frayed Royal York Hotel. It's a three-day celebration of mining capitalism. Prospectors and promoters press the flesh and do deals. Men in cowboy hats and string ties fill the noisy bars, and every single room is rented out. Doors are left open onto the corridors twenty-four hours a day, beckoning players to come in and talk shop. Cases of beer and spirits are drained as the mining men mingle from around the world. It's the biggest mining show on earth.

On March 7, 1987, La Marche spent most of the day in the hospitality suite of his longtime partner and mentor, disbarred lawyer and convicted fraudster Sam Ciglen. La Marche was trying to promote his Vancouver companies to anyone who would listen. The two had a drink in the York Station Bar, and at four o'clock they took the escalator down to the foyer. Right behind La Marche was a childhood friend and former partner, a man named Timmins Bissonette. As La Marche and Ciglen got to the bottom of the escalator, Bissonette pulled out a pistol and shot La Marche in the shoulder. The mining promoter spun around, and Bissonette shot him point blank through the heart. The bullet traveled through La Marche's body and hit a nearby wall. He was dead by the time he hit the floor.

Bissonette fled down the upward-moving escalator, out the front door in broad daylight and ran up a side street where he flagged down a cab. But police cruisers surrounded the taxi before it went three blocks, and Bissonette gave himself up. No shots were fired, but the scene horrified Bay Street brokers and other denizens of downtown Toronto, especially those who were dining at nearby Anthony's, an elegant watering hole frequented by brokers.

Bissonette, convicted of second-degree murder in February 1988, admitted that he shot his friend of thirty-five years. He said he was provoked by La Marche's refusal to repay money he owed and by La Marche's claim that he had a contract out on Bissonette's life.

In the early days, the two had sold aluminum siding and pots and pans. Bissonette later became a carnival operator and bar owner and often went to Las Vegas casinos where his associates included New York mobster Tony Salerno. He said that he had given La Marche between $125,000 and $150,000 in loans and guarantees over the years and that his friend had abandoned him when their fortunes reversed. When Bissonette needed money, La Marche had promised to give him $100,000 and to let him stay in his apartment. But La Marche had turfed him out without a cent after two days.

Bissonette hired a private detective to locate La Marche and found out that he would be attending the Prospectors' Convention. Bissonette met his old friend there twice. At the second meeting, La Marche told him that there was a contract out on his life. Bissonette went back to his seedy hotel, loaded his gun, and tracked down La Marche at the Royal York. "Guy, I need that money," Bissonette said to his friend on the escalator. According to him, La Marche's last words were, "You won't need no money because you're going to be dead in a couple of days, you piece of shit."

La Marche moved in the type of circles where murder contracts are a way of life. The Dutch have linked him to a real estate deal with Colombian cocaine chief Carlos Lehder Rivas, convicted on May 19, 1988, of smuggling cocaine. La Marche traveled the world, but he returned to Toronto three months before his death after establishing several boiler rooms in London, Panama, and Spain. At the Prospectors' Convention he discussed, with several unknown people, setting up a new boiler room in Dublin as well as several mining deals.

8/Following the Trail

Tracing the ownership of the boiler rooms is a frustrating business. First Commerce's sole director was Walter Bonn, the man who accepted the search warrants from Jan Koers and the Dutch judge. Koers arrested Bonn in 1987 and charged him with forgery and with directing a criminal organization. Such charges carry a sentence of six years. It was obviously a ploy to get Bonn to cooperate with police by fingering others, but Bonn said at first that he was kept in the dark and knew nothing.

"Bonn has met Kott a dozen times, but when asked who owns First Commerce, he says he doesn't know," says van Apeldoorn. "Bonn made a 200-page statement to police. Bonn said things were not told to him. He used to sign blank checks without asking questions. He became tied to the company because he got a house loan from Kott of some 180,000 gilders [$70,000]. He is out on bail and has shifted the blame to Kott's controller, Bahir Hussain, and says he can't take responsibility."

In April 1987, weeks after Jan Koers issued warrants against Irving Kott and Bahir Hussain, First Commerce's bankruptcy trustee Jan van Apeldoorn set out to find assets, bank accounts, and share certificates with some value. For instance, First Commerce was owed millions of dollars by an entity called the Austin Smith Corp. in Panama. Van Apeldoorn describes his investigation. "I visited it and it's a file in a law firm. It owes First Commerce money, but where do I go to get it? It is frustrating. The trustee is paid out of the estate, but at a certain stage the money will run out, and I will say that's all I can do. But the good name of Holland is involved, and I'm trying to convince courts of that so they pay us to pursue this."

Van Apeldoorn is tracing the ownership of the First Commerce boiler room and three others. Each one was owned by different, mysterious offshore companies, but all were probably linked in some way. "They used the same salesmen, same trust company, same accountant, and sold the same types of stocks, mostly Vancouver Stock Exchange or NASDAQ [the National Association of Securities Dealers Automated Quotations, a computerized over-the-counter U.S. stock exchange which lists trading in 10,000 small companies]. Most interesting, however, was the fact that their money flowed the same way."

Van Apeldoorn has been trying to follow the money trail in the hopes of finding some assets with which to pay off the millions owed to investors. His search took him to Panama, where he encountered the obstacles that have frustrated white-collar crime investigations for years.

Secrecy is for sale in steamy and corrupt Panama. Like many other underdeveloped countries, it is a criminal's paradise. Tax evaders, crooks, drug dealers, and ex-husbands hiding from alimony payments can find shelter behind corporate shells, which the best law enforcement agencies on earth cannot penetrate.

The Bahamas is the dirty-money pioneer, thanks to secrecy laws which threaten to jail bankers who divulge customers' names. Police can apply to Bahamian courts for information but have to prove that the money in the accounts under investigation is dirty money. (Tax evasion does not count.) Until the Americans took on Canada's Bank of Nova Scotia to force it to disclose information about tainted deposits offshore, every criminal — from drug traffickers to corrupt politicians and inside traders — permanently buried the proceeds of their crimes in exotic climes. All they had to do was deposit money in offshore bank accounts.

To encourage even more of this activity, the Caribbean and Central American secrecy havens have also eliminated corporate income taxes and extended their secrecy laws to include local corporations. "You can set up bank accounts and shell corporations in a dozen jurisdictions in one day that would take police 100 years to unravel," says RCMP white-collar crime chief Rod Stamler. "It's impossible."

Van Apeldoorn discovered that all four boiler rooms were linked to Panamanian shell corporations "in trust with" a company called Citco Panama SA. Such trust companies are run by lawyers and are in the business of renting out their letterheads. Citco will create a company in minutes for a fee. Once a shell company is created, Citco acts as a caretaker for the corporate seal and documents and also handles asset transactions. The Citcos of this world make their money by collecting legal fees for creating companies, administrative fees for running things, and also professional fees when their lawyers act as directors for the corporations. In Panama a corporation needs only one director, and he or she need not be its owner. The only information the corporation must file on the public record is the name of the director and his or her business address.

Tracing ownership from this point is impossible. Panama also allows corporations to issue bearer stock certificates to owners. Unlike normal stock certificates, which bear the name of their present owner and are destroyed when sold to someone else, bearer certificates are like cash. There is no name on them and whoever possesses them can cash them in or sell them.

The boiler rooms used all these tricks to hide their money or to evade taxes in Holland, says van Apeldoorn. For instance, documents in Amsterdam showed a payment of

$6.7 million from one of the boiler rooms to a Panamanian shell called Wilmington Commercial Panama. Wilmington's trust company was Citco, and its sole director was a Citco lawyer, R. Van Der Wall Arneman. Originally from Holland, Arneman is the director of 4,000 similar shell companies, which means he is the custodian of a bunch of file folders. He avoided van Apeldoorn and declined an interview.

Even if he had consented to talk, it is unlikely he would have told van Apeldoorn anything. He probably does not know who owns Wilmington or the 4,000 other companies. As a lawyer, Arneman cannot divulge any information about his companies without his clients' permission because that would constitute a breach of client confidentiality and be grounds for his own disbarment. Even if he did obtain consent, it would likely come from another lawyer in another tax and secrecy haven with another 4,000 file folders as clients.

Van Apeldoorn hit a brick wall trying to find out what happened to the $6.7 million payment to Wilmington Commercial Panama. In each transaction, the boiler room paid Wilmington big bucks for the stock and then resold it for considerably less. The losses were designed to bankrupt the Dutch boiler room in the end, thereby providing its owners with the opportunity to skip town, leaving behind debts to suppliers and workers and tax officials. And operating losses meant that the boiler room had no income and therefore owed no taxes in Holland. Meanwhile, the boiler room owned the Panamanian company it bought the stock from; this company made a profit but paid no taxes in Panama because there are no corporate taxes in Panama. Nice and neat. And illegal.

The pattern was the same for two more outfits. Arneman was the sole director of more Panamanian shell companies that sold shares to Amsterdam boiler rooms. Van Apeldoorn traced the flow of millions of dollars from Panama to corporate accounts sitting in the Bank of Credit and Commerce International in New York City and finally to accounts in the same bank of dozens of corporations in Switzerland, Luxembourg, Amsterdam, Liechtenstein, the Isle of Man, and elsewhere. The only way to unravel where the money went was to spend hundreds of thousands of dollars waging court actions in dozens of countries to get access to potential evidence. But the courts will not get involved unless the evidence is already in hand. It is the classic Catch-22.

Panama provided a haven for fugitive financier John Doyle, formerly of Montreal, who left Canada in 1974 after legal skirmishes concerning his company Javelin International Ltd. In 1986 the Quebec Superior Court found Doyle, Javelin's former chairman, guilty of fraud against the company and ordered him to pay $15.4 million in compensation to the company. The court also seized his Javelin shares as partial payment of the fine. This is under appeal.

Doyle has eluded a few law enforcement agencies. He arrived in Canada from the U.S. in 1965 to dodge a three-year prison sentence for securities violations he received in 1963. Then he left before he was also criminally charged in 1976 with 406 charges of wash trading in Newfoundland as well as several charges of fraud and violating a public trust dating back to 1973. Doyle denies committing any of those offenses.

Canadian authorities obtained an extradition order in Canadian courts, then got permission to extradite him from the Panamanian court. Two RCMP officers flew down to Panama to arrest and bring Doyle back, but when they arrived at his palatial home they were ordered off the property as trespassers. "He had just gotten Panamanian citizenship the day or week before and we couldn't extradite him," recalls an RCMP official.

Canadians are not the only ones stonewalled by regimes such as Panama's. Similar roadblocks also annoyed U.S. officials who accused Panama strongman, General Manuel Noriega in 1988 of drug and arms trafficking, the murder of a prominent opponent, rigging elections in 1984, passing U.S. secrets to Cuba, and forcing out a series of civilian presidents.

Two U.S. grand juries indicted Noriega in February 1988 on narcotics trafficking charges, but he denied the accusations. Unable to extradite a Panamanian citizen, the U.S. government imposed economic sanctions on the tiny central American country in an effort to pry Noriega out of Panama or get him to leave as political leader.

Van Apeldoorn had learned shortly after the second raid on First Commerce in November 1986, that a group of employees took ten boxes of share certificates to Panama. During his short stay in Panama, van Apeldoorn visited Metropolitan Securities, a brokerage firm recently opened by Kott in partnership with a Uruguayan bank. Metropolitan had the ten boxes of share certificates that had been taken from Amsterdam. Van Apeldoorn met with a J.P. Bonino, who represented Kott's partner, the Metropolitan Bank of Montevideo, Uruguay, a legitimate financial institution with branches throughout South America. The bank's partner in Metropolitan Securities was a company called International Portfolio Management, linked to Kott and some of his associates. "I have a statement from J.P. Bonino that the 'parties involved in Metropolitan Securities are Shafiq Nazerali, Irving Kott, and Bahir Hussain, all Canadian citizens.' Bank officials also said they visited Kott many times in the Montreal offices of Janus Financial Consultants."

Metropolitan Securities gave van Apeldoorn the boxes of stock certificates, but not before van Apeldoorn inadvertently created something of a furor. Van Apeldoorn had made the rounds in Panama, talking to police and other officials, because Panama is one of the countries that recognizes the Netherlands' warrants, or subpoenas. When the Panamanian police learned that warrants were outstanding for Hussain and Kott, they moved quickly. Hussain happened to be in Metropolitan Securities' offices at the time, setting up the new firm. He was detained. Koers was notified immediately by telex, but the documents outlining the reasons for the extradition to Holland did not arrive on time. Under the extradition rules, an individual can only be detained for twenty-four hours, until those applying for the extradition can convince a local court that the individual should be shipped back to the extraditing country for questioning. In this case, Hussain spent a night in jail and was released because the documents were late. He took the next plane back to Montreal.

Police released details about Hussain's detention. The next day newspapers carried the full story of the First Commerce swindle in Amsterdam and the fraud and tax evasion allegations. Because Hussain was involved with Metropolitan Securities, which in turn was partly owned by the Metropolitan Bank, the public panicked. The bank was completely innocent of any wrongdoing, but there was a run on deposits that day and the next. Eventually, the bank went into receivership. The Panamanian boiler room never got off the ground and van Apeldoorn returned to Holland with ten boxes of nearly worthless stock certificates.

In May 1987, four weeks after returning from Panama, van Apeldoorn went to Luxembourg and sued First Commerce's sister company there, AIM (Asset Investment Management) Commodities, in order to freeze its bank accounts. AIM's parent company, the Alya Group, had "bought" First Commerce in 1984 from a Bahamian shell company, then had sold it back to a Bahamian entity (Euro Placement Securities) after the Dutch police raids.

While in Luxembourg, van Apeldoorn met a mysterious black man named Altaf Nazerali, a six-foot four-inch former bodyguard whose brother is linked to Irving Kott. Nazerali's brother Shafiq had been named by the Metropolitan Bank's officer as one of the parties involved with the ill-fated Panama brokerage firm, along with Kott and Hussain. Thirty-four-year-old Altaf Nazerali is listed as Alya's owner.

Van Apeldoorn also managed to cause a panic in Luxembourg, which led to AIM losing its seat on the tiny Luxembourg Commodities Exchange. "We arrested AIM bank accounts in Luxembourg, and on May 31, 1987, it countersued and I was served with three writs and claims for damages," says van Apeldoorn. "AIM supplied stock to First Commerce and another Alya company hired the sales force. Michael Kott, for instance, was employed by one of the Alya companies, one called Inter Alya, but worked at First Commerce in Amsterdam. Another firm Alya owned was IDB [Investment Discount Brokerage] and it is bankrupt and under investigation in the United Kingdom."

The month before, in April 1987, van Apeldoorn had been contacted by a Chicago lawyer named J.J. Bellows. "Bellows made an appointment through Professor M. Wladimiroff [Kott's Dutch lawyer and reputedly the best in the country], and said he just wanted to see who I was. He wanted to know if we could reach an agreement if his client could deliver [share certificates] to make sure investors got shares."

Bellows purposely avoided naming his client. "I asked him who his client was and he said, 'Let's say he lives on the North Pole, has a red jacket and a white beard,'" says van Apeldoorn, who nevertheless assumed it was Kott. "I don't know whether Kott's getting a bit nervous. He can't leave Canada because of the risk of extradition and might want to show good faith so he can say he did no wrong. Another possibility is his honor may start to hurt. But I was told that will never happen. That's why Mr. Bellows says he's acting for Mr. Claus. There is no traceable connection. However, Bellows said he could make Hussain available to me and Hussain agreed to talk about accounts.

"Bellows said he represented Alya, then later denied it. When I met with him, he also agreed to a [financial] contribution for all the work I'm doing," says van Apeldoorn. "I told him I want to meet Mr. Kott. He has done some very wrong things, and I want to convince him to make them right. I want to convince Kott he has to do something for these people.

Bellows tells me they want to deliver shares and pay back the credit balances."

So far, this hasn't happened.

But Bellows and Professor Wladimiroff met at the end of the summer in 1987 with van Apeldoorn and Jan Koers in an attempt to make a deal. Bellows said that if Koers dropped his criminal investigations against Kott, Hussain, Bonn, and others involving the activities of First Commerce, investors would be compensated either with cash or by getting their missing share certificates. "He did not want to deal with me at all," says van Apeldoorn. "This is because I am the bankruptcy trustee and whatever money I get must go to preferred creditors. In the case of First Commerce, the preferred creditor is the Dutch government which claims that $30 million in taxes were never paid. They wanted to make a deal directly with investors because I think they are frightened of the investigation and also frightened that once I am finished, and run out of money, then investors will begin to sue Kott and others."

Koers turned down any deal and refused to drop his investigation. He says that Bellows admitted to a link between Kott and First Commerce. "Bellows said to us that he worked for the owners of First Commerce and then in a separate statement said that he worked for Irving Kott. There is no doubt that Kott owned the First Commerce operations."

9/Catching up to One Culprit

Bankruptcy trustee Rodreck Casander has had more success than van Apeldoorn. He was given the responsibility of tracing the assets of three boiler rooms he believes were run by Barney Altwerger and David Winchell. Altwerger operated BA Investor Advisory Services (or BS Advice, as some of his boiler-room boys used to call it). BA would set up a series of shell companies in various jurisdictions to frustrate tax collectors and regulators. In this case, however, Casander tracked down $3 million in a bank account in the Isle of Man and with Koers got cooperation from the local police and courts there. It may be the only money ever recovered.

Barney Altwerger is still a ladies' man, even though he is now in his seventies. A career criminal with as many aliases as convictions, he's passed himself off as Barnett Auld, Stanley Weinreb, Allan T. Barnett, Allen Bennett, Arthur Barnett, Altwiger Barnett, and Bernard Alvey. His last fixed address was a penthouse on fashionable Walmer Road in Toronto. His current whereabouts are unknown.

Altwerger has mob connections and was a long-time associate of the brother of gangster Paul Volpe, who was murdered in 1983. Some police investigators were surprised to learn of Altwerger's involvement in Amsterdam. "We were surprised because he's more of a hood as opposed to a crafty fraud man or a stock market manipulator," says Metro Toronto fraud officer Sergeant Jake Mol. "He's the kind of guy who would get involved in manipulations that were based on threats or deceit, but not this sort of white-collar stuff."

BA Investor Advisory Services was housed in an office close to the twenty-room hotel that Altwerger rented and furnished for his sales staff. Altwerger was always on hand, managing affairs. Like the other boiler rooms, BA was long on hype and short on delivery. Shares for Marco Resources Ltd. ("Potentially one of the largest producers of precious metals in the world," boasted BA's *International Special Situations Newsletter*) were offered at about five dollars each shortly before it collapsed to eighty cents on the Vancouver Stock Exchange. Canadian Industrial Minerals of Toronto sold for three dollars a share ("A guaranteed great future. . . expected to be $8 to $10 within a year") but fell to thirty cents in 1987 after being suspended from trading during part of 1986. Shares in U.S.-based Scherlock Systems ("The finest prospects of any high-tech company we have investigated") were sold for ninety-five cents each but have no market. No one is interested in trading them.

BA was raided in May 1986, along with the other six boiler rooms. All were bankrupted by Dutch officials in January 1987. Compared to First Commerce, BA was small potatoes, with some eight to ten salespeople. In May 1987 the Dutch court tried Altwerger in absentia on a charge of selling securities without a license, but acquitted him on June 5, 1987, due to insufficient evidence. But efforts to get his money did not fail.

Documents scooped from the raids showed that, as Barnett Auld, Altwerger had a number of shell companies on the Isle of Man. After arriving there, Casander and Koers convinced bank officials to open up accounts, with the help of local police. They found a total of $3 million, which Casander asked the courts to freeze. Koers prepared documents to link the accounts to Altwerger, who was under investigation in Holland for fraud, so the money could be seized.

Koers issued warrants to pick up Altwerger for questioning. But in December 1987, a Toronto lawyer named Joe Perbel approached Koers to make a deal about the cash. "I agreed not to charge him [Altwerger] and he paid for it," says Jan Koers. "We made a deal, he paid a fine of 100,000 gilders [$40,000 Canadian] and 75 percent of the other money goes to the bankruptcy trustee and that will be paid to the investors."

Altwerger has a long history of run-ins with the law. He was born in Poland and emigrated to Canada with his parents as a youngster. On April 25, 1952, in New York he got a two- to four-year sentence for attempted burglary. On February 21, 1955, he was found guilty of violating immigration laws and deported from New York to Canada. He was deported a second time from New Orleans on July 20, 1972.

In the 1960s, he appears to have graduated from street crimes to white-collar ones. In 1961 he was investigated by securities officials in connection with a company called Trans-Oceanic Hotels Corp. Ltd. On December 8, 1961, he was arrested in Edmonton and pleaded guilty to failing to comply with a summons issued by the Alberta Securities Commission. He was fined $200. On December 15, 1961, he was convicted of violating the Alberta Securities Act.

Altwerger was implicated in two probes: the 1965 Ontario Securities Commission investigation of United Buffadison Mines Ltd. and the Alberta Securities Commission investigation of fraudulent mailings from Toronto to solicit sales of shares in Cedar Oils Ltd. Both investigations were dropped, but Altwerger was convicted for other offenses. On September 19, 1972 in Toronto, he was convicted of personation, fraud, and absconding bail, and received a sentence of two years. He was paroled on September 30, 1974. On April 27, 1978, he was convicted of keeping a common betting house in Toronto, along with a brother of Paul Volpe. He was fined $2,800 and sentenced to sixty days in jail. On May 9, 1980, in

Toronto, he was fined $30,000 and paroled for two years for conspiracy to defraud in a case involving one of Volpe's brothers and the flogging of worthless parcels of land in Florida. Between these convictions, a number of charges were laid but were either dismissed or withdrawn.

Altwerger continues to enjoy business and romance. The Dutch police found many torrid love letters from women in several countries among his personal effects. "He's short, fat, and a ladies man. He's in his seventies but dresses like a thirty year old, a playboy image," says Casander. "A couple of years ago he went to an Isle of Man trust company and fancied one of the secretaries there. He proudly told the story to the bank manager just before leaving that he had gotten together with the young secretary. Just before he left, he showed a piece of paper to the bank manager and said yesterday he took her to his room. The note said in her handwriting, 'Thanks for a wonderful night, Barney.' He was proud that he could still get a young girl. But he took the paper away so rapidly the bank manager couldn't be sure the signature was the same girl. People thought of him as a good-looking grandfatherly type."

Casander visited the United Kingdom in 1987 to talk to British security officials about an Altwerger operation in London called Greenwood International. It was run by Altwerger's stepson, Gary Anderson, a former Vancouver stock promoter. Greenwood flogged two Canadian stocks, Multi Choice Communications Inc., now defunct, and Campbell-Boys Industries Ltd., a graphic arts company in Ottawa and Toronto. Greenwood was partially owned by GR Investor Relations Inc., which was run by Toronto lawyer and financier George Sukornyk.

In September 1985 Altwerger and Anderson toured the Mississauga facilities of Multi Choice's subsidiary, Home Choice Communications Systems Inc., then agreed to buy stock from its treasury and flog it through Greenwood. Sukornyk told Canadian newspapers that he did not know

Altwerger was involved and said that, when he discovered the connection in 1986, he asked Anderson to resign from Greenwood.

The London fraud police shut down Greenwood in March 1987, and a British high court appointed a receiver. "The company was set up as a legitimate business, but Gary Anderson became involved without telling us [the British authorities], and when we found out we shut them down," said Rowan Bosworth-Davies, the head of the United Kingdom watchdog FIMBRA (Financial Intermediaries, Managers, and Brokers Regulatory Association). "After we lifted the license, we reported the company to the DIT [Department of Industry and Trade], and it went in and petitioned to have the thing wound up in the public interest." (In 1988, Washington securities officials said that they suspected that Anderson was running a new stock promotion outfit from Costa Rica, touting several Vancouver stocks to Americans.)

Virtually none of the money raised for the share sales came back to Canada, says former Ontario Securities Commission investigation chief John Leybourne. Listed over the counter in Ontario, Multi Choice was halted from trading on February 9, 1987, by the Ontario Securities Commission. Besides hyping its shares through Greenwood to investors from Scotland to Singapore, Multi Choice had also tapped into that recklessly dispensed largesse called the Scientific Research Tax Credits, compliments of the Canadian taxpayer. (Fledgling research companies, which rarely pay taxes, claim research credits and "sell" them to bigger companies for cash to give them write-offs for tax purposes. The idea was to encourage research. Instead, the credits encouraged fraud. A total of $3 billion in taxes was written off, and an estimated $1 billion was misappropriated before the program was canceled in May 1985.)

Multi Choice was one of 1,810 Scientific Research Tax Credit projects, and its subsidiary, Home Choice, used up to $14.3 million raised under the program. Several hundred thousand dollars of this went toward promoting Multi stock around the world, through Greenwood. Investors were told the company was a leading manufacturer of microwave communications equipment. In July 1986 Revenue Canada officials seized the assets of Multi Choice and Home Choice because the parent company had not fulfilled its obligation to do $31 million worth of research. Although financial statements indicated that the assets totalled $10.6 million, they eventually fetched only a meager $700,000.

One of BA's earliest stock promotions involved a tiny over-the-counter company called CIM, short for Canadian Industrial Minerals. In 1985 Altwerger approached Robert Opekar, president of Ram Petroleums Ltd., who was trying to raise money for CIM. Altwerger eventually bought $1.4 million worth of CIM shares at forty and seventy-five cents a share. To Opekar, Altwerger was Barney Auld, and the money for the shares came from two Isle of Man companies. Ram Petroleums was involved because it manages CIM in return for a royalty and 3 percent of its shares. "We went to reputable brokers to get financing, and nobody was interested. Auld walked in and said we can sell the shares. My first reaction was skepticism," said Opekar.

BA flogged CIM for five to six dollars a share. On the eve of the raids, Opekar was contacted by John Leybourne's staff, who were concerned about the boiler-room selling techniques. "We got our money, but we became worried about selling techniques in April 1986, when the Ontario Securities Commission contacted us," says Opekar. "We sold the shares at an agreed price, we received our money, and we didn't know what he was saying to people about these shares. We'd given him [Altwerger] all the information related to the project including a geologist's report. When we found out what was going on, we sent him a registered letter disassociating ourselves. The interesting thing is he is incredibly bright and could make money at anything he wanted. He had a reasonably successful tile business in Toronto for some years and he sold it to Olympia & York Tile [owned by the wealthy Reichmann brothers of Toronto real estate fame]. Tile was his business."

Although Opekar was a victim of sorts, at least he didn't lose his shirt, as many other victims did. On February 22, 1987, *Sunday Times* columnist Tony Hetherington wrote to a reader who had lost a fortune in CIM shares: "BA stands for Barnet Altwerger, not your everyday run-of-the-mill stockbroker, but what respectable newspapers sometimes refer to as a man with colourful associates. I am sure Barnet was perfectly frank with his chums about his convictions of fraud and gambling offences. Selling shares in a totally non-existent company would have swiftly attracted attention and been rather daft; Barnet did not get very rich by being very daft. CIM does exist; it's just that Barnet was, well, a little high-spirited about the share price. You probably paid US$1.50 and were promised $8. Vancouver broker Jones Gable makes a market and the last trade [February 4, 1987] was 45 cents Canadian. For some time in 1986 trading in CIM was banned by the OSC because CIM was in breach of the law requiring it to file accounts to the public."

Another BA promotion was Marco Resources Ltd., listed on the Vancouver Stock Exchange. Its promoter, Philip Lieberman, resigned in May 1987 amid a controversy over the meteoric, and unjustifiable, rise in share prices. That month the company had announced that it would put into production a Mojave desert property that could produce up to 500,000 ounces of gold, making it North America's largest gold mine.

But its shares had begun soaring back in June 1984, when another Canadian-owned stock broker in Amsterdam called Frankal Investment Advisory Services boasted in its tout sheet that Marco "should be regarded as potentially one of the largest producers of precious metals in the world." Quite a boast, and identical to BA Investors' boast. It was triply ridiculous, considering a respected engineering company, Bechtel

Civil & Minerals Inc. of San Francisco, drilled the property for Marco and found only "trace" amounts of precious metals, according to its June 22, 1984, report. It added that further exploration was "not warranted."

Philip Lieberman said he knew nothing about Frankal or BA, but an entity called BA Investment was listed as one of Marco's biggest shareholders with a little more than 10 percent of the stock. Lieberman himself owned 1.2 million shares, or a slightly higher percentage than BA, as of October 1984.

(Lieberman is an interesting character. He arrived in Vancouver in 1970 and began launching questionable stock promotions. In 1975 there was Philco Resources Ltd., owner of patents which were supposed to revolutionize the oil business. Philco also boasted of many deals which would catapult it into the big time. Nothing of the sort happened, and Philco hit twenty cents in 1986 and fifty cents in 1987. Lieberman then promoted another company, Nomad Mines. It was suspended in 1979, when he was its chairman, after gold assay reports on a Vancouver Island property quadrupled estimates over previous studies. It turned out that Nomad was drilling on a nearby Indian reserve instead of on its own land. Some shareholders threatened to sue for incompetence.

In 1980, Lieberman and seven other promoters were charged with bribing Chris Caulton, former vice-president of the Vancouver Stock Exchange. Charges against Lieberman and four others were stayed in 1983; another promoter was found guilty in 1984, and two others were acquitted. These and other clouds led Vancouver officials to monitor Lieberman's activities closely. In March 1988 Lieberman had his trading rights suspended for ten years and was forced to resign from Marco and two other companies for securities violations.)

10/ANOTHER ONE THAT GOT AWAY

Rodreck Casander was also in charge of tracking down the assets of Financial Planning Services, a boiler room linked to Toronto brothers Luther and David Winchell. The boiler room had an affiliate in Switzerland, which appears to be where most of the documents and money were stashed. After the boiler-room raids, Casander went through official channels to request copies of some Swiss documents. But because Swiss secrecy laws are so tight, it took one year for the information to arrive.

"We believe there were five partners, but Winchell was the big boss. His brother, Luther Winchell, came to Amsterdam around 1980 and 1981 and spent a good deal of time setting it all up," says Casander. "John King in Nassau is the front man. Money laundering was involved in some cases, carried out by various boiler-room boys. Cash to stocks to cash is ideal laundering."

Financial Planning was started on February 1, 1980, according to Amsterdam Chamber of Commerce documents. Luther came along to set up operations. "He had a heart attack while he was in Amsterdam," says Dutch journalist Tino Bakker. "It was a serious one. David was living in Florida but came to see Luther a few times. This was reported in a number of our newspapers. A Swede, Nils Persson, ran things here for the Winchells."

Financial Planning and its associated boiler room, Capital Venture Consultants, were raided in May 1986 and declared bankrupt in January 1987 by the Dutch. Police believe they sold hundreds of millions of dollars worth of Federal Ventures, the stock bought by Canadian Rick Ellis while he was working in Saudi Arabia.

Winchell's involvement in the boiler rooms was related by his former Toronto lawyer, Enver Hassim of Toronto. Hassim was charged along with Winchell for his role in the International Chemalloy scam, but charges were stayed and he still practices law. In 1985 the Ontario Securities Commission subpoenaed Hassim and he testified in no uncertain terms that David Winchell was the owner of Financial Planning Services.

Hassim described "the organization he [Winchell] had created in Europe through a company called — at that time I think it was a combination of companies — Capital Gains Research, which was a Bahamian company, and another company called Financial Planning Services, which was a Netherlands company.

"Capital Gains Research company produced a weekly newsletter which was sent to a large number of people in Europe and the Far East. That gave him a fairly large market into which he could sell shares of any particular company, always assuming that the shares had some promotional value. The actual selling organization was the FPS [Financial Planning Services] organization."

When asked how it operated, Hassim responded, "Much like a broker-dealer operation in this country. They had lists of people with names and phone numbers and they had salesmen who called them on the phone and induced them to part with their money."

As for the ownership, Hassim made no bones about it. "They [Capital Gains and FPS] were all owned by David Winchell. Capital Gains had been incorporated in the Bahamas. The shareholders of record of that company, certainly at the time [up to 1984] that I knew about it, were Mr. John King and his wife Belle. Mr. King has a trust business in the

Bahamas. He acts as trustee for people. His firm is called Worldwide Trust. There would have been — standard procedure in these countries — there would have been some kind of trust document executed by King and his wife that they were holding the shares in trust — the shares of Capital Gains. FPS was incorporated in the Netherlands. To the best of my recollection, the shares were held by Capital Gains Research. The directors of FPS were John King and a lawyer by the name of Hans Friedrichs, who lives in Amsterdam. But he [Winchell] has never done anything directly."

When asked whether he could comment on any further sort of relationship between King and Winchell, he responded, "I have been at numerous meetings at Mr. King's offices in Nassau. Mostly David Winchell was there, as well. They would discuss together what business was going on at the moment, with Mr. Winchell giving instructions on what was to be done on any given matter."

Similarly, Walter Claudio Fantin acted from September 1984 to April 1985 as the managing director of Financial Planning Services, taking over operations after Guy La Marche invited him to come on board. During a 1987 hearing into whether he could have his broker's license reinstated, Fantin told Ontario Securities Commission officials about operations at Financial Planning Services. The Commission refused his request and denied him a license because of his involvement with Winchell. "The purpose of the hearing related to Fantin's activity with Financial Planning Services BV, incorporated on February 1, 1980, with Luther Francis Winchell as the owner/founder," said a statement published June 25, 1987, by Ed Goad, the Commission official who refused Fantin's application.

"The evidence of Enver Hassim is in part relevant to this hearing. Hassim identified that FPS [Financial Planning Services] and Capital Gains Research were owned by D. [David] Winchell but operated through Worldwide Trust, a

Bahamian corporation. 'D. Winchell never did anything directly,' Hassim said. The operations of FPS were nothing more than a high-pressure boiler room," said Goad.

In 1984, La Marche approached Fantin for the job in Amsterdam, and flew him there for a free holiday so that he could consider it. Fantin took the job. "Fantin's duties were to take all incoming calls from clients whose salesmen had left or were not there. In particular he was to deal with the concerns of investors in Portinax Development Limited. Fantin denied selling, but later it was obvious that Fantin sold," said Goad in his decision.

Portinax's products did not warrant the value at which Portinax was sold, as high as US$8 a share. Portinax lost substantial sums of money and on December 1, 1983, the share capital of Portinax was raised from 10 million to 25 million shares for one cent each. That month one million penny shares were issued for $5 million cash, $4.775 million of this from J. Stroere & Co., underwriters. "The same people who directly or indirectly controlled Portinax also controlled J. Stroere & Co. and FPS," said Goad.

Then he said Portinax lent $2.6 million to two B.C. companies, repayable in shares of Night Hawk Resources Ltd., on the Vancouver Stock Exchange. "The beneficial owner of the two British Columbia corporations was again the same Winchell group whose members were also the principals of Night Hawk," said Goad. "Portinax was cease traded in July 1985 at the request of its officers and resumed trading as Federal Ventures in December 1985."

Fantin testified he took orders from John King and got money from him to prop up Financial Planning during a troublesome time. He admitted selling some "worthless shares," as Goad put it. "Fantin has knowingly fronted for stock fraud artists and convicted fraudulent individuals. Canadians who have operated in Amsterdam or any other unregulated jurisdictions in a manner similar to Fantin must not be allowed to re-enter the market in Ontario. They are unworthy of their nationality," concluded Goad.

I couldn't have said it better myself.

Winchell lives in a mansion near Palm Beach where he enjoys the good life with all the toys — a Rolls Royce Corniche and a seventy-foot yacht named Night Hawk after a Vancouver stock he once controlled. The yacht has a full-time crew of two, a king-sized bed in the master stateroom, and a telex.

Winchell's flamboyant lifestyle has never flagged, even though in 1980 he left behind a bankrupt company and pleaded guilty to theft. He did not go to jail, but agreed to pay the largest individual fine ever levied in Canada — $1 million plus $600,000 in restitution for looting the treasury of International Chemalloy, which was listed on the Toronto Stock Exchange until 1974.

"He asked me to sit next to him in court in 1980," recalls Alistair Dow, formerly a *Toronto Star* investigative reporter. "He was shaking like a leaf. He was scared to death of jail. After it was all over and he was fined, we went to the Westbury Hotel to celebrate over a few drinks." Dow, now a freelance financial writer, worked for Winchell after 1980, writing newsletters for a mutual fund called FPS, short for Financial Planning Services, the same name as the Winchell-linked Amsterdam boiler room.

"Winchell was making a pisspot full of money even while the Chemalloy thing dragged on for five or six years [from 1974 to 1980]. He paid me $1,000 U.S. a week to write a weekly newsletter about FPS, which did well during the high-tech boom in the late 1970s. He would call me every Sunday night from New York to give me the FPS net asset values. I would put that into the newsletter, and apart from that he had nothing to do with what went into it. John King, his guy in the Bahamas, did most of it. But they were sloppy buggers who didn't know anything about administration. They were on their boats most of the time drinking. I started to get worried about these net asset value figures, and in a meeting I asked King for a copy of the portfolio, and he never sent me one. I went to a lawyer and he told me I had done nothing illegal, but if I was uncomfortable to drop it. I did."

Dow went down to New York to tell Winchell that he was quitting. At the time, Winchell was renting a mansion on Long Island Sound next door to Charles Lindberg's widow. "I told him I had bad vibes, there was no portfolio, and I said I quit. He said, 'I understand.' We had a few drinks and went to dinner."

The Winchell brothers immigrated to Canada from Ohio with their mother, who married a wealthy Canadian tire magnate. David Winchell married Irene Orpen, whose father Fred owned the Dufferin racetrack in Toronto. The couple have lived apart for several years but remain friendly. A huge man with huge appetites, Winchell lives life to the fullest and drinks Johnny Walker neat. He is a great raconteur and has an eye for the ladies. He reportedly had a lengthy friendship in New York City with beautiful red-headed movie star, Rhonda Fleming, who met him in an elevator in the posh Waldorf Towers where they both lived.

David Winchell's younger brother Luther is married to Susie Walwyn, whose father J.F. Walwyn founded the Walwyn Stodgell brokerage firm in Toronto. Luther promoted a company called Magicuts, which recently signed a deal with The Bay, Woolco, and other department stores to install dozens of its franchised haircutting shops. He now lives in Toronto.

David Winchell began his stock-market career as a phone clerk on the floor of the Toronto Stock Exchange. Luther worked as a salesman for Irving Kott. By the early 1960s, David felt his education was complete and decided to graduate from selling shares to other people to owning shares himself. He bought a shell company called Chemalloy Minerals Inc. from a prospector. Its only assets were claims at

Bernic Lake in eastern Manitoba for a mine which contained tantalum, a corrosion-resistant metal used in the manufacture of computers, jet-engine components, and nuclear reactors. A mine had been sunk years before to recover other minerals but was under several feet of water. Winchell could not put the mine into production without a great deal of money. So, in the well-worn tradition of many stock promoters, Winchell went about the business of finding cash.

In 1966 he approached one of Canada's most important investors, the late Jack Pullman. Cited as a courier for the mob, Pullman left the U.S. to become a Canadian citizen and set up many businesses in Canada and the Caribbean. Pullman was an important person to court because he could summon a great deal of buying power to support a stock promotion. He also knew everybody who was anybody.

Winchell went to Monte Carlo, where Pullman lived part time, to tap the money men. There Pullman introduced him to a U.S. stock promoter named Charlie Beigel. Beigel and another American stock promoter, Richard Chadwick "Pistol Dick" Pistell, agreed to pay $6 million for a 60 percent interest in Chemalloy's subsidiary, called Tantalum Mining Corp., which owned the Manitoba claims. Such financial wherewithal meant Chemalloy was big enough to become listed on the prestigious Toronto Stock Exchange. But the money from Beigel and Pistell never came through, and the parties ended up feuding in court.

After that, the stock was kited, promoters' parlance for boosting prices by fanning speculation. The stock soared following hype about five discoveries of cesium ("a wonder metal") and huge sales to the USSR and China. These sales never took place. Winchell also added credibility to Chemalloy, now called International Chemalloy, by getting such blue-ribbon directors as Charles A. Sullivan, special assistant to U.S. Treasury secretaries Douglas Dillon and Henry Fowler.

Winchell's flamboyant style paid off as well. He lived high

on the hog while promoting, staying in the Presidential suite of Geneva's largest hotel and hiring entire orchestras and dancers to entertain clients all night long. The stock hit five dollars and then began falling. Pullman made money as it fell by selling short (betting that the stock will go down in price), but others, such as Toronto real estate tycoon Angelo Del Zotto, chairman of Tridel Enterprises Inc., hung on and lost their proverbial shirts.

By August 1974 things were desperate. Winchell's brokers threatened to dump his stock because its price had collapsed and he owed them money. He had to come up with $600,000. On August 29 he had his company borrow $600,000 from the New York company using a Chemalloy subsidiary as collateral. Then he paid the money to his personal company. Two months later he borrowed another $1.4 million from a Liechtenstein company and used the same collateral again. "The lender was impressed with the speed with which Winchell got documentation for the loan. Little did he know that it wasn't due to efficiency but due to the fact that it was exactly the same transaction that had already been done," says a lawyer who was close to events.

Throughout the summer of 1974, Winchell was desperately trying to prop up the stock's price, but by September it had collapsed to eighty cents. Brokers unceremoniously dumped stock by the boatload because owners could not immediately repay loans against the stock. In an effort to stop the fall, Chemalloy announced plans to sell $15 million of tantalum to Japanese investors. This pie in the sky brought in the regulators. Trading was halted, and an investigation was announced by the Ontario Securities Commission. In January 1975 Winchell sold half of his shares; in February, an unhappy Angelo Del Zotto called in loans he had made to the company. They could not be paid, and the insolvent Chemalloy was pushed into bankruptcy.

After a long investigation and bankruptcy tangle, in December 1977 the Ontario Securities Commission charged

David Winchell, Toronto lawyers Sam Ciglen (who was with Guy La Marche the day he was murdered) and Enver Hassim, as well as two others, with making and circulating false statements, and fraud and theft in connection with International Chemalloy. Hassim was Chemalloy's lawyer and Ciglen was its financial adviser. Charges against Hassim were stayed and those against Ciglen were dismissed. In 1980 Winchell pleaded guilty to "converting" the $600,000 for his own use, thus looting Chemalloy's treasury. He also pleaded guilty to having pledged half of Tantalum as collateral to two separate companies.

But during the investigation a number of other skeletons came out of the closet. Some of the findings "bore the well-known imprint of the financial mafia," according to a Swiss prosecutor involved in part of the case. A Swiss bank bought $8 million of Chemalloy convertible debentures, or Chemalloy IOUs bearing a rate of interest and convertible into common stock. The debentures were sold in two lots: $3-million worth in 1971 which could be converted by the owner into two million Chemalloy shares, averaging out to a per share cost of $1.50, and $5-million worth in 1972 to the Swiss bank, which were also convertible into two million shares for $2.50 each. It was only after bankruptcy trustees started rummaging through Chemalloy's records that they discovered that the Swiss bank, for instance, paid only $825,000 of the $5 million for the second lot of debentures. Then the Swiss bank sold the two million shares to the public on the open market for $4.20 each for a total of $8.4 million. Charges against Winchell concerning the debentures were stayed as part of his arrangement to plead guilty to theft. "We spent a fortune gathering the evidence for that and the crown stayed the charges," recalls Angelo Del Zotto's brother, Elvio. "We were pretty upset."

Winchell easily wrote a check in 1980 for his $1.6 million fine. Police believe he left the next day for Amsterdam, where he spent a few weeks getting a boiler room organized, before heading back to his Florida estate. But one of Winchell's fatal mistakes may have been to upset one of his long-standing business partners, Fred Otash, a former U.S. Marine and policeman from Los Angeles who lost his police license for being involved in horse-race fixing. Otash, now a private eye, has gone to police officials with information about Winchell's role in the Amsterdam swindle. "He screwed me and I'm going to screw him. Winchell was behind the operations. I was on the board of directors of a bunch of his companies, and I can prove it," says Otash.

We will see whether he can.

11/Bit Players

Guy La Marche may have been the master of the telephone, but the master of the tout sheet is Canadian Peter Jefferey. He loves to be called "Pete the Pen" and considers himself the slickest newsletter writer in the business. Employing top-notch researchers and quoting from the classics, Jefferey considers his newsletters works of art, and himself an artist. Although he is a disciplined wordsmith who meets any deadline, he has often been undisciplined, gambling and drinking too much. He lived in Amsterdam off and on, but mostly on, for three years until the party ended in May 1986.

Jefferey was born in 1929, grew up in Toronto, and worked for various Canadian media outlets such as the *Globe and Mail* and the CBC. Among aliases he has used are Peter Jeffries, Peter Turner, or Mr. Ritter. In July 1968, he paid $101,515 in back taxes and a $2,500 fine for late payment after Canadian tax officials took him to task. Before that, in 1963, he ran afoul of Washington's Securities and Exchange Commission over statements in one of their "Dynamic Letter" publications. Its registration as an advisory letter was revoked.

But his creative writing activities are only a lucrative sideline and his real fortunes may have been made, and lost, by setting up mutual funds and trust companies in tax havens. He sold mutual funds to Nova Scotians, then to Britons, then the money flowed into an offshore insurance company for tax purposes and was, in turn, invested in companies set up by or under Jefferey's influence.

His vehicle for these maneuvers was Guardian Trust Co. Ltd. in the Bahamas, also used by Colombia cocaine dealer, Carlos Lehder Rivas, "Jefferey was afraid of Carlos Lehder," says Bakker who interviewed him in 1987. "Jefferey told me he found out only later how dangerous these people were. He said he had done his affairs through the same financial institution as Lehder and Jefferey feared they felt he knew too much."

Police sources say Jefferey left his white stucco Nassau mansion hurriedly in 1983 because of the impending liquidation of Guardian Trust which went bust in May 1984 with some $15 million in assets on the books. What followed was a police investigation which determined, as did a Royal Commission Report in the Bahamas in 1984, that Guardian's purpose was to launder drug money for Rivas. Indications are that Jefferey also used Guardian to carry out some of his own transactions with clients' money.

Rivas was using Guardian to launder money in a variation of the old money-laundering routine of Meyer Lansky: dirty cash from drug deals is deposited into an offshore trust company, mutual fund, or bank, then lent back to drug dealers. Clean deposits are also made to the institution. Then the assets of the trust company are siphoned off by lending money to drug dealers or other associates who will never repay their loans. For a while, interest on deposits are paid but the company is being slowly looted.

Jefferey is believed to have started another mutual fund in Britain in 1985. He left under a cloud for Amsterdam, and is now in Spain involved with other Canadian-operated boiler rooms. He has a live-in girlfriend whom he met in Florida, an American beauty named Laura Brandeis. She has a major influence on him and has convinced him to stop drinking and to eat health foods. The two lived in a splendid Amsterdam apartment and were frequent patrons of l'Europe Hotel where the chef prepared a special seafood salad named after Jefferey from a recipe created by Brandeis. Wherever he was, she was. "She sits there silently like a cat. She's dangerous," says Bakker.

While police in the Bahamas and Britain continue to try to unravel Pete the Pen's tangled mutual fund affairs, van Apeldoorn has enlisted help from Swiss authorities concerning the bankrupted Amsterdam boiler rooms of Tower Securities and United Consultants. Van Apeldoorn claims that millions of dollars were funneled from these Dutch operations to Panama and back to Swiss bank accounts. In spring 1987, van Apeldoorn filed complaints in Switzerland against Tower and in February 1988 the Swiss police arrested and jailed Tower's Swiss trustee, David D'Albis, and agreed to freeze $6 million worth of deposits in two bank accounts while a criminal investigation into possible fraud proceeded in Switzerland.

The Swiss are also being pressured to do something about those behind Tower and United because one of their victims is a well-connected Saudi Arabian businessman named El-Anjou, who lost $14 million buying some of their stocks. He has been lobbying members of the powerful Saudi royal family and pressure has been placed on the Swiss to investigate these Canadians. El-Anjou's lawyers filed a criminal complaint in Geneva and took action in Saudi Arabia too. His executive assistant in Saudi Arabia, who bought stock from the boiler rooms on his behalf, has been jailed ever since in a Saudi prison.

The first directors in Amsterdam of Tower Securities were Herb West, Steve Polon, and Sollie Kaplan. Herb West was born in the U.S. in 1928 and Polon was born in about 1917 in Poland. Indications are that they may share a piece of the action, but are surrogates for considerably larger, more well-heeled, but unknown, entities. (The second set of directors who took over Tower's operations toward the dying days were also Canadians: Harvey Roth, Al Lindzon, and Lloyd "Butch" Caplan.)

West is a fast-talking salesman who graduated from selling stocks to peddling diamonds and back again. In the early 1970s, his brokerage firm, Herbert West & Co. Securities Ltd., closed following a probe by the Ontario Securities Commission. A diamond peddling outfit he was part of, International Diamond Merchants, was shut down in the late 1970s by the RCMP. He was charged, along with his brother Phil West and others allegedly involved in Amsterdam boiler rooms such as Gordon Resnick. Herb's charges were dismissed, while his brother, Phil West, went to jail for fraud, along with others. (Phil West in spring 1988, voluntarily went from Toronto to Syracuse, New York, to plead not guilty to charges of mail and wire fraud laid by U.S. postal authorities concerning the selling of a hair tonic to cure baldness.) Polon, who still speaks English slowly with a thick accent, owns a silver Rolls Royce and lives like a king, commuting between two posh Toronto apartments. He has never been charged or convicted of any crimes.

The last three directors of Tower — Caplan, Roth, and Lindzon — cooperated with Swiss police and in affidavits said they were acting on behalf of a company called Gardina Overseas Corp. in Panama. "They said they do not know who owns Gardina and it may be impossible to find out too," says van Apeldoorn. The Dutch would like the Swiss authorities to place the onus of showing where the money came from on the owner of the two bank accounts. Van Apeldoorn says the Dutch boiler rooms stripped themselves of cash by buying the shares from Panamanian companies at a high price and selling them to investors at a lower price. The Panamanian proceeds were then funneled to Swiss bank accounts.

12/THE END OF THE TRAIL

The three Dutchmen — Koers, van Apeldoorn, and Casander — and a handful of others continue to chip away at the perpetrators of the boiler-room swindles. But they are running out of time and money. With criminal investigations and civil suits launched in several countries, only Barney Altwerger's money has been snagged, along with roughly $2 million. No more money has been found and the probes continue to be plagued with delays, red tape, and even bickering.

Koers made a secret trip in late 1987 to visit with Canadian police and extradition officials who promised help. Paradoxically, the best way Kott, Hussain, or Bonn can be convicted in Holland is to get them criminally charged here in Canada. Nothing so far has happened.

"The reason I have not formally charged Hussain and Kott," Koers explains, "was because of some trouble I have with the Montreal RCMP. They promised me that in early 1988 there would be some searches of Kott's businesses and homes. That was canceled and another date canceled. At this moment, I may prepare a letter for the government of Canada to point out my opinion about this kind of operation. The problem is, I guess, the members of the RCMP have some trouble formulating a request for a search warrant. But our opinion is that we have given them enough material to start a conspiracy case against Kott and others. But they have to prepare a document themselves for the search and to ask the judge for a search warrant. And the more weeks I have to wait, the older my case becomes. There is a statute of limitations in the European treaty in terms of criminal charges and, like your Charter of Rights, a matter must be dealt with in a reasonable time."

The same problems plague van Apeldoorn and Casander in Luxembourg and Switzerland. "Van Apeldoorn has some troubles in Luxembourg and the government has refused, not officially, but is very slow to help us," says Koers. "I sent them a request two years ago, a request for mutual assistance. Until today, they have not even answered formally whether they will help or not. I have the same problems with my criminal investigation in Luxembourg. My opinion is, at Alya we can find some evidence. But the longer the delay the greater the chance there won't be evidence and everything will be destroyed. We need the help of these countries because a lot of the money flowed from the Netherlands to Luxembourg or Switzerland and so did share certificates."

Van Apeldoorn has launched his criminal case against Tower Securities, and an investigation is under way. Casander, meanwhile, must now go over all the shareholders lists from Barney Altwerger's operation to determine who will get how much money and for what. The big fish Koers and the Dutch police are after is Irving David Kott. To this end, they have been feeding Canadian authorities with all of the evidence they have garnered in their effort to link Kott to First Commerce Securities. Hopes are that a Canadian conspiracy charge of some sort may eventually be laid because extradition may be impossible. Searches in the Bahamas and Bermuda yielded splendid evidence of a connection, as has more evidence gathered in Europe and contained in Koers's files.

Koers figures he has until the end of 1989 at the latest to put a case before the Dutch courts, or he will have to drop the whole matter. After our interview he said to me plaintively, "This is a tremendous scandal with a lot of people deliberately damaged financially. You can say I'm naive, but nevertheless these people have a responsibility to make that good. I want to meet Mr. Kott. He has done some very wrong things, and I want to convince him to make them right. But I know that may never happen."

In May 1988 van Apeldoorn stopped over in Canada on his way to Japan. He went to Montreal, Toronto, and Vancouver in a last-ditch attempt to meet and confront Kott, Hussain, and Nazerali. He did it at his own expense because the public well is nearly dry. "I went to Janus in Montreal and Electra told me to call back later that day because Mr. Kott was in meetings. I called twice then I gave up. She told me Mr. Hussain was no longer with Janus so I called him at home and his son gave me a business number. I called it and it was a meat market in Montreal that had never heard of him. I finally got through to him and he was abrupt and not helpful at all. In Toronto, I saw two lawyers who did the legal work for Tower in Switzerland but they said it was not their problem as to what the firm did over there. They just did the legal work and had no knowledge of anything else. And I hope to see Mr. Nazerali who I understand is living with his father in Vancouver and just applied for Canadian citizenship."

He never got to see Kott, Hussain, or Nazerali.

II

The Stock Jockeys

13/THE COP

George Wool looks every inch a cop. Standing over six feet, he has a deep cleft in his chin and a nose that has been broken a handful of times. He is built like a linebacker and looks younger than his forty-seven years. Muscles bulge beneath his three-piece blue suit.

It's February 1988, and we are meeting at a Vancouver hotel over breakfast to talk about his earlier career as a RCMP officer. He has just been called to the bar as a lawyer. The night before he celebrated the occasion with a group of lawyers and cops he has worked with and he is slightly hung over. He orders coffee black, drinks lots of it, and describes his life.

While he was a Mountie, Wool was a hotshot, a white-collar crime specialist who traveled around the world investigating cases involving such people as notorious Chicago money launderer Jack Pullman and prominent victims such as British author Jeffrey Archer and King Hussein of Jordan.

To Wool and other observers, the Amsterdam boiler rooms were simply another Canadian swindle, albeit on an unprecedentedly large scale. For generations now, Canada has been a popular staging ground for white-collar crimes, financial frauds that involve an element of money laundering and stock-market manipulation. And just as the Canadians have set up shop in Amsterdam, so American criminals have come to Canada to do their dirty work. American fugitives and crooks establish operations in Canada to frustrate police and securities regulators by placing a border between them.

Canada is an excellent venue for crime, just as Amsterdam was. Criminals cash in on our good reputation and naivete. It has always been easy to flog shares in Canadian mining or oil stocks because of Canada's track record as a resource-rich country with great potential for future discoveries. But the world never realized that in many ways Canada is no better than Panama or any other banana republic where secrecy, and sleaziness, is for sale. Here, a more sophisticated version of the same game operates. Because of stupidity or a misguided laissez-faire philosophy, Canadian stock markets have allowed scoundrels to hide behind shell companies listed on their exchanges or to manipulate the price of shares artificially. Even when trouble is detected, little is done. The bad guys simply move to another Canadian stock market or country. It is capitalism's cancer and a national disgrace.

Wool came to Canada with his parents and brother in 1948 as refugees from Estonia. His real name is Juri Vool, but the immigration officer in Halifax found the family's names unpronounceable and changed them on documents. "That's how I became George. This was 1948 in Canada and we couldn't speak a word of English. We didn't know our names had been changed, more or less forever."

The four were sent by train to Vancouver, where his father worked in the lumber trade and his mother ran a rooming house. Wool grew up around the Vancouver area, finished high school, and joined the RCMP in 1961.

In the 1970s, Wool became involved in cleaning up Montreal, where unholy alliances between stock-market manipulators, stock exchange officials, and mobsters led to jail sentences and closures. Around this time, Irving Kott was charged and the brokerage firm, L.J. Forget, was shut down. Estimates at the time were that the Forget brokerage firm was responsible for half of the entire trading volume in Montreal. L.J. Forget's president, George McPhee, who linked Kott to an Amsterdam boiler room in a statement given to Dutch police, went to Bermuda, establishing a beachhead for a decade of offshore business activities.

Although Kott, Winchell, La Marche, Altwerger, and others stayed put in the east, a large number of stock-market promoters moved out west after the 1960s Toronto Stock Exchange scandal involving Windfall Oil and Mines Ltd. (Those revelations, about insider trading and illegal manipulations, led to jail sentences and a Royal Commission which, in turn, led to a securities act in Ontario in 1968.) The stock-market boys who moved west turned the already wild and woolly Vancouver Stock Exchange into a financial slum. It became the favorite haunt of the sleaziest promoters and hucksters from around the world and the scene of some gigantic scandals. Recently, American fraudsters have been moving in by the dozens to avoid the more stringent securities regulations south of the border. Once here they take over shell companies and flog junk stocks through so-called legitimate exchanges, mostly to Americans.

As an embarrassed Vancouver Stock Exchange tries to mop up the mess, the boys are turning their attention toward Alberta or the over-the-counter market in Toronto. The word is out among white-collar criminals, and Alberta has been getting two to three listing applications daily since early 1987, when the exchange became virtually deregulated. It is more than mere coincidence that many of the stocks flogged in Amsterdam are traded, and virtually all the perpetrators do business, on the Vancouver and Alberta stock exchanges. And it is more than mere coincidence that money laundering and mobsters are still involved behind the scenes.

George Wool was posted to Fort Smith in the Northwest Territories in 1966. There, of all places, he found more examples of white-collar crime and made his name in the force as a tough-minded cop.

Shortly after arriving in the north, Wool spotted an advertisement in the Yellowknife newspaper about a mutual fund registered in Panama. It smelled like a scam and he investigated. The case eventually took Wool all over Europe. Convictions followed and catapulted him into the so-called big time in Toronto and Montreal, where the sharpest criminals in the country operate.

The Panamanian mutual fund was called Allied Fund Capital Appreciation and claimed to be listed on the International Stock Exchange. As proof of this, its promoters, William ("Bud") and Cliff Bennett, told Wool that the exchange's prices were published in the prestigious *International Herald Tribune*. Sure enough they were. But nobody had heard of this International Stock Exchange. Saul Froomkin (now Bermuda's attorney general and then a crown prosecutor) joined Wool on the case and set off for Paris to track down the mysterious exchange.

In Paris he met with *International Herald Tribune* officials, who said they got the mutual fund's numbers from a stock distributor in Munich. Froomkin went to Munich, where the stock distributor said he got the information from a trustee in London, who said he got the prices every day in a phone call from a bank in Panama. The bank, owned by an impenetrable Liechtenstein anstalt (a company that need not disclose its ownership), had some $39 million on deposit, probably from sales in this stock.

"The bank consisted of two Americans in a small office, and I asked them where they got the information, and they said, 'We get a call every day from Miami,' " says Froomkin. What was so amazing was that such a chain of communication ended up in one of the most respected newspapers in the world, as well as in local ones like Yellowknife's *News of the North*. All the better to entice investors.

Bud and Cliff Bennett, the promoters of Allied Fund Capital Appreciation, got three and five years respectively in 1971 for false pretenses, a fraud which netted them only $1,500. But Froomkin and Wool suspected it was simply the tip of an iceberg and that millions have been bilked, mostly from Americans. "The Bennetts had the Yukon franchise, so to speak," says Froomkin. "Allied was small but had worldwide implications. The stock was floating all around the world after the early 1970s, when the stock market went into the sewer. They used some brilliant techniques. Ads would offer to swap stock for legitimate stocks and then culprits would disappear. The Bennetts had only been in Yellowknife one year. They weren't the brains. There were two U.S. guys behind it. Big fraudsters."

THE BIG STING

In 1971 Wool was posted to Toronto, where he became part of a brand new RCMP unit investigating stock-market manipulation. In his first year, he did the unit's first prosecution under the new Ontario securities act and then became involved in a series of cases which fell into the RCMP's lap one after another.

In 1971 RCMP squads in Toronto tapped the telephones of a number of people, including the offices of Stanley Bader, a loan shark, and those of lawyer Sam Ciglen, where Guy La Marche and Ciglen's son-in-law, Syd Rosen, also worked. In Montreal the RCMP was also monitoring the calls of Irving Kott and his brokerage firm as well as those of Montreal mobsters, Vincenzo Cotroni and Paolo Violi. It was later discovered that Cotroni was the godfather of the Montreal mob at the time; his successor was Violi.

Wiretaps are one of the most important tools the police have, but they are an expensive proposition. Installation is easy enough. Once a court has okayed a phone tap, a police team, disguised as telephone repairmen, can get access to a line by hooking into wires several blocks away. After it is installed, however, a wire tap eats up the time of fifteen to twenty people. There are three shifts daily, seven days a week.

Someone must be listening; typists must be on hand to transcribe the tapes regularly; and crown prosecutors and police must evaluate the findings regularly to determine what evidence, if any, has been obtained.

More often than not, wiretaps are inadmissible in court, but they provide leads essential to cracking a case. Police use incriminating information they overhear when they question players, who are sometimes persuaded to cooperate. Tapes are admissible in court only if one of the parties involved consents or if there is a judicial authorization. Even then, tapes must relate directly to the allegations police presented to the courts when they requested permission to place wiretaps. If, for instance, police have wiretaps in a murder case and overhear evidence of a massive fraud, they usually cannot use the fraud evidence in court.

Wool was involved in the many 1971 Toronto investigations of stock-market manipulation. While John Beer worked on the Somed Mines case against Irving Kott and Syd Rosen (described in chapter 7), Wool was tracking the efforts of Jack Pullman, Toronto lawyer Sam Ciglen, and Ciglen's stock promotion partner, Morris Black. That's when Beer discovered wiretaps which contained conversations about extortion payoffs being made by Rosen and Bader to Hamilton godfather Johnny "Pops" Papalia via Toronto mobster Sheldon "Sonny" Swartz. Papalia was using the names of Montreal gangsters Paolo Violi and Vincenzo Cotroni. Violi and Cotroni heard about it and wanted some of the money. The taps in Violi and Cotroni's offices showed that the mobsters were blackmailing boiler rooms in Montreal and Toronto and using their services at the same time. Like holding up an illegal poker game, it was a perfect crime because the victims couldn't complain to the police without incriminating themselves.

One of Rosen's associates, Stanley Bader, told police about the extortion and eventually testified that he made a payment of $300,000 in 1973 to Papalia and Swartz. The two told him that a contract to murder him had been put out by Cotroni and Violi, but they would "fix it" for a fee. By 1974, Bader thought there was no contract and he'd been the victim of a swindle perpetrated by Swartz. Papalia said he had been given $40,000 and Swartz pocketed the rest. Violi and Cotroni felt they were entitled to a share because their names had been involved. All four were convicted initially, but the appeal court judges ruled that Violi and Cotroni had been merely opportunistic and had not been part of the conspiracy to dupe Bader. They were acquitted years later. Along the way, the Mounties obtained evidence from wiretaps that Paolo Violi was also involved in manipulating the share prices of a company called Buffalo Oil & Gas Ltd., a stock listed on both the Toronto and Montreal exchanges. In this particular manipulation, Violi joined forces with a duplicitous duo of U.S. fugitives, James Danielson and Stephen Dinneen, who had operated for a couple of years on the fringes of Canada's financial world. Both were wanted in the United States by the police and by some of their enemies, who were concerned that Danielson and Dinneen might incriminate them if they were caught. Their concern was well justified because that is exactly what happened.

Conspiracy cases are almost impossible to prove in court without the cooperation of one of the conspirators. Wool and the Mounties desperately needed a turncoat to crack the Buffalo Oil caper. So they set up an undercover sting operation, with an officer posing as a crooked lawyer. He got in touch with James Danielson, met him in a sleazy hotel room to make a payoff, and then arrested him. "Danielson turned and talked like a duck's rear end," recalls Wool. "We only had a marginal case against him, but he turned and said, 'I'll tell you everything I know.' He wanted to become a Canadian version of Valachi in the U.S. That was his ego. He loved the attention and wrote a book about his experiences. He was difficult as hell to handle, his ego was ten miles high. But he provided the key pieces of evidence."

In 1972, with information from Danielson, some hundred RCMP officers raided the homes and offices of thirty-six brokers and mining promoters and eighteen company offices across Canada. The raid was part of a widespread sweep investigating the use of bribes to get brokers and floor traders to peddle and hike the prices of stocks. Danielson and Dinneen both testified against their Canadian accomplices in return for immunity from prosecution in Canada. However, both faced long jail terms in the United States. In December 1974, when he handed down sentences to Buffalo Oil conspirators, Mr. Justice Melvin L. Rothman called it a "systematic program of bribery and corruption of professional traders."

Danielson, who was forty in 1974, testified that Violi's accomplices asked him in 1972 to use bribery to "distribute" and illegally control the price of Buffalo Oil shares. Danielson said that he and his partner Stephen Dinneen worked only one week for the accused until they were fired. Danielson admitted that he "bribed" floor trader Robert Broadley by offering him a secret commission of 10 to 15 percent and that he knew it was illegal. "Everyone was doing it in those days. I don't believe the public gets a fair shake anywhere in Canada in this business. More than half the people I dealt with were crooked," he testified, adding that he had "promoted or distributed stock of more than a dozen issues here and in Vancouver."

Montreal mobster Paolo Violi was described as the conspiracy's "umpire," and Sessions Court Judge D. Reilly Watson called Violi the "essential personage in the conspiracy," but admitted that the proof was "to a great part circumstantial," permitting a view of "only the tip of the iceberg." During testimony, the judge said that Violi had described numerical entries in a notebook that showed stock prices as formulas for ice cream. "This is virtually an insult," said the judge.

Danielson's partner, Stephen Dinneen, a self-described

con-man in his fifties, also began to sing. He told the court he had "turned a new leaf and stopped lying." He admitted that in Canada he had used the alias Steven James and that he faced a ten-year prison sentence in the U.S. for fraud and embezzlement. Dinneen said he and Danielson were hired to get two-dollar shares up to five dollars by "creating a market" in return for $2,000 each and a 20 percent commission.

In four days during January 1972, the two managed to get the stock up to $3.30 a share before the partnership ended on January 31. On that day Dinneen was told, "The big man wants to see you." In court, he identified "the big man" as Paolo Violi, vice-president of Reggio Foods Ltd., a Montreal meat-processing firm owned by Vincenzo Cotroni. "He and his friends were in Buffalo [shares]," Violi had told Dinneen, "and he was there to see that they weren't going to get screwed around. He also told us to bring to him anybody that wanted market play." The next day, trading in Buffalo Oil stock was shut down, suspended by the Quebec Securities Commission because of the price jump and wiretap information about the manipulation.

Danielson testified for days at the Buffalo trial. He also blew the whistle on many other scams, including one in Vancouver in which he did deals with Robert "Bobby the Slick" Slichter and Alan Savage. (Both are still active in Vancouver as promoters or market makers.) With an ego as large as his bribes, Danielson boasted of dozens of manipulations on the Vancouver Exchange, but the one involving Pace Industries became the most celebrated and cost Slichter, Savage, and others their brokerage licenses.

Danielson's contacts and connections are detailed in an eye-opening book called *Under Protective Surveillance*, written in 1976 by Danielson under the *nom de plume* Marlis Fleming. According to the book, Danielson, who skipped $35,000 bail in the U.S. and fled to Canada, was an experienced crook in the States but learned some new tricks here. "The slow-witted are soon separated from their money. From 6:30 in the morning, Monday through Friday, it [the Vancouver Stock Exchange] is thronged with the fastest guns in the Western world," the book noted.

The book also talked about the Pace Industries manipulation and how Slichter was used to gather floor-trading intelligence and to execute buy and sell orders. Pace was eventually delisted as a result and the British Columbia Securities Commission booted Slichter out of the business. "To reform Slichter was doomed to failure," concluded the commission. But Slichter never left. He is still acting for himself or clients as a market maker in controversial deals in Vancouver, such as Technigen Corp. and ChoPP Computers.

"Danielson was a sonofabitch to deal with. A real demanding jerk," says Wool. He and Dinneen were kept in protective custody for months, hidden away from hired assassins who had been paid a great deal of money to silence them permanently. By 1976 both men had been relocated and given new identities, probably in the United States. The whole operation was so covert that the men were moved constantly from houses to motels, in and out of the province of Ontario. Security was so tight that other police forces, such as the Ontario Provincial Police and Metro Toronto Police, were not briefed about events.

During a one-month stay at a Toronto home, police women and men were coming and going in shifts on a regular basis, guarding Danielson and his family. A neighbor became concerned, when he saw so many people coming and going, that the house was being used as a bordello. So he called local police. They staked out the house and tapped the phones, without knowing what was up. Luckily, procedure dictates that forces must inform other forces about their plans. The RCMP were able to veto the raid, just in time to prevent Danielson and his police guards from being arrested by an ignorant, overenthusiastic local police force.

THE KING AND THEM

In the 1970s Danielson led the RCMP to another scam, this one involving a company called Jordesco Resources Ltd. and a Toronto lawyer named John Hargrave, who belongs to one of the city's blue-blooded families. The scheme began when Hargrave and Donald Smith, president of Jordesco, got a concession from King Hussein to drill for oil in Jordan. For years major oil companies had ignored Jordan, for all the right reasons — it had been left out of the geological sweepstakes, according to drilling and scientific data. But such scientific evidence didn't stop Hargrave from using a concession there as a promotion ploy. And King Hussein accommodated them by throwing a lavish party in Amman to celebrate the signing of the deal.

Jordesco never actually drilled, but plans were stalled while stock was unloaded by Hargrave at inflated prices onto an unsuspecting public. Along the way, Hargrave enticed many members of the Toronto police force into buying Jordesco's shares. He threw a gala party when the company finally became listed on the Vancouver Stock Exchange and chartered a jumbo jet to fly non-stop from Toronto to Vancouver for the celebration. Along for the ride were members of the police force and a contingent of Jordanians.

During the months of promotion, Hargrave and his accomplices pocketed profits as the stock soared. Danielson and Dinneen were busy forcing prices upwards. But the bubble burst when Arab investors became suspicious. Jordesco had not done any drilling in Jordan, but money raised from share sales for exploration had all but disappeared from company coffers. The RCMP received a complaint via Interpol, and Danielson filled in the details.

The Arabs wanted swift and exacting punishment. For a while some of the perpetrators were afraid that the Jordanians had hired hit men to bump them off. Even more annoying to the Arabs, however, was that a mysterious "Mr. Boni" from

New York had accompanied the group to Amman and participated in the festivities. "Boni and the others were literally taken through the streets of Amman in Cadillacs and wined and dined," says Wool. "Boni was sitting there eating grapes and sitting to the right of Jordan's minister of resources who asked him at one point where he was from. He replied he was an American. They persisted, intrigued as to his nationality, and he said he was Italian."

When the party was over, the Arabs were furious to learn that Boni was Jewish. They wanted to kill him. That was the height of scandal. The Arabs didn't mind losing face or millions of dollars. But a Jew in the Palace? That was too much. The whole incident tumbled into the diplomatic arena, and Canada was severely chastised by Hussein and his cabinet. Hargrave went to prison, Smith was charged but acquitted, and Mr. Boni was never charged.

During the trial, some sensational testimony pointed to a Toronto police scandal. Hargrave paid a policeman bribes in the form of shares of Jordesco, then used him to rough up unhappy shareholders and prevent investors from complaining to the authorities. Even more interesting was the venue for the payoffs. Hargrave met the policeman in the men's room of the Bacchus bar, where he handed him stock certificates as they stood at the urinals.

JEFFREY ARCHER'S INSPIRATION

In 1975 Wool was sent abroad once more, this time to London to investigate another phony Canadian stock deal called Aquablast Resources Ltd. Wool was tipped off that Aquablast, listed on the Montreal Exchange, was a complete fraud. It became his priority after Stanley Bader linked it to organized crime through notorious money launderer Jack Pullman.

Aquablast, a modest company located in a Toronto suburb,

originally sold a brick-cleaning process that blasted a building with water under high pressure. Like other Canadian companies, it languished on the stock exchange, was bought out, and became a vehicle for stock-market manipulation. But it had no sex appeal, so its promoters announced that Aquablast had picked up the world rights to a wonder-widget known as the Wyman Idler Adjuster Valve. The stock ran up as high as eight dollars a share before collapsing to pennies. Since most of the victims were in Europe, Wool set off to meet some of them and build his case. His efforts resulted in some convictions, but they also derailed one of Britain's most promising political careers.

It is a beautiful spring day in London in 1988. Jeffrey Archer, a handsome and gregarious man, meets me for an interview in the pink and green splendor of the Savoy Hotel. His chauffeur waits to take him to Cambridge, some two hours away, where his wife, a Cambridge professor, and his children live. Archer lives during the week in a posh flat on the Embankment near the Houses of Parliament and commutes home on weekends. He writes most days between 5 a.m. and 8:30 a.m. "so I can do my politics." He is an unpaid adviser and a confidant to British Prime Minister Margaret Thatcher.

In 1987 Archer was plunged into controversy as the plaintiff in a sensational libel case involving one of London's raciest tabloids and a prostitute. Archer sued following a story in the newspaper about how he had given the prostitute £2,000. After days of titillating testimony, the jury agreed that the woman had lied in order to sell her story to the newspaper. The jury awarded Archer £500,000. "I was naive. It seems to be a failing of mine, but I think I have finally learnt my lesson after this latest trial," he now says. Archer was also naive in 1975. He was left penniless by a handful of Canadian swindlers who duped him out of his entire fortune. It was a wrenching experience, which not only robbed him of wealth, but also cost him his political career as a Member of Parliament and his social standing. He found himself virtually unemployable with enormous debts. "I resigned my seat and was down £427,000. With an income of £11,000, it would have taken me 300 years to repay. I couldn't get a job because no one would hire someone with such debts. So I decided to write a book. It took me eighteen months because I'd never written a thing in my life before."

The book was titled *Not a Penny More, Not a Penny Less* and was a novel based on his own experiences. The dedication reads "To Mary and the Fat Men," a reference to his wife and two sons who were toddlers at the time, "little tubby things that I couldn't afford to feed." The crime described in *Not a Penny* was the same he fell victim to, but the outcomes were different. Archer's four protagonist-victims got their pound of flesh by swindling the swindler. That did not happen to Archer in the Aquablast affair. "It was a travesty what happened, really. I came to Canada to testify against the culprits, but they got off completely or got off with very light sentences or something. I attended every single minute of the trial. But I was very disappointed."

The only compensation was that *Not a Penny* did very well which encouraged him to continue to write. Two books later, Archer hit paydirt with the publication of *Kane and Abel.* "I eventually made £3 million out of *Not a Penny More*, but only after *Kane and Abel* made me a millionaire overnight and they republished all my books. Those successes allowed me to pay everyone I owed money to. Every single penny. It took me seven years and three months to do that. Then I celebrated by buying a BMW 320 Si."

Archer's misfortunes began just after Sergeant George Wool checked into a cheap London hotel back in 1975 and called him to arrange a meeting to talk about Aquablast. Hours later Archer tendered his resignation to his party whip. "I did not actually resign because there was to be an election in four weeks. I simply agreed that I would not stand for re-election," he says.

Archer learned for the first time from Wool that he had been duped by seasoned criminals. Archer told Wool how he, as a thirty-three-year-old rookie Member of Parliament was independently wealthy from a sizable nest egg he had accumulated after years of running his own film production and public relations firms. While in office, he met Michael Altman, vice-president of the First National Bank of Boston, who introduced him to Aquablast, the Wyman Valve, and a line of credit to buy lots of stock.

Archer was sucked in by Aquablast's promoters, who boasted that the Wyman Valve would revolutionize the car business. The scam was that the perpetrators controlled virtually all of Aquablast shares from the beginning. Archer and others bought stock on the advice of other dupes, like Altman, who put out the word to their friends, associates, and clients. As the stock rose in price, the perpetrators unloaded their shares to Archer and others and promoted its great future. When the bubble finally burst, the stock collapsed to cents, and victims were left holding the bag, which was full of the swindlers' stock they had purchased.

Archer and the others kept buying because Altman repeated the promoters' lies about Aquablast's prospects. They were told that the Wyman Valve was a gadget which, when placed in any car, would all but eliminate pollution. In fact, the valve had been invented in 1923 by a German con-man named Kurt Wyman and actually increased the emission of dangerous gases. The scam had gone around before, in the 1920s, but most people had forgotten about it. And Archer was too young to know.

"I felt as vice-president of a Boston bank, Altman would be of a pedigree acceptable to do deals with. I believed him. I was told the German police used the Wyman Valve on their cars, and the Germans would be putting it on their cars. I figured it was just a matter of time before New York followed suit. It looked like a winner."

Behind the scenes were some interesting characters. There

was Jack Pullman and Manny Silverman, Sy Stewart (son of Las Vegas founder Bugsy Siegel), and Jerry Sperling, a notorious Monaco promoter tied to David Winchell and Chemalloy. Allegations are that the promoters planted the story with Altman and others, who then spread the word; manipulated the stock upward through wash trading, which attracted even more attention; then recruited a former Chrysler executive who endorsed the valve. This was key to Archer's commitment. "I met with Manny Silverman once at a club. He said they were employing some man from Chrysler to be the chairman of the company," says Archer. "That reinforced its credibility."

Unfortunately, Archer not only staked all of his assets on Aquablast, but borrowed against them to buy the stock. If he had sold before the scam was up, he would have become a rich man. He didn't. "I overinvested. I would have made a fortune as the stock soared. But they kept reinforcing the fact I should stay on for even greater profits. I later learned that it was in order to get the price up so they could unload their own shares along the way before the truth was discovered."

Archer eventually came to Toronto and testified as a crown witness in 1977. Altman fled Britain after Wool began his investigation and was never charged. Sperling died before the trial began. Archer's testimony in Toronto was critical to the crown's case. But Wool remembers that Pullman's lawyer, J.J. Robinette, declined to cross-examine him. It was an unusual move for a defense attorney to leave crown evidence on the record without rebuttal. Wool asked why. "I went up to Robinette and asked him why he didn't take on Archer. Robinette said that when you get someone on the stand who is so brilliant and so well spoken you don't tangle with him because he'll simply destroy the defense."

Archer says he was hoping for a cross-examination. "Robinette had a mind like a razor, and I was hoping he would take me on. I was right, had been a victim, and I wanted to make that point to the jury. Robinette knew he had to get me out of the mind of that jury. So he got me out of the stand. The next witness after me was some poor fellow who simply fell to pieces and was totally inarticulate. By lunchtime, the jury had completely forgotten about my testimony."

Pullman was acquitted. Silverman testified as a crown witness in return for immunity from prosecution, and two of Aquablast's officers, who also testified against Pullman, received relatively light sentences. The bank manager, Michael Altman, was also punished. He fled Britain and now ekes out a meager existence as a copywriter in Jerusalem. Archer landed firmly on his feet, once again wealthy and back in politics in an unelected capacity. "My attitude is when you have made a fool of yourself or done something wrong, you can curse for about three minutes, and then you must get on with things. There is nothing to be gained by looking over your shoulder. Take Altman, living in Israel, an innocent man. He should have stood up and apologized and taken his punishment. Instead, he just disappeared below the stones. Very sad."

THE GODFATHER

Wool's investigation into Aquablast led him to Jack Pullman and to Monaco and Switzerland, where Pullman kept two homes and lived with his attractive Swiss wife. Pullman had been a lifelong friend of Mafia money launderer Meyer Lansky. The two men had been bootleggers in Chicago during Prohibition and, some reports say, had spent time in jail together. Pullman was arrested in 1931 and served six months of a fifteen-month sentence for bootlegging. But, like Lansky, he was too presentable and too intelligent for a lifetime of street crimes. So he turned to white-collar scams.

John Pullman immigrated to Chicago from Russia as a young man. But he left his adopted country for Canada in 1949, renounced his American citizenship, and became a

Canadian as soon as he qualified in 1954. He realized what many have since, that the ultimate citizenship of convenience for a white-collar criminal is Canadian citizenship. Canadians enjoy the right of free, and unrecorded, access to the United States. They can slip across the border and return with suitcases full of cash or stock certificates. They also enjoy an enhanced status in the United Kingdom and the Commonwealth. This is particularly important because mobsters and money launderers use their Canadian contacts to set up secrecy and tax havens as well as gambling casinos in the Caribbean. Canadians have a vast network of contacts and businesses there. During Prohibition, liquor made on the islands was often routed through Canada's east coast on its way to New York or Chicago speakeasies. And Canadian banks enjoy the lion's share of island business.

There is another very good reason why a criminal might want to become a Canadian citizen. If they set it up right, including spending more than 181 days outside the country, Canadians are taxed only on their Canadian earnings. Americans must pay tax on their worldwide income. Even when Americans live abroad permanently and earn all their income outside the U.S., they must still file an annual income tax return. If they earn money and pay taxes in, for instance, Canada, the U.S. credits them for Canadian taxes paid, but if the Canadian taxes are lower, they must pay the difference between what was paid in Canada and what would have been paid in the U.S. (even if it is all to do with strictly Canadian income.) To avoid people renouncing their citizenship just to get around these rules, the U.S. tax laws may apply for ten years after the date of renunciation of U.S. citizenship, if tax officials have reason to believe that the renunciation was made for tax evasion purposes.

Canadian citizenship also insulates criminals from extradition because Ottawa has fewer extradition treaties with other countries than the U.S. does. For instance, the Dutch warrants outstanding for Irving Kott and the others do not apply in

Canada but are in force in the States as well as in most other countries.

Soon after he arrived in Toronto in 1949, Pullman set up a mortgage and insurance business. He made many contacts and became a mentor and a partner to a generation of Canadian criminals. They became his fronts in schemes that brought casinos, hotels, and cash to the Bahamas. Canadians led the way in developing most of the Caribbean, now the world's dirty-money mecca. But Canada was just one beachhead for the peripatetic Pullman. He left his Toronto business and apartment behind in 1969 and moved, more or less permanently, to Lausanne and Monaco.

There, on the beach in his green-and-white-striped tent, he held court for the likes of David Winchell (alleged owner of boiler rooms in Amsterdam and Switzerland), Allen Manus (who pleaded guilty to manipulating the stock market price of Consumers Distributing shares in the early 1980s), and the late Lou Chesler (a colorful Canadian from Belleville, Ontario, who obtained the first gambling license in the Bahamas in the 1950s, then invited Manus and various mobsters to participate).

U.S. attorney Robert Morgenthau of New York charged Pullman in 1969 with being a "courier for years for the mob" who "now handles their investments in Swiss bank accounts." Pullman called Morgenthau "a liar" and told the *Wall Street Journal*, "I never carried five cents for anybody except myself." He said he dealt with Swiss bank accounts only for his own benefit. "People come to see me in Switzerland and ask what bank to put their money in, and since I'm familiar with Swiss banks, I tell them. But I haven't made deposits for others."

According to George Wool, "Pullman was in charge of Canada, and anyone who wanted to run a crooked deal here had to get his permission. You know, you had to pay him off and involve him in the deal. Pullman had great Swiss contacts, and he could bring immediate buying power to any stock manipulation. It was money laundering for the mob and for Europeans. German professionals were hiding cash away for tax reasons and depositing it with brokers and banks in Switzerland. Pullman had arrangements with these brokers and banks, and he would get the brokers to buy Canadian stocks with some of the funds under their control. Those stocks would be run out of Toronto or Montreal or Vancouver and involved phony mining claims from up north, where nobody could double-check. Guys would go to Pullman to get his blessing for a manipulation. He would supply buying power in return for a slice."

Some of the money was dirty money, mob money, and Pullman provided a perfect money-laundering vehicle. The European deposits were converted into Canadian stock, which was manipulated on Canadian stock exchanges until it was high enough to sell off to the unsuspecting public. It was money laundering married to capital gains.

Pullman said in press reports that he was a victim of guilt by association. He also denied that he was an associate of Meyer Lansky. He said he had met Lansky and other mobsters while awaiting a divorce in Las Vegas two decades before. "When you're in Vegas for six weeks, you meet casino owners and their associates. So because of that, and because I played cards with various characters" he claimed he had been unfairly linked to the mob.

Pullman also had accounts in the mob-related International Credit Bank of Geneva in Switzerland and he used to solicit business for it in return for a one percent finder's fee. The bank was eventually shut down for fraud. He had another account with the Exchange and Investment Bank, also of Geneva, which was owned by two Americans who, along with Pullman, were implicated in 1974 in the first insider-trading case in the United States.

These two Americans were also officers of a bra manufacturer called Exquisite Form Industries. The company had purchased control of Corporation of Americas, another fashion business, and in 1968 Exquisite Form decided to buy all the shares of Corporation of Americas it didn't already own. Bogus rumors were floated by persons unknown that the stock was all but worthless. The various remaining shareholders, which included the Catholic Archdiocese of Detroit, cashed in their shares for up to $1.25 each. Most of these were snapped up by a Florida banker for about $60,000. He resold them to Pullman, who flipped them back to Exquisite Form six months later for $375,000. In 1974, when the case came to trial, a Miami federal judge ruled that Pullman had bought the shares on inside information that Exquisite Form wanted them badly, then ordered Pullman to return his $315,000 profit to the shareholders who had sold their shares. He never did.

Pullman showed his cleverness by becoming a Canadian expatriate living in Europe. "Pullman sits out grand jury subpoena powers in Lausanne, Switzerland. He is even further insulated from the government's inquisition by the fact that he renounced his U.S. citizenship and became a Canadian citizen," said a *Wall Street Journal* news story in 1975. "Pullman is believed to be the banking expert for mobsters, specializing in hiding their dirty money in coded Swiss bank accounts and then processing it in the form of loans back to the mobsters so that it comes out clean. The funds are then invested in legitimate business enterprises and real estate holdings, providing the gangsters with untainted income."

Wool arrested Pullman in the Aquablast case in 1975 as he was checking into the posh Sutton Place Hotel. He was charged with participating in the $5-million Aquablast international stock fraud, with defrauding Aquablast itself of $1.6 million, and with a $100,000 fraud in connection with the purchase of the Wyman Idler Adjuster Valve. But within hours of his arrest, he wrote out a personal check to cover his $250,000 bail. Then he hired Canada's best lawyer, J.J. Robinette, to defend him. A year later, Pullman was acquitted of all charges, even though two others pleaded guilty and two more cooperated as crown witnesses. He was also acquitted of income tax evasion charges in Canada several years later.

After the Aquablast case, Pullman told associates that he would not return to the U.S. to testify because he feared he would be jailed if he didn't disclose the identities of Swiss bank account holders. If he did disclose them, he added, he would be jailed in Switzerland.

Pullman was kicked out of Monaco after the Aquablast charges were laid. Wool was also able to penetrate Swiss officialdom for the first time ever by any country which does not have a mutual assistance treaty with the Swiss. Wool accidentally divided and conquered the Swiss legal front. He obtained a search warrant from a judge in Lausanne, a French canton, one of the dozens of counties in Switzerland. He presented the document to Ernest Hieber, the man in charge of the suspected bank, which was in a German canton, where Pullman kept his safety deposit box and other assets.

"I went to see Hieber and he turned me away, saying that the judge had no authority to order him to divulge information about banking clients," says Wool. "I went back to the French judge who became furious, and he called the local chief of police. The cop who came with me the second time was also French, and he arrested Hieber then and there. He said to the banker, 'You are under arrest and cannot go anywhere out of your office until you give Mr. Wool every single piece of information he desires.' The cop and the judge were furious. They were French, and Hieber was pulling a stunt because he was in a canton where Germans were in control. It was a rivalry thing. I couldn't believe that Hieber had absolutely no rights whatsoever. But he cooperated and we even became friends after that. He told me how the scams worked."

The result was that in 1975 Wool gained access to Pullman's safety deposit box. In keeping with rules of gathering evidence in other jurisdictions, Wool had French, German, and Swiss police present when he opened it. Inside was a king's ransom. "It was about one cubic foot in size. It was crammed full of high-calibre securities, blue-chip New York and London stocks, and U.S. government bonds. We counted all of it. I can't remember the figure, but it was tens of millions of dollars' worth."

There was probably more money somewhere, but it was never found. Wool interviewed Pullman extensively in Europe and in Canada. The two got along very well, and Pullman would pour tea or drinks for the policeman during his visits. Pullman's homes were magnificent, with Dalis and Picassos hanging on the walls and luxurious furnishings everywhere. He was always immaculately tailored and spoke with a faint Russian accent. He was always polite to the police, and rarely lost his cool, but he never said anything of substance.

The secret of Pullman's success was his ability to keep a low profile. So it is hardly surprising that when he was featured in a 1977 CBC documentary about the mob called "Connections," produced by Jim Dubro and Bill Macadam, he reacted with uncharacteristic anger. He sued over two extracts that linked him to Lansky and money laundering for the mob. The program also said that after his acquittal in the Aquablast affair Pullman began to invest millions of dollars in Canadian real estate, hinting it was mob money. The lawsuit claimed millions in damages, but was dropped one month later. Pullman died in Toronto in 1982. So did his secrets.

ARCTIC ANTICS

In 1977 George Wool was sent back up north to set up a commercial-crime unit, this time in the Yukon. During his five-year stay, he had a field day. The place was riddled with economic crimes, from corruption to bribery and influence peddling. As he puts it, "The Arctic is like a Third World country. Lots of scams are run through there, like mining claims and stuff, because the area is too remote to double-check things. And at that time, the federal government was just pouring millions of dollars into an empty pit, and I wasn't there long before I got caught up in an investigation involving the commissioner of the Yukon himself, Arthur Pearson, who had been running stock deals through the north for years."

Pearson received his Privy Council appointment as Commissioner of Yukon Territory in 1976. In 1978 Wool charged Pearson with forging mining claims that were used and promoted by a Vancouver Stock Exchange company. A professional biologist who had promoted many companies in Vancouver over the years, Pearson resigned from the Yukon government and was sentenced to six months' probation.

Next followed charges against a lawyer in Whitehorse who was convicted of charging a client $7,000 for contacting his biological mother on Mars. "The client was a miner and the guy honestly believed he was a Martian." In 1979 Wool started a fraud investigation into the activities of an Australian-born real estate developer, Barry Bellechambers. The developer was being investigated for buying more land lots in the Yukon than he was legally entitled to own. Bellechambers lobbied Yukon's minister of justice, Douglas Graham, to get Wool off the case.

"Bellechambers was convicted of fraud. His case was no problem. Straightforward. Some of my superiors in the RCMP gave me orders not to pursue it any further, and I said you have no right to tell me who I can lay a charge against," says Wool.

Wool laid charges for obstructing justice against Bellechambers and another against Graham in 1979. The developer was convicted, but the charges were stayed against the minister. (Staying means the charges remain on the record for one year and may be resurrected.) "The stay was entered after normal court hours," says Wool. "There was a great deal of criticism at the time. The whole thing stank." Embittered and frustrated, Wool left the force to attend law school after twenty-one years of service.

Wool now works for a Vancouver law firm, occasionally defending white-collar criminals on the wrong side of the law. It is an intellectual leap for him to be on the other side, against his buddies who are still cops and crown attorneys. He did his time and served his society, but the reasons for his departure are troubling. Losing experienced white-collar cops like Wool costs a country. Such officers are the thin blue line separating capitalism from the jungle, and their departure can sometimes make all the difference in the world.

14/THE EXCHANGE

Despite the scandals that hit the Vancouver Stock Exchange in 1987, Don Hudson, the exchange's president, maintained in a mid-year interview that,"the incidence of improper behavior by market participants is relatively rare." That is poppycock. The dubious press releases which flow daily from the exchange's 2,400 listed companies boast of huge sales by companies promoting everything from Chinese-language Ouija boards to tea-leaf cures for cancer and AIDS to King Solomon's mines (discovered by a shady billionaire arms dealer). Many are lies. Most contain omissions. Some are wishful thinking. If these press releases were advertisements (which technically they are), the companies could be charged with misleading advertising. But not on Vancouver's Howe Street, where permissiveness encourages ex-cons and greedy brokers to devise investment scams. Unless Vancouver's laissez-faire philosophy is replaced with tough-minded and close regulation, the exchange should be shut down.

A 1979 report on the exchange, commissioned by the province, was never released to the public (for obvious reasons). Conducted by Brown Farris & Jefferson Ltd. in Vancouver, it revealed that the vast majority of investors lost money trading in Vancouver. According to the figures, the public and brokers invested $994.6 million in primary and secondary issues between 1965 and 1976; the market value by 1977 was $419.6 million, for an overall loss of $574.9 million.

Put another way, investors put up $1 a share each and ended up with an average of 42.2 cents on that dollar. The report concluded that, generally speaking, 84 percent of investors lose some money and a staggering 40 percent lose *all* their money.

"The further back one goes, the worse the performance," reads the report. "What is striking about this conclusion is that several interviewees told us that it was the sophisticated buyers who consistently make money and that these typically are those who buy new issues and sell fairly soon thereafter. It seems true that these buyers do profit. However, they can only do this because there is an available 'market' buyer — who, as it happens, more often than not, loses (and fairly heavily)."

Laissez-faire proponents point out that exchanges like Vancouver's are risky because the companies are young and prospects uncertain. They maintain that the social justification for allowing people the freedom to blow their financial brains out is that these young companies create jobs and economic activity, and some even hit it big, thus adding to the nation's wealth. Unfortunately, the report debunked that myth when it came to Vancouver. "A relatively low proportion of the funds invested by the public ever gets to the company."

The unpublished report did not even touch on the fact that the exchange is sometimes used as a money-laundering and swindling vehicle by the world's crooks. In 1984 regulators in Ontario slapped the first insider-trading charge ever made on a Vancouver company whose shares were selling in Ontario. Rea Gold Corp. Ltd., its president Larry Reaugh, and two others were fined. Ontario investigator Sara Blake remarked tellingly, "We were fortunate in this case because they used their own names for the trades. Most insiders are smart enough to trade through other names."

Obviously, even simple or obvious scams work in Vancouver, otherwise Rea Gold might not have been quite so sloppy. Such horror stories began filtering into the media following some large-scale scandals, and subsequent pressure from the provincial legislature led to some improvements in 1987. Neil de Gelder became the stock market watchdog as the new Superintendent of Brokers and began taking tough action, as others had done before him. Unfortunately, the superintendent's tenure may not be long enough to make serious changes to exchange rules and provincial laws.

A fundamental shift in philosophy is needed to clean up the financial sewer that the Vancouver Stock Exchange has become. Otherwise, Ottawa may have to move in to regulate the securities industry. This, in fact, seems to be the only way of preventing sophisticated scam artists from playing one exchange or securities commission or even country against another. Howe Street's entire brokerage community, which consists of many of the same players working the Toronto Stock Exchange and others, must clean up its act or lose its right to govern itself.

HOW MARKETS ARE SUPPOSED TO WORK

The stock market is a relatively new innovation, historically speaking. It is derived from the English common-law concept of limited-liability entities, better known as corporations. Limited companies divorced proprietors from responsibility for the actions of their corporations. This separation also enabled proprietors to sell parts or all of their companies. This was done by dividing the company into pieces, then issuing paper, or stock certificates, entitling holders to pieces of the company. Names on certificates were evidence of ownership and began to be swapped for cash or for other pieces of paper informally in open-air street markets. That practice gave birth to the phrase "curb market," now applied to stock exchanges where shares of fledgling companies are bought or sold.

Nowadays, stock exchanges are highly sophisticated, electronic auctions. Buyers and sellers never meet, nor do they even know one another's identities. They operate through intermediaries, called brokers, who run the stock markets as non-profit cooperatives. Revenue to run the exchange's expensive facilities is derived from annual fees as well as transaction fees.

There are several layers of stock-brokerage regulation in Canada. At the very bottom is self-regulation, a privilege that doctors and lawyers also enjoy. This is supposed to mean that stockbrokers impose, and enforce, certain ethical standards on themselves and their colleagues. Stock exchanges are also self-regulated and have bylaws governing the behavior of the companies, brokers, and brokerage firms that trade on the exchange.

At a slightly higher level are professional organizations like the Investment Dealers' Association of Canada, which consists of sixteen of the biggest brokerage firms with more than half the business. This association has the power to conduct spot audits of brokerage firms to assess their financial strength; to levy brokerage firms for a national contingency fund, which protects investors in case of a brokerage-firm failure; and to discipline firms and individuals for transgressions.

Above this level are the custodians of our laws governing stock-market activity: the provincial securities commissions. These autonomous bodies are both police and judges when it comes to the enforcement of provincial securities laws. The Superintendent of Brokers in British Columbia and the directors of the Ontario and Quebec Securities Commissions are appointed by the chairman of the provincial securities commissions, who are themselves politically appointed.

These regulators have sweeping powers. They can shut down firms, stocks, and listed companies and can discipline or lay criminal charges against brokers, traders, officers of companies, and any others involved in shady dealings. Regulators must also investigate complaints and double-check self-regulatory efforts, and they can call hearings to investigate problems. Hearings are adjudicated by commission chairmen and their fellow commissioners, who are also political appointees. Regulators also come up with new policies or revisions to old ones. (It was the lack of securities commissions in the Netherlands that allowed the boiler-room boys to flourish in Amsterdam.)

At the very apex of controls, however, is the federal Criminal Code which describes a number of stock market offences which can, if proven, net jail sentences, fines or both. Enforcement of the code is left up to police and crown prosecutors.

Canada has five stock exchanges: Montreal, Toronto, Winnipeg, Alberta (in Calgary), and Vancouver. Some 5,000 companies are listed on these exchanges. In addition, there is a lively over-the-counter or curb market of several thousand more companies, which can be listed on an exchange if they meet the exchange's criteria. These criteria differ slightly from one exchange to another.

The best exchanges follow the types of rules found on blue-ribbon markets such as New York's, because exchanges that do not play by these rules lose credibility worldwide. And this costs money. Rules are essential because, as in any other game or auction, players want to be sure that there is no cheating going on and that the odds are not stacked in favor of the house, a rival, or a stranger. An exchange without credibility misses out on its portion of the billions of dollars that move around the globe in search of the highest return. That's why swindlers vie to get their worthless companies listed with legitimate exchanges.

To be listed, companies must show a certain amount of capital (the sum of cash and assets) and sales, and they must meet "distribution requirements" (or have a minimum number of shareholders) in order to demonstrate to an exchange that the company will be attractive to investors. Once listed, companies must regularly disclose detailed information about operations, performance, prospects, and participants. They must also put up with the inconvenience and expense of publishing annual reports and quarterlies and issuing press releases whenever there is a material fact to disclose to the public. A material fact is defined as any information which, if known by the public, would affect the price of shares. There is one postscript to that requirement: to protect public companies from predators or competitors, the companies can withhold privileged or highly confidential material about future strategies or plans that, if revealed, could jeopardize operations.

This is where insider trading rules kick in. Insiders — suppliers, officers, or directors — must not use privileged information to buy or sell shares in a company whose prices will be affected once the privileged information is released to the investing public. To prevent such abuse, legitimate exchanges require insiders to disclose any transactions they execute with their company's shares by filing an insider-trading report, usually within fifteen days after the end of the month in which a trade was made. Anyone who owns more than 10 percent of a company's shares must do the same.

Despite such invasions of privacy, companies listed on stock exchanges enjoy advantages over their private counterparts. Publicity is constant, and prices (and the company name) are quoted in newspapers around the world every day of the week. More importantly, however, companies can raise additional funds by selling more shares to the public, which means they don't need to go into debt to acquire or build assets. This is the biggest single benefit derived from going public.

The higher the share price on exchanges, the fewer new shares must be issued to raise the same amount of money. So share prices are very important, as are the exchange rules governing prices. Supply and demand drive prices up or down. More buyers than sellers means a price hike on an unfettered exchange floor. More sellers than buyers means the opposite. However, few exchanges are completely unfettered anymore because history has shown more than once that panics can destroy prices or entire economies.

To reduce dangerous volatility, exchanges appoint members to act as market makers for individual stocks. When there are too many sellers, their job is to buy the stocks to prevent a precipitous fall simply because no one is interested in them. Conversely, they also take the heat off stocks by selling shares when buyers are clamoring for more and more. Technically speaking, it is a form of legalized stock-market manipulation. If it is properly supervised, it removes the peaks and valleys that can create the kind of unjustified panic that has needlessly destroyed companies in the past.

Brokers worldwide lost billions supporting stocks during the panic in October 1987. Two days after the crash, many were running out of money and could not continue to prop up stocks. Several firms went under and the government announced that it would "provide liquidity" (lend money) to prop up the brokerage firms which were, in turn, propping up the stocks. If the crisis had dragged on much longer, the exchanges would have been forced to shut down, brokers would have gone broke, and exchanges might never have reopened, thus wiping out values for all involved, from individuals to pension plans.

Supply and demand for stocks are driven by information, which is spread by word of mouth, corporate press releases, and the media. Poor prospects or poor profits ahead make stocks fall in price. Good prospects or profits increase prices. Information is key, so exchange rules require "full, plain and timely disclosure." This requirement is designed to ensure that one player does not enjoy an unfair advantage over another.

Another set of rules tries to protect investors against overenthusiastic, or downright fraudulent sales tactics. These are called know-your-client rules. When an account is opened, the client must describe his or her investment strategy and disclose personal financial details. This ensures that a salesperson's lust for commissions is not on a collision course with the client's best interests, that a widow who should be buying Blue Chip Corp. is not put into High Flyer Inc.

More rules apply to the underwriting, or financing and selling, of new shares on exchanges. Brokerage firms vie for this sort of business because they collect huge fees up front. Firms offer two underwriting deals. In a straightforward underwriting, the broker takes the full risk by guaranteeing to buy the shares from the company even if there is no buying interest. In a best-efforts underwriting, which indicates lukewarm interest, the broker will try to peddle the shares but will not guarantee purchase.

During underwritings, brokers with stock to get rid of behave like promoters, singing the praises of the stock and the company involved. It is at this stage that many abuses occur. For instance, Praxis Technologies in Toronto, which makes compact discs used by recording companies, forecasted sales in its prospectus of $23 million for the year ending December 1987. Actual revenues by June 30, 1987, were only $2.2 million because of operating delays. Even though operations were lagging badly, the $23-million forecast was not withdrawn until July, shortly before the actual performance was reported. Although all this was perfectly legal, the Praxis matter raised eyebrows. Fueled by unrealistic forecasts, shares shot up from eight dollars to thirteen dollars, before falling back to four dollars and eventually to cents. Investors bought stock based on bullish, or unrealistic, forecasts published in the prospectus and orally hyped by brokers. Although the Praxis case involved no illegality, illegal manipulators intentionally publish unrealistic forecasts to hike the price of a stock artificially.

Before shares can be sold, a company and its underwriter must prepare a detailed sales document called a prospectus, which contains information about the past, present, and future of the company and is available to anyone upon request. The prospectus is vetted by securities commissions as well as by exchanges, but only for completeness, not for accuracy. The underwriting broker is on the hook for accuracy, legally speaking, and this responsibility is known in the business as due diligence. The broker is responsible for verifying the validity of the statements and facts in the prospectus. If the prospectus is incorrect or misleading, the broker and the company can be sued.

This happened in 1986 when Enfield Corporation sued the Campeau Corporation. Enfield bought $18 million worth of Campeau preferred shares in August 1986 using a prospectus that did not mention any plans for a major takeover in another field. Some six weeks later, Campeau launched a $5-billion takeover of Allied Stores of New York. Enfield was upset because it said that the huge takeover reduced the value of the preferred shares and that the takeover plans should have been mentioned in the prospectus. Campeau said plans were not disclosed because they were not known at the time the prospectus was drawn up.

Due diligence has been a myth in many cases, as shown by a particularly shabby example involving Banco Resources, a company that is now no longer listed on the Vancouver Stock Exchange. In August 1986, Banco hired Vancouver's brokerage king, Peter Brown, and his Canarim Investment Corp. Ltd. to undertake a $9.6-million underwriting of 1.2 million shares at eight dollars each, the biggest single issue that year. The money was to be used to build a pipeline in Tennessee. Rules required Banco to prepare an abbreviated prospectus called a statement of material fact, containing financial information and business plans. Such statements must be signed by a bona fide underwriter who is supposed to double-check facts and make sure all pertinent information is disclosed. This is what due diligence is all about. In this case, Canarim (which does about half of all Vancouver underwriting) picked up an underwriter's fee of $340,000 for attesting to Banco's statement.

Banco announced that 634,000 shares of its 1.2 million were sold. It was later discovered that 610,000 shares had been sold to Banco's president, Eurrell Potts of Nashville, Tennessee. Banco then said the shares had been given to Potts free of charge to settle a debt. However, the statement of material fact and a previous financial statement failed to show the outstanding loan to Potts. Also missing from the statement was the truth concerning the pipeline development. Banco said its "experienced" pipeline contractor was "ready, willing and able to proceed" with the project. Yet just months before the share sale, Banco had sued this contractor, citing in its court documents "poor, substandard work."

When all this came out in 1986, the company was delisted and B.C. Superintendent of Brokers Neil de Gelder held a hearing which obtained severe penalties for some of the culprits. The three-member Securities Commission panel imposed a twenty-year trading suspension against Eurrell Potts, a three-year suspension against prominent Vancouver lawyer Don Cameron, and a two-year suspension against accountant Anton Drescher, all Banco directors. The three-member panel of Commission members criticized the exchange, disregarding arguments put forward by Canarim's Peter Brown that the regulators acted as a backstop for companies and underwriters. Brown claimed that, "The high cost of extensive due diligence is impractical for a broker active on a junior stock exchange."

The Securities Commission remained unmoved by these arguments, and in December 1987 announced trading sanctions. "This was a sorry episode in the history of the British Columbia securities market. The due diligence process, under which an issuer, its directors and underwriter are expected to ensure that a prospectus or statement of material facts contains full, true and plain disclosure before signing certificates to that effect, broke down in the largest distribution of 1986 on the Exchange." Canarim and Brown were taken to task, charged a $90,000 fine, and ordered to return the $340,000 underwriting fee.

There's another side to delisting. It means that values disappear, and shareholders are left holding worthless pieces of paper that cannot be sold. Even so, delisting was the only appropriate action to take. Although the exchange acted swiftly in the Banco matter, this case illustrates a fundamental problem in Vancouver and elsewhere in Canada: the brokerage community does a haphazard job of protecting investors and the system from scalawags.

PRIMITIVE SCAMS

There are dozens of ways to manipulate the stock market, but one of the grand-daddies is a classic fraud pulled off in Toronto in 1965 by con-man extraordinaire Elias Yassin Rabbiah (a.k.a. Eduardo Rabi). It is a shockingly simple scam, but one that could easily be, and undoubtedly has been, repeated.

Rabbiah landed in Canada as an immigrant in 1956 with a phony Israeli passport. False papers hid his long record of criminal convictions in many countries. In 1960 he incorporated a company called Racan Photo-Copy Corp., which he said held the exclusive patent for a revolutionary new process of optical scanning that produced a dry copy on any type of paper and at a lower cost than any competitor. This photocopier was called the Racan 1015 Dry-Copy Machine, and Rabbiah's public relations efforts were so convincing that even Xerox Corp., IBM, and 3M sniffed around its allegedly advanced technology. In June 1962, Rabbiah sold 100,000 shares of Racan's 400,000 outstanding common shares for two dollars each. By January 1963 they were worth five dollars, and almost exactly one year later they were up to twenty-five dollars.

Not only did Rabbiah pull off a stock-market manipulation, he also pulled off a debt scam, bilking Atlantic Acceptance Corp. of an estimated $1.24 million, equivalent to nearly $10 million in today's dollars. (His lawyer and adviser was Sam Ciglen, confidant of Guy La Marche.)

Rabbiah bilked investors and lenders by lying and stonewalling. Although the machine never worked, Rabbiah hosted public viewings. One took place in a New York hotel in 1963. His presentation ended after he produced only two copies and claimed the machine had broken down. The stock declined only slightly after that, possibly because Rabbiah immediately announced another preview at Toronto's Royal York Hotel, scheduled for June 3, 1963. Four days before it was to take place, the event was canceled because of "imminent negotiations," which Rabbiah never explained.

The next show took place in July at Toronto's King Edward Hotel. Rabbiah produced fifty good copies from one master sheet. He postponed a request from an investor in the audience who wanted to operate the machine himself, saying that he wanted first to show a film and then demonstrate another Racan wonder product, a wheelchair capable of climbing a stairway. Rabbiah reassured the investors that members of the audience would be allowed to operate the Racan 1015 following these presentations.

The lights went out. When they came on again, the photocopier had disappeared. Rabbiah apologized, saying that the factory was closing and needed the machine returned immediately. The stock halved in price to $3.50, newspaper accounts were critical, and yet fraud charges were not laid until a year later. Rabbiah was arrested in 1964 and bail was fixed at $100,000. Rabbiah "became at once afflicted by a virus infection acquired, as he said, in the course of a visit to the Congo, and he spent the next six weeks under guard in hospital, appearing at the preliminary hearing in a wheelchair," says the Royal Commission report on Atlantic Acceptance's collapse. Rabbiah was eventually ordered to stand trial, and his bail was reduced to $30,000. But he skipped town, wheelchair and all, by driving to New York via Niagara Falls.

(As Eduardo Rabi, Rabbiah was paroled from a New York prison in 1987 after serving five years of a fourteen-year sentence for grand larceny. He had bedded a Mexican heiress thirty years his junior and defrauded her of millions by selling her a bogus chicken franchise in California and an abbatoir in Colorado. When she found out, she went to police, taped conversations with Rabi, some including their bedtime pillow talk, and testified against him. For the trial, Rabi resorted to his old tricks. Married to someone else and in his sixties, he feigned illness to garner juror sympathy and came to court in a wheelchair.)

TODAY'S CLASSIC CANADIAN SCAM

"When an outsider, a member of the public, reads price quotations of a stock listed on the exchange, he is justified in supposing that the quoted price is an appraisal of the value of that stock due to a series of actual sales between various persons dealing at arm's length in a free and open market on the exchange, and so represents a true chancering [appraisal] of the market value of that stock thereon under the process of attrition due to supply operating against demand." So stated the judge in the case of Hams v. United States, New York, 1931.

This is the classic legal description of how stock exchanges are supposed to work. But there are a variety of manipulations, some of them laughably simple, that undermine the system. Some are perfectly legal, most are not. Essentially, it's a financial version of Hans Christian Andersen's story, "The Emperor's New Clothes."

The idea is to create the illusion that a company has prospects or operations and is a popular and broadly owned business. Perhaps in reality, the company is a mere shell, and its manipulators directly or indirectly control the trading of

90 or even 100 percent of the shares, buying and selling to themselves at ever-increasing prices and volumes. To spirit things along, they also issue fraudulent press releases until they are ready to cash in, or "blow off" the stock to the public at the highest possible price. Once as many shares as possible are sold, the stock begins to plunge and ends up virtually worthless because the emperor really has no clothes. What follows is a swindler's lexicon of manipulation.

Backdoor Listings

Manipulators buy shells, or dormant companies, which rarely trade and have no operations. Such inactive companies still remain listed on exchanges because there is a lively marketplace for just selling, and buying, shells. Manipulators look for shells with a "thin float," or small number of shares outstanding, which trade for pennies. Once they have 80 to 90 percent of shares, the manipulators are ready to go to work. Buying shells allows them to get control of a listed company without being subjected to the rigorous scrutiny and minimum requirements necessary to get a new company listed.

Taking over shells also obviates the need to prepare a prospectus and do an underwriting. In 1987 the Vancouver Stock Exchange partially sewed up this loophole by requiring the filing of more information before a takeover can occur.

Rollback or Reverse Split

In the case of RTOs (for reverse takeovers), manipulators reduce the number of shares outstanding to increase their control by shaking out other shareholders. For instance, a typical RTO may be an offer to shareholders of a five-for-one rollback, which means they can get one share for every five they own. Thus a company with three million shares would end up with 600,000 shares and prices should theoretically go from ten cents a share to fifty cents. This is legal and is also necessary to overcome the fact that new shares in Vancouver cannot be sold to the public unless shares cost at least twenty-five cents. (Since 1987, however, Alberta has allowed the selling of nickel stocks.)

Wash Trading

Large-volume trading attracts interest in a stock from investors and brokers because it is an indication of interest and heightened demand. But it may simply be wash trading, a practice in which buyers and sellers are actually the same and shares don't really change hands. But the transfers are recorded as though they were legitimate trades between different entities, a fraudulent illusion created to engender interest in a stock. Techniques vary. In wash trading, manipulators open up a number of accounts in different brokerage houses in a variety of names. More sophisticated wash traders open dozens of accounts in many different cities and countries. By going international, wash traders frustrate detection and prosecution and enhance their chances of pulling off a stock-market manipulation.

One of the first wash-trading cases successfully prosecuted in Canada involved a prominent Toronto mining promoter, Viola MacMillan. In July 1964 she instructed her broker to sell 244,000 shares of a Toronto Stock Exchange listed company, named Golden Arrow, from accounts she owned or controlled to certain other accounts she owned or controlled. This transfer was reported as a large trade on the ticker tape of the exchange and sparked more buying and a price hike from twenty-five cents to fifty-eight cents. She then sold out many of her shares for between fifty and fifty-five cents each. She was eventually charged and went to jail for a few months.

Matched Orders

This is a variation of wash trading. Shares change hands to falsely increase prices, but the buyers are accomplices of the seller. This is illegal. Theoretically, when customers place an order to buy or sell with their brokers, they are not supposed to know who is on the other side of the transaction. In a matched order, buyers and sellers know they are placing buy and sell orders of the same size at the same time and the same price. Corrupt floor traders are usually involved to make sure the price is right.

Taking Out the Offerings

As a stock begins to move upwards, manipulators must stop the general public from taking profits or selling on a mass basis. However, if sell orders remain outstanding, prices will fall, so manipulators mop up all available shares by giving their brokers standing orders to take out the sell offerings. They will also buy small amounts of shares at prices slightly above the current market price to nudge prices upwards. This allows them to move the price up and gain control over even more shares.

Warehousing

To ensure control over share prices, crooks must accumulate most of the shares themselves or know where all the stock is located. It is not necessary for them to buy it all, but the shares must be in accounts that will not sell at the wrong time. Most manipulators don't have enough money to buy all the stock anyway, so they often set up warehousing arrangements by paying brokers secret commissions of up to 15 percent to convince their clients to buy and hold the stock for sixty to ninety days. Clients have no idea they are part of a manipulation and are simply acting on the recommendations of their brokers.

Warehousing, however, leaves manipulators open to back-dooring, an illegal scheme perpetrated by crooked brokers who outfox the manipulators. Brokers take their secret commissions, get clients to buy or hold, and then break away from the conspiracy. By using other brokerage firms to make the trades, brokers get their clients or themselves out at a profit before manipulators start to sell off the stock and its price plummets. In this way, brokers pocket a secret commission and also pick up a legitimate commission for the sale, without manipulators knowing exactly who's selling. They even make money for their clients. Needless to say, even though it is itself illegal, backdooring destroys more illegal promotions than rules, regulators, or police.

Painting the Tape

This strategy is designed to create the illusion of a price rise. Newspapers publish stock market tables that list prices, but these are closing prices only, that is, the last price paid by the last buyer each day. So manipulators paint the tape by getting a floor trader to watch trading. Just before the bell tolls ending the day's trading, the floor trader puts through a trade with another floor trader, thus nudging the price upward at whatever price manipulators want. By doing this gradually over a few weeks, manipulators create interest among members of the public who then buy the stock and push prices up even higher.

False Underwritings

This technique helps manipulators get control of more shares and also creates the illusion of a public demand for the stock. The manipulators issue a prospectus but covertly buy up all of the shares offered to the public. In a pre-arrangement with a broker and a floor trader, all shares offered on the floor are bought and channeled into the manipulators' accounts, or into those of their accomplices. This precludes the public from buying the stock and allows manipulators to create a false price through wash, or matched, trades. This type of manipulation is difficult for regulators to detect.

Fiction, Not Fact

During a scam, manipulators try to get reporters to write glowing stories on their latest find, such as a gold mine or a new machine. Most large-circulation papers do not fall for such bait, so manipulators are left to sing their own praises through the creative use of press releases or advertisements. Stock exchanges get copies of press releases and financial statements, but they do not have the staff to go out in the field and actually check the veracity of these statements.

Misleading or downright deceitful press releases are commonplace, particularly in Vancouver, where 300 releases are issued daily. Often releases are cunningly phrased. For instance, when George Wool was investigating the Allied Fund Capital Appreciation case in the Arctic, he came across a line in the company's prospectus that described one of the directors as "an expert in oil and gas." As it turned out, the expert was the brother-in-law of the perpetrators, who pumped gasoline for a living. Sometimes omissions are more important than statements. One example was the statement, "We have hit favourable mineralization," but the company failed to say that the minerals were found in such small quantities that they would never be recoverable.

Distribution

Also called an off, this is the technique manipulators use to sell their shares at a high price just before abandoning the stock at the end of an illegal promotion, when the manipulators feel they have pushed the price as high as they can and when they have gathered as many shares as they can. The distribution will be preceded by several price hikes and followed by news releases to create public interest. At this point, manipulators start to unload their shares gradually because dumping a huge volume would cause prices to plummet. Many floor traders can spot this and will start to unload shares they have accumulated. During this period, there is a high volume of trading, then interest falls off, and shares plummet to pennies.

Dutch police believe the boiler-room boys "blew off" billions of worthless shares to a greedy or foolish world. Distribution through a boiler room is most effective because detection and prosecution are difficult across borders. But it also requires more organization, money, and contacts.

Media Manipulation

Timing is crucial to manipulators. If promoters leak good news too early — whether it is bogus or true — they will have to pay more to buy the stock themselves than if they pick shares up cheaply before the news is out. For instance, officials of a company are informed first about drilling results, and if the news is good, manipulators can instruct brokers to start buying a lot of stock in other peoples' names as nominees. Once enough stock has been accumulated, a press release is issued. In the famous case of Texas Gulf Sulphur, the company's geologist telephoned the president in New York on April 12, 1965, and reported excellent results. Some insiders bought stock for between seventeen dollars and twenty-nine dollars and the company stated that drilling had occurred but was not conclusive. On April 16 the company announced a major discovery and the price shot up, hitting seventy-one dollars by the end of the year. The reverse can happen when insiders temporarily withhold bad news in order to accumulate short positions, which is a complicated method of borrowing stock to make money on it when it falls in price.

There are as many ways to manipulate the news of a stock as there are manipulators. In one amusing example that occurred during the 1970s, the culprits got away scot-free even though the victims knew they had been cheated. A small oil company listed on the Alberta Stock Exchange was drilling for natural gas, and competitors sent out scouts to see what was happening. (Scouts are private eyes who gather corporate intelligence for oil companies. They trespass onto drill sites, hang around bars, and bribe roughnecks or workers to get information about results. Oil companies never admit they use scouts, but all of them do. If they know about a discovery before others do, they can snap up adjacent land in the hopes that it shares a pocket of oil or gas.)

The scouts swarmed around the rig and listened to speculation in Calgary bars about a huge natural gas strike. So the company officials decided to give the scouts something to phone home about. Under cover of night, they hauled in a tankful of propane and flared it the next morning. (Flaring occurs when there is a discovery because excess gas rises to the surface and must be burned off before the well is capped and tested.) The scouts took off in all directions, phoning their oil companies and brokers, not necessarily in that order. Adjacent lands were snapped up. The stock tripled in days. Insiders steadily sold.

The stock exchange halted trading along the way and asked the company to explain the sudden jump. The company issued a press release that claimed it had no idea why stocks had jumped, because the drilling results were incomplete. Finally, two weeks later it announced that the well was dry and contained no oil or gas. Then the officials left town and returned to Denver. The stock plunged. Companies and individuals that had bought adjacent land or shares were out of luck, but no securities law was broken. Technically, the flaring was intended to defraud, but the scouts were breaking the law by spying. They could not complain without getting themselves into trouble.

Besides manipulating the press, sometimes there is out-and-out corruption. Promoters vie to get their companies mentioned flatteringly in important financial publications. A common practice in Vancouver was for promoters to hand out to reporters cheap, or free, shares in new companies that were about to be listed.

I once interviewed Don Duguid, promoter of Aero Energy Ltd., for *Canadian Business*, about the costs of taking a company public. He offered to let me buy a tranche of shares in another promotion he was about to take public and mentioned that a Vancouver journalist who wrote for the *Financial Post* on a regular basis had bought shares in the past. I wrote about this in *Quest* some months later, after interviewing the reporter and Neville Nankivelle, publisher of the *Financial Post*. The journalist felt there was no conflict in taking stock in new issues of companies about which she wrote. The woman was dropped from the roster of *Financial Post* freelancers.

This incident resulted in tighter rules at the *Post* and other papers. Now *Post* reporters cannot buy new issues (except for Canada Savings Bonds), and they must declare any conflict of interest when writing about a company whose shares they own. There are also restrictions on the trading of stocks mentioned in the managed portfolio features, in corporate stories dealing with exclusive information, or in sensitive news stories that might affect stock prices. The trading ban extends until the Thursday following the story's Monday publication date.

Although most financial journalists take their responsibilities seriously, some do not. Sometimes articles can actually be bought. For example, in the early 1980s there was the case investigated by the Quebec Securities Commission involving Kott-linked Belgium Standard company (later renamed Amertek), which was listed on the NASDAQ exchange. By accident, Quebec investigators found out that a Kott associate named Arthur Dalfen lent US$30,000 to a journalist at a U.S. publication called the *Penny Stock News* around the time it published a bullish article written by Dalfen. The article was reprinted and used to tout Amertek in Amsterdam by boiler rooms.

Sometimes photocopies of articles are fabricated, as allegedly happened during 1986 in the Audit Resources affair (now before the courts). Promoters circulated an article apparently from the prestigious U.S. publication *Barron's*, which sang the praises of Audit and a related company, North Sun. *Barron's* says it has never mentioned either company in its columns or in advertisements.

In July 1987 concerns about the ethics of journalists led to new rules in Quebec. Journalists are required to hold onto the stocks of companies they write about for seven days before the article or broadcast and for thirty days afterward, unless a special exemption is obtained. Quebec also requires non-journalists whose recommendations about trading are published or broadcast without any revisions by the media to disclose their holdings in those stocks. This rule does not extend to recommendations made in the course of interviews because the non-journalist has no control over what is used, but it does apply to publications that invite brokers, analysts, or counselors to make recommendations that are reprinted without changes.

The rules are the subject of a running battle between the Quebec Securities Commission and Jacques Forget, former owner, publisher and columnist of *Finance*, a weekly business newspaper. "The new policy is silly," says Forget, who has a personal portfolio worth $5 million. "We started a new monthly [publication] called *La Bourse*, and we were ordered to register it as a financial counselor or cease publication. We have told the Quebec Securities Commission to jump in the lake and nothing has happened."

Forget has a history of battles. A few years before, the Quebec Securities Commission charged that Forget profited personally from stocks he wrote about and fined him $1,000. Currently, he is under orders to disclose his monthly trades to the commission, a restriction now under appeal in the courts. "It is harassment," says Forget. "We have criticized the Montreal Exchange and heavily criticized the Quebec Securities Commission for its interventionism, arbitrary decisions, favoritism and weakness."

Forget only hires journalists who play the stock market because he feels that gives them the insights and knowledge they need to write astutely about markets. He imposes no internal rules. "We treat the reader fairly, and the real sin is to not publish news," he says. "I don't see why a journalist should be at a disadvantage to other market players. The players are guys on the floor surrounded by rumors, institutional guys, brokers on phones all day long. That's the real public we serve."

Moose Pasture Mines, Limited

In light of all the loopholes available to stock-market manipulators, some people, including Rupert Bullock, former Superintendent of Brokers for British Columbia, remain unconvinced that stock markets really work. An expert on such manipulations, Bullock says it's easy once you know how. "Moose Pasture Mines Ltd., founded by Tom Hardworker, is approached by Joe Crook who offers to take over the company for ten cents a share. Rumors designed to make a stock rise or fall in price are purposely floated in conversations and on the trading floor. Then Crook does a rollback, offering one new share for five old ones, to squeeze out small shareholders. This gets the price up to fifty cents, above the minimum required for a new underwriting or sale of shares. Crook renames the company United Moose Pasture, sells it worthless assets at an inflated price which he directly or indirectly owns in return for more shares of the company.

"Crook makes a deal with a crooked broker who helps him prepare a false prospectus and underwrite more shares. Rules require that the underwriter must allow at least 25 percent of the stock to be sold to other brokers. On the day the underwriting is available, 75 percent of shares are sold and repurchased by Crook and a deal is struck with a floor trader who asks other traders interested in buying the stock to lay off and not buy. The next day, the broker gives Crook a check for so many shares at forty-five cents a share, and Crook gives the broker a check for slightly more as payment.

"Crook now has control of virtually all the shares. Public interest is generated because the underwriting was snapped up quickly and prices rise. Crook then arranges warehousing deals with brokers, then he jiggles the market to encourage other shareholders to sell out by arranging for a drop in price to fifty-five cents. These people sell off, he snaps them up or has warehouse brokers buy, prices rise quickly, preceded by some bogus news releases. Then there is a period of stability, followed by a short dip again to shake out any others not in cahoots with Crook. He issues more fraudulent press releases, then the stock goes up again through wash trading and warehousing. (When you wash trade, it's better to use the U.S. and Canada, and not to do it all in one town. So he trades in Los Angeles, New York, Montreal, Vancouver, Toronto, and leaves a horrendous paper trail for police which would take months to unravel who bought and sold. It might even be impossible.) After a few months of this he has gotten a ten-cent stock up to two dollars or so, has almost all the shares under control, and then launches his distribution to convert shares into cash.

"Ideally, he arranges with a newspaper for a major article about a mining prospect, issues a false press release with good news from exploration, then sits back safe in the knowledge everything is ready to go, traders and brokers have gotten their payments. Then he releases an engineering report showing good results, followed by assays [appraisals of gold or other mineral content from exploration samples] of high value. He states major mining companies are interested in looking at the claims, which creates fantastic public interest and buying pressure. He gradually begins to sell and prices begin to fall gradually because supply outstrips demand. In the end, he dumps most of his shares at an average price of $1.50, not bad because his costs, secret payments and other expenses ended up totalling twenty-five cents a share. If he controlled 500,000 shares, then he made $625,000 after paying bribes. Not bad for three to four months' work."

THE YANKEE SCAM

The Racan Photo-Copy caper pulled off by Elias Rabbiah in the 1960s was one of the more primitive forms of stock-market manipulation. It seems hard to believe that journalists, stock brokers, and stock-exchange regulators were all gullible enough to be duped into believing in a revolutionary photocopier that no one had ever seen work. But the same primitive scam still works. It was pulled off, with slightly different twists, in Vancouver in 1980 and again in 1986. The scams involved New Cinch Uranium Mines and Carolin Mines Ltd. The scandals hit the headlines, but no one went to jail. In fact, rather than leading to reforms or legal precedents, the New Cinch and Carolin Mines assays scams made things far worse. After New Cinch, a lawsuit prompted changes in the Vancouver Stock Exchange's way of doing business, changes that left the market open to even greater abuses.

It all began in the late 1970s, when New Cinch's promoter, Albert Applegath, approached well-respected Toronto mining financier, Arthur White, of the Dickenson Group, for funds to drill on some New Mexico claims. As with any mining operation, samples were taken from underground, and these were tested to determine their gold or silver content. These assay results were sent to a Texas firm called Chem-Tec Laboratories.

Chem-Tec told New Cinch that the test results were promising, and that enough ore might be buried beneath its lands to develop a mine. However, a Vancouver mining consultant who examined the drilling samples told the company there were only "negligible" amounts of precious metals, too little to warrant developing a mine. The company submitted both reports to the Vancouver Stock Exchange, for its eyes only. For some unknown reason, the exchange allowed New Cinch to publish only the optimistic Chem-Tec results.

Not surprisingly, after these results were released, New Cinch shares skyrocketed from less than four dollars on

November 10, 1980, to twenty-seven dollars on November 25. A medium-sized Toronto mining company, Willroy Mines (now part of Lac Minerals), snapped up 16.7 percent of New Cinch's six million common shares, preparing for a possible takeover. But in early January 1981 Willroy publicly questioned New Cinch's assay results, then unceremoniously dumped all its New Cinch holdings, thereby losing $21 million overnight. In February Willroy sued New Cinch's chief shareholder, the Dickenson Group, for the $21 million.

Despite these events, the exchange allowed the trading of New Cinch shares to continue and took no action against officers or directors. In December 1981 the New Cinch shares slid to new lows when New Cinch admitted that the Chem-Tec 1980 assay results were inaccurate because they had been contaminated, or salted. (This is mining jargon for samples to which gold has been added. It is the oldest trick in the mining scam book, equivalent to printing counterfeit cash.)

A year later one of Chem-Tec's employees, Michael Opp, was found murdered in an apartment in Phoenix, Arizona. After the funeral, his father gave newspapers his son's eighteen-page statement about the New Cinch assays. Opp's parents were quoted as saying that their son Michael Opp "knew the assays were being salted."

Dead men can't testify, but civil litigation ground its way through the courts until Willroy (Lac) agreed to an out-of-court settlement of $4 million. The stock exchange, which had behaved so ineptly by allowing New Cinch to publish only one glowing mining report about the New Mexican properties, contributed $275,000 toward Willroy-Lac's legal costs. New Cinch itself paid another $1.3 million to Willroy. Albert Applegath was quoted in the press as saying the salting of the assays was a mystery. Currently, he is promoting two Vancouver companies, New Beginnings and Tundra Gold Mines, and several others in Toronto and Montreal.

The New Cinch affair showed a scandalous mishandling of

affairs by the Vancouver Stock Exchange. It not only hurt Vancouver's already tainted reputation, but also changed its procedures — for the worse. Now press releases, all 300 or so published daily, bear a disclaimer that the Vancouver Stock Exchange is not responsible for their contents. As a result, the exchange is legally off the hook, so it never has to vet or double-check releases. It has indemnified itself from responsibility, legally speaking, if not morally. And in March 1988 it took another step back from responsibility and issued a new edict that companies must distribute press releases themselves, rather than through the auspices of the exchange (as was the case for years).

The lessons learned in eastern Canada have never really been understood by the westerners running virtually unregulated stock markets. What the Royal Commission into the Windfall Oil scandal said back in 1965 will always apply: "The listing of a security on an exchange is, in the mind of an investor, a stamp of approval regardless of how the exchange itself may look upon it. It follows that minimum standards of performance which are meaningful with respect to the securities must be established and adhered to."

Vancouver has yet to learn this basic lesson, so it comes as no surprise that crooks were once again able to use the exchange for a similar scam. Just six years after New Cinch, a company named Carolin Mines boosted the price of its shares on the basis of salted assays. This time the scam involved the resurrection of a spent gold mine and brought in the British Columbia Securities Commission immediately. The commission held hearings and imposed a permanent cease-trading order on Carolin because there was no evidence whatsoever to support the company's claims of rich gold deposits. A commission spokesman issued a strong statement in April 1987: "News releases to date present technical evidence in a misleading fashion. I am concerned those public disclosures may cause a prospective investor in Carolin shares to assume value which has no evidence to support it."

But it was too little too late. The fun had begun months before, in January 1986, when Carolin issued a press release stating that its 800,000-ton tailings pond (the mine's dump) at its dormant mine contained valuable quantities of gold and platinum. The company quoted test results from a Nevada assay firm called Intergold U.S.A., owned by Martin Fife of New York, which stated that the tailings contained an ounce of gold and half an ounce of platinum per ton. Intergold estimated that the dump was worth some $240 million. Carolin planned to reopen the operation and mine the dump.

Hearings were held in which an expert government witness said the reopened mine would lose $62 million, not make $240 million, because there were only trace amounts of gold and no platinum to be found anywhere. Expert mining witness William Stevenson, a consultant geologist and chairman of the provincial government's mine-evaluation committee, said that the assays were wrong, and revealed that Intergold owner Martin Fife owned 240,000 Carolin shares, according to documents filed in the U.S. In his defense, Fife claimed that Intergold had used a "secret" assay method which was better able to reveal gold content than more traditional methods.

Carolin was eventually kicked off the Vancouver and Toronto stock exchanges but continued for some months to trade over the counter in Ontario until a fifteen-day trading ban was imposed in September 1986 and an Ontario hearing announced. Undaunted, Carolin's promoters peddled their stock south of the border on New York's over-the-counter market. It had risen from $1.40 to $5.60 a share by December 1986 because of the credentials of Martin Fife of New York.

The company in 1988 resurrected plans to study whether to reopen its mine, but at greatly reduced possible estimates of one million tons at 0.125 ounces of gold per ton. That would work out to 125,000 ounces of gold worth roughly $80 million, a far cry from boasts of $240 million. For the once-bullish mining company Carolin, it was a dreary anticlimax.

At peak production, Carolin had hit fifty-eight dollars a share. In 1988, it traded for pennies a share.

THE GERMAN SCAM

Vancouver's biggest scandal occurred on October 19, 1984, when a dozen companies associated with a massive fraud lost $40 million in paper value in ten minutes. The crash (ironically the same date as the global stock-market crash of 1987) was locally dubbed Black Friday. Within minutes, a company called Beauford Resources crashed from $11.50 to $1 a share. At the same time the shares of eleven sister companies, such as Rencon Mining Co. Ltd. and Marathon Minerals, Inc., also plummeted.

It was estimated that two hundred innocent West German investors, local brokerage firms, and personal creditors paid out $3.2 million, for which they will never receive restitution. Their paper losses (or the highest prices all the shares reached before crashing) totaled $40 million, the highest loss up to 1985. But worse losses were to follow.

The case was broken wide open by a German broker named Jurgen Horschelt, who was both a victim and an unwitting accomplice in the scam. He had been peddling Beauford stocks in Germany when the crash occurred. After the crash, Horschelt went to Vancouver to get money out of Beauford's promoters for his furious German clients back home. When he failed, he went to the Vancouver headquarters of the RCMP and, in sworn statements, incriminated the German-born promoters of Beauford, Erich Brunnhuber and Engelbert Roosen. He agreed to become a crown witness and came back to Vancouver for the jury trial.

Despite his own questionable credibility, Horschelt's version of events was believed by the judge and jury. During the seventeen-day trial, he described how he had sent $1.3 million to Brunnhuber and Roosen to buy 600,000 shares of

Beauford Resources, which the two had used for personal purposes, including the purchase of a Cadillac and a Porsche. At the same time, the two had artificially increased the volume of share trading and forced prices up by selling shares back and forth to one another, in a complicated scheme involving 160 trading accounts they controlled at twelve different brokerage firms.

The court learned that the two had secretly taken over Beauford on April 12, 1984, for sixty cents a share, without disclosing their control to the public, as is legally required. On the day of the crash, Beauford started at $11.50 a share and plunged to $1, dragging down related stocks. Prices collapsed because the promoters ran out of money for wash trading, and brokers who had lent them money to pay for stock (called margining) panicked and dumped their stock. (Brokers who lend money to pay for stock in this way give investors little time to make up shortfalls. If an investor owes half, or $500, against $1,000 worth of stock that suddenly is worth only $500, he or she must come up with $250 to bring the borrowings to only half. This must be done within hours or the stock is automatically dumped at any price into the market.)

The defense maintained that Brunnhuber and Roosen were entitled to use the German money and that if any was misappropriated it was by Horschelt, who had peddled the stock for them in Germany. The lawyers argued that Horschelt had agreed to buy the 600,000 shares for $2.3 million and that Brunnhuber and Roosen didn't have to turn over any of the stock until that sum was paid. Only $1.3 million was paid, so they claimed they were forced to trade stocks between their accounts to keep the deal alive. "If this was meant to be a scheme to defraud why didn't they [the accused] sell the stock and run? They were waiting for the money to come from Germany, and their brokers were waiting for payment of accounts," says one of the defense lawyers.

Even if Brunnhuber and Roosen were right, it was outrageous that they should use as a defense an illegal activity such as wash trading to "keep a deal alive" when a customer failed to pay up. Horschelt told the court that the German promoters were lying. He said $1.3 million was all he owed them for the shares. He said Brunnhuber had come to Germany in the summer of 1984 after Horschelt's customers had bought Beauford stock and boasted that Beauford's Alberta oil properties were worth $16.2 million. The estimate was subsequently rejected by the Vancouver Stock Exchange and the property was revalued at only $1.7 million.

Other charges resulted from the trial. In the middle of the Black Friday trial, on December 9, 1986, the RCMP also charged Vancouver promoter Earle Ball with six counts of fraud involving $97,425.50, which had gone missing from Rencon sometime in 1983. Ball is still at large but is believed to be in the U.S.

Horschelt, of course, did not get off scot-free. He had a prior criminal record for misappropriating client money in Germany. His German brokerage firm skimmed 40 percent commissions off the stocks it sold. A theft charge against Horschelt was dropped in Canada, but he was convicted in Germany for investing some Beauford share money in other Canadian stocks. He said he diverted the money to save the other companies and turned himself into German authorities immediately after he visited the RCMP in Vancouver.

Thanks to Horschelt's cooperation, Brunnhuber and Roosen were charged a year later. By January 1987 they had been tried and convicted and were sentenced to seven years in prison on each of several counts, the sentences to be served concurrently. Now under appeal, these are the longest white-collar crime sentences ever imposed in Canada, longer than some armed robbers get. It was proof at last that some judges were prepared to send stern messages to white-collar criminals and that the courts had finally realized that more money can be stolen in minutes by these crooks than blue-collar robbers can steal in months.

Black Friday shocked the world and provided more proof that the Vancouver Stock Exchange should be avoided by investors. Even more alarming was the fact that the exchange's pervasive immorality was actually used as a defense for the two Germans.

Brunnhuber's twenty-seven-year-old lawyer, Roger Cutler, told a local newspaper after the trial that the accused's actions were commonplace. "They were playing by the rules of the game, and they didn't make those rules. . . . The impression being portrayed is that this was an isolated situation," he said. "I think it's significant that nobody from the brokerage community came forward [during the trial]. Based on the evidence, there were obviously a great many people in the brokerage community involved."

There were many accessories to their crimes. One analyst even told a newspaper that many people knew Beauford's shares were worth only $1.47, not $11.25, even before the crash. Police added that a routine probe by the Superintendent of Brokers would have revealed trading irregularities and nipped the scheme in the bud. But these critics were nowhere to be found before Black Friday. The crash blackened Canada's financial reputation, particularly in Germany. It is a reputation that's likely to stick for many years to come.

When all was said and done, British Columbia Supreme Court judge Mr. Justice John Bouck said to the jury: "Ladies and gentlemen, I don't know how many of you are going to rush out and invest in the stock market after this. I suspect not many."

THE INSURANCE SCAM

Just months after Black Friday, a company called International Tillex Enterprises Ltd. was listed in Vancouver. By June 1986, its trading was halted after officials noted discrepancies in financial statements. Finally, it was delisted eighteen months later by the exchange on April 3, 1987, ending months of regulatory mishandling and erasing overnight a staggering $172 million in paper value of its shares. The affair has been under investigation by the RCMP.

According to an April 11, 1987, *Vancouver Sun* story, American ex-con Sam Ford was behind Tillex. In 1978 a district court found Ford guilty of fraud and perjury in connection with the promotion of a penny stock in the U.S. between 1975 and 1977. He received an eight-year sentence, went to a minimum security prison in Pennsylvania, and was paroled in 1981.

Police say Sam Ford and his allies got a backdoor listing by taking over an inactive shell company, which had been a mining exploration company, in early 1984. Then they did a reverse takeover to reduce the number of shares outstanding, ending up at one point with some 97 percent of the outstanding float of the company.

Officials got disturbed by Tillex's creative bookkeeping. In 1985, Tillex said it made a profit of $3.95 million on revenues of $16 million, then quadrupled that in the first quarter of 1986, saying it earned $3.8 million in three months on revenues of $16.3 million. The company did not account for adequate reserves set aside for insurance claims, which would have meant greatly reduced profits. (Reserves are important because insurance companies usually make no money on premium income but only on investing it until they pay most or all of it out again to policyholders in claims.)

In December 1985 Tillex bought British Insurance Management Co. of the Turks and Caicos Islands, for a questionable price, paid for with unquestionably overpriced Tillex treasury shares. Shares of Tillex took off, going from thirty cents to the equivalent of seventy-seven dollars a share (before a three-for-one split) in just eighteen months. The excitement was that, through British Insurance, Tillex owned stock in New York-based American Motor Club, which allegedly provided alternative insurance to high-risk clients in New York against fire, theft, and other physical damage. The club boasted 20,000 members who paid $1,400 a year plus a deductible of $350 for each accident.

Exchange officials protested behind the scenes about the bookkeeping and the fact there were no reserves set aside, but a Tillex spokesman said concern was unnecessary because club memberships were not technically insurance premiums and therefore did not require the setting aside of reserves in accordance with the insurance industry standards. He added that the company had established a small fund with which to pay claims. Exchange officials did not accept that explanation and pressured Tillex into agreeing to prepare new six-month audited statements. The company failed to produce the statements. Tillex explained that a delay was necessary because its auditor had to have a kidney transplant operation. Then on February 24, 1987, just as independent auditors were completing a review, Tillex told the exchange that the audit papers had mysteriously disappeared from a strongbox locked inside a New York office, adding that its directors were baffled by the theft "as there were no signs of forced entry to the premises." That incident was the last straw for the exchange. In March 1987 the RCMP searched houses and financial institutions and started a lengthy investigation.

It was another black day for Vancouver. In April 1987 a Vancouver *Province* article quoted investor Jim Kelly of Philadelphia who spoke for many when he said, "Personally I'd like to see somebody go to jail." He had invested $56,000 in Tillex, which had grown to $140,000 on paper when trading was halted. Now his shares are worthless. Others were more fortunate. An investor tipped off about Tillex by a drug dealer made a mint. "I was losing money on another stock which an expert told me to buy," said Bruce Singer, a twenty-six-year-old physical education teacher in Brooklyn, New York. "Then a drug dealer told me about Tillex and I thought, what the hell, I'm losing money with the expert, why not listen to him?" Singer quadrupled his $500 Tillex investment and got out just in time.

Shortly before delisting, American Motor Club's New York office was shut down by the New York State Insurance Department and was put into receivership. Clarkson Gordon audited the company and found unreported transactions, including a $1.4-million loan from American Motor Club made without the knowledge or approval of Tillex directors. Tillex subsequently dismissed three U.S. officers, who sued for wrongful dismissal. Dale Ciochetti, a broker formerly with Continental Carlisle Douglas, was fined $100,000 and suspended from trading for his activities — he had handled the initial stock distribution for Tillex.

Like the New Cinch affair, the phony Tillex distribution raises an interesting legal question. What are the legal responsibilities of brokerage firms when their employees go astray? Recent rulings by the Ontario Securities Commission say that Toronto Stock Exchange brokerage firms are responsible for the actions of their brokers. But it remains to be seen whether British Columbia regulators will follow suit. Tillex also shows that the changes resulting from New Cinch — a disclaimer on all news releases and the establishment of a mining-evaluation committee — allow promoters to make virtually any boast they wish with impunity and to escape evaluation as long as they stay away from mining companies. So they buy mining companies and turn them into "high tekkies," as Howe Street brokers call them. In 1975, 97 percent of the companies listed on the Vancouver Stock Exchange were natural resource companies. Now only 70 percent of them are.

Equally interesting is the fact the Vancouver Stock Exchange has been sued by investors over Tillex, as was the case with New Cinch.

THE SAUDI/MALI SCAM

The Vancouver Stock Exchange had barely recovered from several scandals in 1986 when along came the king of promotions deals, the jet-setting Saudi Arabian arms dealer Adnan Khashoggi. The Khashoggi promotions show how easily smart operators can play Canadians in general, and Vancouver in particular, for suckers. It's all stock-market sleight-of-hand, the creation of value out of illusion. The Khashoggi capers also show how the Vancouver Stock Exchange is one of the handiest ways to sidestep U.S. regulators, exchanges, and courts.

This series of schemes began when a Vancouver shell company, Skyhigh Resources Ltd., suddenly announced in July 1986 that Adnan Khashoggi would be its chairman. Founded in 1983 by Surrey, British Columbia, geologist Ron Philp, Skyhigh was just a speculative stock which was housed, along with Philp's other shells, in a rundown Vancouver office tower. But Khashoggi's appointment worked magic in the markets. Shares surged, and months later Philp moved into posh offices in Vancouver's expensive Stock Exchange Tower.

Skyhigh's stock went soaring skyhigh from seventy cents to sixty-eight dollars a share. Khashoggi's appointment was followed by another announcement that Skyhigh would swap its treasury shares and borrow $125 million to get controlling share interest in a highly profitable oil company owned by Khashoggi in California. As it turned out, the oil company, Edgington Oil Co. of Long Beach, was controlled by Khashoggi's troubled Triad America Corp., and Triad was eager to get assets out of the U.S. and away from creditors. Despite Khashoggi's reputation as one of the world's wealthiest men, Triad was tottering on the brink of bankruptcy. This became evident during the Iran-Contra controversy, involving the White House in the fall of 1986, when Khashoggi's role as a deal-maker became a matter of public record. Newspapers then began digging into his affairs, and Skyhigh's purchase of Edgington was blocked by one of Triad's creditors, the Sheraton Corp. hotel chain, which obtained a court injunction.

The Boston judge who ruled on the case in December 1986 said that the Edgington-Skyhigh transaction would "defraud" creditors. When the swap was blocked, Skyhigh's Ron Philp asked for a trading halt, as he did with another Khashoggi promotion called Tangent Oil and Gas Ltd. Tangent, another shell, reopened four days later, and its shares fell from its high of $22 to $3.75. Skyhigh did not trade until December, then collapsed in January 1987 to eighty cents.

Khashoggi's involvement in Tangent as a shareholder had been announced in November 1986. The scheme announced involved Tangent buying an obscure Spokane company called Johnson Geneva (USA) Ltd., which allegedly had a joint venture with airline giant Pan Am Corp. to recover a satellite in mainland China and relaunch it. Three days after Khashoggi became involved with Tangent, its stock catapulted from ten cents to twenty-two dollars, reaping a fortune for the Arab and others.

Khashoggi paid ten cents per share, or $26,590 for 265,900 shares. Overnight his investment grew to $5.85 million on paper. Peter Brown of Canarim Investment Corp. bought half as many shares at ten cents each. "This is not moose pasture in Saskatchewan," Brown told the media during the promotion. But profits disappeared for those who hung in until the beginning of 1987, when it became apparent that moose pasture was exactly what Tangent was. Khashoggi was persona non grata after all the adverse Iran-Contra publicity, and prices collapsed. Tangent was renamed Pacific Star Communications Corp. after announcing that the satellite deal was off and that Khashoggi was no longer a shareholder.

The next Khashoggi deal involved three Canadian public companies and two Denver promoters, Frank Grey and

Charles Stidham. Stidham is a former Texas lawyer who pleaded guilty in 1978 to stealing $80,000 from his clients. He served twenty-two months in prison, resigned from the Texas bar association, and agreed to make restitution. Then he moved to Denver. In 1985 he and Frank Grey formed a partnership which called itself an investment counseling company.

Stidham and Grey have a simple strategy: they make outrageous announcements, promote stocks on that basis, then cancel the deals without explanation. They are masters of promotions and press releases and have made a mockery out of the regulations of the Vancouver and Alberta stock exchanges. When they get involved with a company, prices rise until a delisting or trading halt. But by that time, fortunes have already been made.

These two are rather partial to the Vancouver and Alberta stock exchanges. Little wonder why. They have yet to be fully taken to task by regulators there over their questionable activities. Their first big promotion was NCN. In two years the company announced and canceled eleven major projects before trading was halted in December 1986, "pending clarification." Clarification never came, and trading remained halted.

Along the way, Stidham and Grey drafted hockey star Gordie Howe as a director of NCN. Before the fun ended, prices were propelled skyward for no reason at all. Among NCN's more preposterous schemes were the marketing of a revolutionary new portable bidet for travelers called the Hydro-Douche and the takeover of a firm that made "super rolls of bathroom tissue," which were ten times larger than standard household rolls and came complete with theft-proof packaging. Needless to say, the deals never came off.

Altar Gold was another of their companies. In 1986 it announced that it was about to buy a mining property in the U.S. "where the gold was so common you could bag it." That deal never came off, nor did a scheme to buy producing Texas oil wells at a bargain price. True to form, Altar Gold veered into other areas such as horsebreeding, and finally into the manufacturing of a wonder tool called the Rist-Rench. Trading in Altar Gold was halted in November 1986, a month before trading in NCN was halted, pending clarification. As in the NCN case, clarification never arrived. Both stocks were delisted.

Undaunted, in late 1986 and early 1987, the dynamic duo became entangled with the ubiquitous Khashoggi, in a questionable deal involving a Denver-listed company, Mali-American Mines. The mastermind behind this was Oliver Reese, Mali's president, an acquaintance of Stidham and Grey, resident of Albuquerque, and a born-again Baptist. The Securities and Exchange Commission took Reese and another Mali officer, Charles Richards, to court over this, eventually obtaining civil injunctions in October 1987 against the two concerning Registration and Anti Fraud violations.

Years before, in 1965, Reese had been taken to court by the commission for fraudulently marketing unregistered securities in connection with a clay pit in New Mexico. He claimed at the time that it had an inexhaustible supply of top-quality clay; it actually contained only a small supply of low-quality clay. The commission won its case and he agreed to cease and desist from what he was doing before. Authorities dogged his tracks in the U.S. for a decade, and Reese ended up in the African country of Mali in 1982, where he convinced the government to give him the right for three years to hunt for gold in a massive concession of 413 square kilometers. In return, he was to spend at least $1.9 million on exploration and give the government 30 percent of whatever he discovered.

In 1986 Reese approached Stidham and Grey to get a Canadian merger partner for Mali to help him raise money to meet his promises to the Mali government. The two suggested a merger with a Vancouver shell company called Vault Explorations. Stidham had already approached Maurice

Hamelin, promoter of Vault Explorations, with a scheme to buy a Nashville record company, Sun Entertainment, in a share swap deal. (Hamelin was a small-time promoter who owned Vault and another tiny shell company and listed his occupation in corporate documents as manager of the Kelowna Elks Club. Other Vault directors included the manager of a Kelowna produce store, the owner of a pub, and a geologist.)

To seal the deal, Stidham and Grey each bought 23,000 Vault shares at sixty-seven cents each. The proceeds from their share purchase were to be used to pay for the legal and accounting costs of negotiating a merger with Sun Entertainment. Hamelin told the world about his agreement to buy the Nashville record company for six million Vault shares on December 18, 1986. News that Stidham and Grey were talking with Vault about an even bigger merger leaked out. Vault trading jumped to 100,000 shares a day from its average of 9,000 daily and prices doubled to $1.36.

At the time, only two million Vault shares were outstanding, but the company had authorized up to 100 million shares for issuance. That was one of its attractions as a Mali merger partner. Meanwhile, in Denver Mali-American's president, Oliver Reese, desperately wanted to hike the value of his company's shares, so he asked Khashoggi to hype them. Four days before Christmas, Reese and others met with the arms dealer in his posh New York apartment and signed an agreement giving Khashoggi 5 percent of Mali's net profits in return for his public endorsement and financing help if mines were to be developed. For effect, Reese also invited along a local television camera crew from Denver. While the crew was there, actress Elizabeth Taylor popped in for a drink, and the television cameras caught the event.

In Canada Stidham got hold of the Denver camera crew's footage of Khashoggi and used it to prove the Arab's involvement in order to promote a Mali merger to Vault's board of directors. The film made the rounds of Vancouver brokerage houses too, as did Mali press releases quoting Khashoggi as saying its mining claims had "absolutely enormous potential. It has been speculated that these are in fact the legendary King Solomon's Mines."

Stidham convinced Vault's president Maurice Hamelin to merge with Mali-American. Then trading went crazy. On New Year's Eve, 1986, some 149,000 shares traded hands, prices hit $1.40, and there were so many buy orders that Vault was suspended before noon. It reopened on January 5, 1987, and 200,000 shares were sold that day for up to $2.85 a share, but on January 16 trading was halted again after 160,000 shares traded hands in only twenty-six minutes for up to $3.50 a share. Then Hamelin announced a proposal to swap 95 million Vault shares for 48 percent of Mali-American, followed the next day by an announcement from Khashoggi that he would serve as Mali's chairman and that its mining claims contained enough gold "to bring prosperity to the country of Mali and help stabilize world finances." He also said money was available to develop mines there.

Exchange officials were ready to release the stock for trading once more, but the Superintendant of Broker's office extended the cease-trade for another fifteen days until more information about Mali's mining claims could be obtained. Officials also found it impossible to verify Khashoggi's Mali involvement, much less the existence of the claims. "How the hell do you pick up the phone and call Adnan Khashoggi?" asked investigator Al Dilworth.

Hamelin, Stidham, and Grey met in Denver with Reese and others and the deal was terminated after a U.S. accountant told the group that a letter from him verifying Mali's financial information had been altered and that he did not trust the numbers. On January 23, 1987, Hamelin said the merger was off, and shares reopened January 26 at ninety-five cents. The merger with Sun Entertainment proceeded weeks later and Vault was renamed Sun Entertainment Corp.

Francis Salazar, a disbarred Colorado lawyer and an associate of Reese, blamed the canceled merger plans on Vancouver's Peter Brown of Canarim. In an interview with Denver's *Westword* magazine, he said, "Brown had helped arrange major business transactions with Khashoggi before and he was jealous that some upstarts from Denver were invading his turf." He also claimed Brown pressured B.C. officials to issue the 15-day cease-trade order.

The article elicited an angry reaction from Brown. "There's an easy way of telling when the people you're talking to [in Denver] are lying," he said. "Their lips move." He denied the allegations.

Just four days after the Vault deal vanished, Stidham and Grey met in Vancouver with Hamelin's friend Walter Berukoff, the managing director of Miramar Energy Corp., to sign a new merger deal. On February 4, 1987, a deal was struck, and the company teased the market by saying it would acquire an American mining company "with a large precious metal concession in Africa." Miramar shares jumped from ninety-five cents a share to $3.40, and on February 19 Miramar announced it would be taken over by Mali. Trading in Miramar was halted on February 25, 1987, by the B.C. Superintendent of Brokers because officials were upset that Mali had issued 733,160 shares of new, unpriced shares to persons unknown on the eve of the merger announcement.

Miramar director Walter Berukoff did not drop the merger plans and decided to double-check things in Africa himself. Not surprisingly, he found that Reese had stretched the truth. The mining permit was half the size he had been told; the so-called $1.5 million in mining equipment on site was worth only $200,000; and boasts by Reese that he enjoyed a good relationship with the Mali government were untrue. In fact, Miramar executives had to bail Reese out of jail after he was arrested for bouncing a check.

Miramar's lawyer made Reese sign a statement on April 15, 1987, saying that he had made sixteen misrepresentations to

Miramar, then both sides worked out a new deal. Miramar would give Mali 2.5 million of its shares to get its African mining claims. Eventually that deal was scrapped. Mali-American needed a new merger partner. They found a prospect in Alberta.

In January 1987 Stidham and Grey had taken over Aldershot Resources Ltd., which promptly became the hottest stock on the Alberta Stock Exchange that year. Aldershot had climbed from fifteen cents to four dollars by April 1987, after the company announced a plan to take over a Texas oil refinery. Not surprisingly, Alberta securities officials shut down trading, pending clarification.

This was to be Stidham and Grey's new vehicle for a merger with Mali-American. However, when Aldershot president Richard Westbury announced on March 11, 1987, that he was negotiating a Texas oil deal, he didn't mention that Onyx (Stidham and Grey's firm) had bought an option on 600,000 shares of Aldershot stock, as well as 176,000 for Stidham personally and 164,000 for Grey. Those transactions should have been disclosed because their shareholders were equivalent to 40.2 percent of the outstanding Aldershot shares and they were insiders obliged to file insider trading reports, according to the Alberta Securities Commission decision in September 1987.

The decision followed a commission hearing into Aldershot's affairs after officials felt company press releases were inaccurate. But before the hearing, Stidham and Grey tried without success to convince Aldershot's board to merge with Mali-American. After the hearing in August, the commission said that Stidham and Grey had also failed to disclose their Aldershot shareholdings by filing insider trading reports. The two were banned from trading on the Alberta Stock Exchange for twenty years.

Indefatigable, the two went back to Vancouver and became involved in two more questionable deals. Finally, in late 1987 the Superintendent of Brokers instructed members of his new investigative team to probe several Stidham and Grey promotions. Unfortunately, their affairs will take months to untangle, and even if they are booted out of British Columbia, or charges are laid, they can still orchestrate deals in Canada as they have always done — by telephone from downtown Denver.

15/The Regulator

Like George Wool, Rupert Bullock was a white-collar crime investigator with the RCMP, and he left because he had suffered many of the same frustrations as Wool. Before giving up the chase, however, he did an equally frustrating stint as the chief market watchdog in British Columbia, the Superintendent of Brokers. He left in January 1986 "because you can't move governments." Bullock now makes six figures a year as a partner with chartered accountancy giant, Peat, Marwick, Mitchell. His ability to analyze trading and white-collar crime now commands big fees, and he appears as a professional witness or accountancy consultant. His job is called forensic accounting because he follows the paper trail left by swindlers or stock-market manipulators, a trail of trading records and financial documents. While he was superintendent, Bullock brought in many reforms, but he couldn't stem the tide of white-collar crime in British Columbia. He left in 1986, and since then the superintendent's job has been a revolving door. Four replacements have tried, but none has yet been able to mop up the mess.

Bullock's career is typical of many of Canada's white-collar cops, who are relatively untrained and poorly paid compared to the crooks they are up against. All too often the best ones leave for private industry (or the other side of the street). The work is often thankless, the bureaucracy is annoying, and the budget is too small to ensure adequate training and research.

"I joined the Mounties in 1960 and had an interest in business, not in a uniform job," says Bullock. "But I was married with two kids, and I didn't want to quit. So I got a cushy job in the force so I could go to night school four nights a week plus Saturdays for several years to get my Commerce degree. I gave the force a five-year commitment for that and spent my last five years setting up the stock market manipulation department. Then I left four days after my twentieth year."

Bullock says training is mostly on the job. "'Commercial crime' is a two-week course in the force. In the mid to late 1970s, commercial crime was only one day in the course. They spend only half a day on stock-market manipulation. It's too complicated to teach in one day, much less half a day. They really need an expanded version of the course on market manipulation on the job."

In 1975 Bullock was asked to head up a new market-manipulation section within the RCMP's commercial crime unit. At the time, the RCMP was so short of personnel and expertise that complaints about stock-market shenanigans were not followed up. Before taking the job, Bullock insisted on undertaking an unorthodox self-education process before launching his special unit. "I worked three months anonymously at a brokerage firm, Odlum Brown and T. B. Read. Two weeks in each department: brokering, trading floor, back shop, compliance."

When Bullock created his new manipulation squad he had to pick and choose from among dozens of complaints to decide where he could do the most good. "We started the section in 1975," says Bullock. "There were 1,500 listed stocks and virtually no limit to the amount of work, so we had to select areas of most impact. And to get impact we needed the most publicity. I looked around and came up with three interesting cases between 1975 and 1977. We chose high-profile promoter Murray Pezim and charged him in 1977 with fraud. He was acquitted, but we chose 'Pez' because he was so well known and we had been given information by an insider.

"The second was Canterra, a situation where the underwritings in our opinion were false. We had about one dozen people on a list of persons buying off the underwriting, and we found it was all engineered by one person, so we charged Ben Hunter with issuing a false prospectus. He had down as buyers his wife, mother-in-law, and friends. Persons unfamiliar with the relationships didn't realize this was not a real distribution supported broadly by the public. He was convicted and went to jail for a few months. This achieved what we wanted, and stopped false underwritings for a while. Now you need 150 shareholders to get listed in Vancouver.

"The third case was Seneca Developments involving [the late] Joe Romano [linked to several crime families in the United States] and Gino Cicci, who were charged and convicted of fraud. After those cases we let people know we were a factor. Before that it was hit and miss. We also installed terminals in the Vancouver Stock Exchange to monitor trading. The Pezim investigation lasted eighteen months and involved thirteen wiretaps on Pez's telephone lines and boardroom. We had the tapes at the RCMP headquarters, went through all the transcripts, and matched them with the trading.

"Even though we won only two out of three cases, it had a deterrent effect. To Joe Schmo off the street it does not mean too much. In the case of Canterra and its false underwriting, it changed the rules. It also built up our credibility. We learned how to talk knowledgeably, set up files on all suspects, and build a library containing all public information about each company so that if we monitored unusual trading we could refer to a file on the company involved."

There was no such police surveillance of trading activity in Vancouver until the late 1970s. Now police as well as exchanges have internal surveillance departments which watch prices and question companies when there are sudden changes up or down without explanation. They also have the authority to shut down trading until they receive answers. They often do.

AN OUNCE OF PREVENTION

Bullock took the job of Superintendent of Brokers because he wanted the opportunity to change policies in order to keep crooks out. "When I took over, the emphasis at the Vancouver exchange was on promotion, not development, of genuine business ventures. Emphasis on business was secondary, and the stock exchange was only there to give legitimacy to promoters. The first year I spent trying to get the system in shape and then trying to get policies which would force improved disclosure and reporting.

"Manpower was a serious problem. Out of sixty-eight employees, one-third were temporary employees. We needed more. We needed to computerize the system and get away from paper. The market was moving ahead faster than us. There were budget freezes, and it was one frustration after another at times," says Bullock. Among the many important legacies Bullock left behind was the establishment of a mining committee. It went a long way toward banishing the more outrageous moose pasture that was being peddled on the Vancouver Stock Exchange.

"The problem was there were too many companies without assets except for a land claim which was an extra long shot. The problem was no one could say there was no gold there and never would be, and most people accept the fact the chances of finding any were remote. But unfortunately, as a regulator, I realized people do not read prospectuses or buy on the basis of the promoter," says Bullock.

Unfortunately, many scoundrels have moved into so-called high tech and other speculative vehicles, particularly those located outside Canada, which are difficult to check. Bullock's mining committee should be emulated everywhere and should also be set up for industrial and other companies.

The superintendent's office, called appropriately the SOB's office, has expanded rapidly as a result of Bullock's momentum. In the summer of 1988, Doug Hyndman, a career civil servant from the Department of Finance in Victoria, became the chairman of the British Columbia Securities Commission and promptly hired Vancouver securities lawyer Neil de Gelder to clean things up. The two were able to get a 50 percent budget increase for the fiscal year 1987-1988, and they started a special fraud squad to conduct intensive investigations into certain companies or promoters. They have also held three times more days of hearings than ever before. Still plaguing the superintendent's office, however, is the fact that, although a few lawyers and accountants are paid good wages, the majority of investigators earn $30,000 a year. They could get $45,000 working at the Vancouver Stock Exchange and even more working in private industry. Mounties are also poorly paid; they make about $40,000 even after many years of experience.

"You are looking at hiring people who could get more money elsewhere," says Alan Dilworth, former director of investigations at the superintendent's office, who left in 1988 for a job in the private sector with an accounting firm. "In 1982, the RCMP had only five commercial crime guys in B.C. and now there's eighty. In that time in the SOB, we went from ten to twenty-three investigators. That's short of what we need. Not to catch all the world, but to keep on top of these guys."

Even so, Dilworth points out many successes in the past. "Once we start looking at you and you do it, we'll get you. It's a small market. The potential people number about two dozen guys and they are not all active at the same time. Between April 1, 1985, and March 31, 1987, we estimate we saved the investing public $451 million by stopping various schemes or prospectuses."

After Bullock left, Earl Jewett was interim superintendent

until Michael Ross was hired. Ross, an eccentric who composed music and did handwriting analysis in his spare time, accepted a jet ride from Vancouver promoter Nelson Skalbania to the Super Bowl Game. "It was in the RCMP mess and we were there having a few drinks and Ross just couldn't resist opening his mouth and bragging about going to the Super Bowl," recalls Alan Dilworth. "I just about fell off the fuckin' chair. Here he was talking about taking a plane with Skalbania and the Royal Red [Mounties] were just about to exercise search warrants as part of a criminal investigation into Skalbania."

Skalbania was never charged criminally, but Ross's actions were considered unethical, given his knowledge about an ongoing criminal investigation at the time as well as the fact that his own office was putting Skalbania and several of his companies under a microscope as part of its investigation into Skalbania's affairs. The controversy that ensued forced him to quit. He was followed by a provincial civil servant, Jill Bodkin, who left abruptly amid rumors that her tough-mindedness annoyed powerful brokers balking at more reforms. In 1987 Neil de Gelder became superintendent.

PLUS ÇA CHANGE . . .

During the two years since quitting as superintendent, Bullock has been a highly paid consultant for an American victim of what is one of Vancouver's latest and greatest scandals. The case began as a civil lawsuit and has resulted in criminal charges being laid against a number of individuals. These charges are now before the courts. The civil trial concluded in the spring of 1988 and B.C. Supreme Court Justice Mary Southin found all six defendants liable for damages for defrauding millions of dollars from a U.S. mutual fund by wash trading and bribing a fund official to create artificial buying power to hike prices before selling off shares to the fund and the public. She ordered all the defendants to pay $17 million to the fund and criticized directors for not living up to their responsibilities. Because of contempt of court restrictions, the names have been omitted to protect the parties found guilty in the civil action. This is because some of them are charged with fraud and with illegal bribes and details cannot be published while the criminal trial is proceeding. This trial is scheduled for fall 1988.

Back on May 17, 1988, Judge Southin pulled no punches in her judgment. "It is clear that A and B embarked in May 1984 on a scheme with C and D by which they were all to be enriched at the [mutual] fund's expense. The scheme succeeded beyond, I suspect, their wildest dreams. Had they all been less greedy it might never have been discovered. But they went once too often to the well," she said.

"A and B were stock promoters. I say this advisedly. There is in my opinion a world of difference between persons promoting a company in which they invested their own money and which they truly intend to make into a successful business enterprise and the practice of persons promoting stock as it appears to be carried on by some people from time to time in British Columbia. Promoters such as A and B have no interest at all in getting a business going. Their only interest is running up the price of the stock and unloading it to others."

The case provides a bird's-eye view into the type of manipulations that probably go on every day of the week in Vancouver, Alberta, and possibly Toronto and Montreal too. The most damning testimony came from one of the promoter's executive assistants who described the manipulation during the trial. "There were basically two patterns. One was for shares in companies that they formed themselves from scratch and so therefore seed stock was raised and shareholders were, or nominees basically were, used to make up the share base — the shareholder list for the shares. They in fact generally owned 90 to sometimes 100 percent of the shares. In the case of purchased deals, they were usually shares that were just about to go public where a prospectus had been filed. In that case, whoever had accumulated the shares would sell the deal, sell what share issue they had to A or B," the court was told.

Judge Southin also blasted the brokerage community for its role "related in spirit to the three monkeys," a reference to those who subscribe to the "see no evil, hear no evil, speak no evil" school of business ethics. As for the Superintendent of Brokers' office and the Vancouver Stock Exchange, she said that they lacked the resources to detect unusual dealings on the market in their early stages. She was being kind. The Superintendent of Brokers was alerted to trouble, but chose to ask one of the marketplace's biggest participants — Peter Brown of Canarim Investment Corp. — to sort it out. Brown blew the whistle on the mutual fund's purchases, but not before getting sucked in himself.

Even after Brown called attention to the affair, he himself got sideswiped during the court proceedings, which ended in spring 1988. Court testimony dragged his name through the mud, and the newspapers faithfully, and foolishly, reported every detail.

Former Vancouver Stock Exchange listings vice-president, Doug Garrod, agreed that Brown was given a bum rap during the civil court case. "I was the vice-president of listings at the time, and there was a meeting [that I] and Rupert Bullock attended where the whole fund problem was laid out by Peter. He had already blown the whistle to the fund itself. Brown has not been criminally or civilly implicated in this case and I think that speaks for itself." Garrod felt so strongly that he wrote letters to the editors of local Vancouver newspapers to complain about their treatment of Brown.

During the trial, the court was told that in 1984 and early 1985, the fund did two-thirds of all the buying for fifteen of A and B's companies, exceeding its own 10 percent ownership-limit rule and rules against buying pure speculations. Brown told me his version of events in an interview with the *Financial Post*. "Bullock came to me in January 1985 with concerns about A and B's companies, which were the high-volume action in 1984. So I thought I could help out the situation by turning them from strictly a promotion to real assets and get some business too. I had no idea what was going on.

"I said to A and B, 'What's going on?' They said, 'It's buying pressure from Europe.' When I looked at their trading, it made sense because X [the main brokerage firm they dealt with] is where a lot of European trading does come from, and most of the trades appear to come in first thing in the morning, which is what happens with the Europeans. Orders build up overnight on the wire and all come in during the first part of the day. I believed them. So I said to them, 'If you have this kind of financial support, why don't you buy some more substantial assets and build some real companies?' They said that was great.

"Now I look back and realize they must have thought they'd died and gone to heaven. They are in the middle of this scheme and in walks Brown. I did three deals. I sold land to Y Resources next to a discovery. I negotiated it, charged a cash fee plus the right to buy 100,000 shares. The fee was not paid and I got the shares for forty cents on March 18, 1985." On March 19, shares hit $2.75 after one of A and B's proxies got on its board.

Judge Southin cited the largest single loss to the mutual fund, which involved a Vancouver company incorporated in March 1982. By December 1983, it had $85,224 in assets and 1,332,001 shares outstanding. Also, 750,000 shares were held in escrow: two defendants had 162,500 shares each, an officer had 325,000 and a director had 100,000. The director was a former Vancouver Stock Exchange official.

In April 1984, a prospectus was circulated that offered shares for sale at thirty cents each. In May 1984 shares were listed on the Vancouver Stock Exchange for the first time because the shareholder distribution requirement of 150 shareholders had allegedly been met. This was not true. A, B, and their associates held virtually all of the shares. On the first day of trading in May, B bought 2,000 shares for one dollar each and by the end of the day there were many sales by trading accounts controlled by A and B, and the price hit $1.30 a share.

Within seven trading days, A and B ratcheted the stock price up to $2.39 per share. Every day's last trade was a new high, that is, A and B were painting the tape. By the seventh day, they began unloading their stock onto the U.S. mutual fund, which dominated trading from then on. For instance, on the seventh day of trading, 191,400 shares changed hands. The fund bought 150,000 and the companies controlled by A and B bought 27,400 for a combined total of 177,400; outsiders bought only 14,000 shares. Gradually, the public began taking a bigger piece of the action as hype and buying power from the fund attracted the public to the stock.

Volume dropped off in June and July, and prices fell to $1.35 by August 1984. Then A and B's companies began buying again, along with the fund. By the end of August, prices were $1.85 and the fund and promoters owned 73 percent of the outstanding stock. The price dropped again steadily as they unloaded, hitting forty cents in October 1984. On this same day, A and B purchased 812,800 shares privately from the fund at forty cents a share, then began running it up again to make more money. In November prices hit three dollars a share, thanks to a well-orchestrated campaign of press releases and trades among A and B's group which owned 68 percent of the stock. The fund held 512,000 shares, considerably more than the 10 percent it was allowed to own in any single company.

"On November 27, 1984, the schemers produced their first false document," said Southin. The first was a press release and the second a bogus quarterly financial report about the company. The press release boasted about a private placement of $180,000 and said that four million escrow shares were being swapped for gold mining prospects, bolstered by a favorable engineering report. "This press release, not found in the public record of the company, was found in the files of the fund. It was false. Had it been true, the company would have had more than six million issued shares. The fund would then have been within the 10 percent limitation," said the judge.

The quarterly financial report was partly false too, in order to satisfy the fund management and its auditors and protect the portfolio manager from detection. By the end of 1984, the fund owned 859,600 shares for which it had paid $1.93 million, or $2.65 a share. In August 1985, 700,000 of these shares fetched forty cents apiece. "The fund, having bought these large numbers of shares mostly from A and B accounts essentially twice, had, by the end of its dealings with the company, lost US$3 million," concluded the judge. The court cited two more examples of manipulations in the judgment, which awarded the fund some $17 million from all of the defendants.

When the fund eventually sued, the suit triggered a criminal investigation and the charges that are still before the courts. The fund also turned to Rupert Bullock as an expert witness after he had left his job as Superintendent of Brokers. It hired Peter Brown to get them out of A's and B's stock positions as expeditiously as possible.

A FINANCIAL BLACK HOLE

Bullock and others have been responsible for making many people realize how the Vancouver Stock Exchange has been used by scoundrels. Despite efforts to stem problems, the scandals are increasing, particularly those involving offshore players and companies. Everyone admits that only a few are ever getting caught, much less investigated. The scams are becoming more sophisticated and considerably more international. Increasing cross-border activity in Vancouver renders probes and punishments all but impossible. Paper trails disappear into thin air, misleading information can be floated with impunity, and extradition, if it ever comes to that, is mostly out of the question because of the costs and legal complexities. Worse yet, as Vancouver cracks down on culprits, they move to Alberta or to over-the-counter markets in Toronto and Montreal, playing one jurisdiction off against another.

Clearly, British California's Casino, or the Vancouver Stock Exchange, is just catching on to the problem of white-collar scams. The fact that it has not tuned in to the well-worn scams, from Rabbiah's fake photocopier to promoters stealing money from Europeans and Americans, is an indictment of both regulators and the brokerage community itself. But the problem is not confined to the Vancouver Stock Exchange. The same brokers who dominate Howe Street dominate Bay Street. Many big brokers, such as Dominion Securities or Burns Fry, do not encourage their brokers to solicit trading in Vancouver or Alberta stocks, but brokers are free to do so if they choose, and some do. If they really feel that the exchanges did not give investors a fair shake, they should ban any trades and withdraw their membership in the exchange. Not encouraging trading is a cop-out. Successive regimes of regulators have shown that the two stock markets have not straightened themselves out. In fact, the Alberta Stock Exchange is getting worse. If stock markets refuse to tighten up regulations, they must be shut down. If provincial regulators won't do it, then the federal government must step in.

Canada needs some kind of super securities cops, preferably recruited from the ranks of the brokerage community; after all, it takes one to know one. Canadian policymakers have yet to do what American policymakers did back in 1929 after the crash sent the world's economy careening. Bootlegger Joseph Kennedy had been bugging Franklin Delano

Roosevelt to appoint him to the Court of Saint James, as U.S. Ambassador to Britain. FDR knew Kennedy for what he was: an ambitious Irishman with a big chip on his shoulder, an overweening desire for legitimacy, and millions to contribute to campaign coffers. So he made Kennedy a deal. Kennedy was to set up the first Securities and Exchange Commission and come up with laws that would close all the loopholes that ruthless traders like himself had used to manipulate stock markets, then he would be on his way to the Court of Saint James. Kennedy agreed to the deal, and the Americans instituted some of the toughest and smartest securities laws around. It's time Canada found itself a Joseph Kennedy to devise strict national legislation.

16/THE CROWN

Len Doust is the doyen of Canada's lawyers specializing in securities scams. He's certainly had enough practice, both as a defense counsel in private practice in Vancouver and as a switch hitter, or ad hoc crown prosecutor. Depending upon what day it is, Doust is fighting either for or against the police. His agility and ability to fight from both sides of the street, combined with all the scandals in Vancouver, has meant that business has been brisk. Even so, he's not pleased. "It's a disgraceful situation, and no one seems to be doing much about it. The exchange has been out of control for a number of years now, and courts, the government, and even cops don't seem to do enough about it."

Born in 1941, Doust is a short, ginger-haired barrister from Geraldton, Ontario. He attended the University of British Columbia Law School, rather than Ontario's Osgoode Hall where he was slated to go, because his railway engineer father got him free fare out to British Columbia. He fell in love with the place and started his own firm in Vancouver in 1977. Now he has twelve lawyers on board plus support staff and is one of Vancouver's most successful lawyers.

The offices of his busy litigation practice, Doust & Smith, are conveniently located close to the court house, the Superintendent of Broker's offices, and a number of brokerage firms. Doust is, by most accounts, a dazzling courtroom performer. "You've really never seen anything like it until you've seen Doust. He's unbelievable," comments RCMP Sergeant John Beer.

Doust admits that his job can be frustrating because of judges. "I had another case in Prince George [B.C.] involving a simple stock fraud case. I argued it, and the judge said, 'I cannot understand it and I can't convict this man.' In another one in Burnaby, we had a complicated two-week preliminary hearing, and the judge said afterwards, 'I don't understand it, but I will commit it to a trial to let a higher court look at it.'"

Another problem is that policing is a hit-and-miss affair, and the RCMP seconds its commercial crime units to special duties such as security and surveillance or special projects. "The problem last year [1986] was everybody was busy with Expo '86. There was a lot of counterfeiting, mostly involving the passing of fake U.S. dollars at the exhibition," says Doust. About half of the stock market manipulation group spent months at the fair, followed by two-week long stints guarding VIPs at the first ministers' conference held shortly afterward.

Worse yet, just as RCMP officers are getting the hang of commercial crime, many are transferred somewhere else. In Toronto in spring 1988, the commercial-crime unit there lost a talented leader, John Beer. Faced with a promotionless future in that unit, where he had worked for fifteen years, Beer accepted a posting in the immigration unit. Another officer left to go to law school, two more were transferred elsewhere to get ahead. Months before, intelligence expert Derek Hatfield, who had helped the Dutch in their boiler-room raids, left the RCMP and is now a private sector investigator with the Toronto Stock Exchange.

After devoting years to studying the players and scams involved, Hatfield and the others were, and still are, routinely pulled off their regular duties for a night, a week, or even months. In Hatfield's case, he had to neglect his intelligence activities for several months while he guarded Sikhs in southern Ontario whose lives had been threatened following a sensational murder and conspiracy trial in Hamilton, Ontario. Similarly, Sergeant Rick Bowlby, who worked closely with Doust in the Audit Resources case, was back into uniform to head a detachment at the Whistler Mountain ski resort. They never complain, but the waste of their talents is appalling, in my opinion.

No business could be run like the RCMP. Even when experience and talent come to the fore, it seems as though the RCMP is bent on squelching or transferring it. If the stock-market scams are ever to end, the Mounties must offer permanent career opportunities to encourage individuals to specialize in this important area. More money and time must be devoted to training lawyers and accountants to join them as a team. Too many hours are lost in training or reinventing wheels. Doust says this plagues criminal investigations as well as prosecutions. It is something that also bothered George Wool and Rupert Bullock. It is something that should bother lawmakers.

THE CORRUPTION OF CHRIS CAULTON

One of Doust's greatest frustrations involved the biggest scandal ever to hit the Vancouver Stock Exchange. Christopher G. Caulton was vice-president of listings at the exchange until his sudden resignation in 1977. The job is a hotseat in any exchange because listings officers are the most important single gatekeepers in the stock-market system. Many sleazy promoters need, and vie for, a listing on a bona fide exchange. It gives them credibility and society's stamp of approval. But because bylaws don't cover every situation, vice-presidents of listings must often make snap decisions or judgment calls. And therein lies the opportunity for abuse, particularly abuse of the public's trust. This is what the case of Christopher Caulton was all about.

Chris Caulton was employed by the Vancouver Stock

Exchange from December 1970 until he was forced to resign on July 31, 1977. His duties included the review of listings, the approval or disapproval of statements of material facts, and the release of shares in relation to escrow or other agreements. These functions were the sole responsibility of the exchange until the day after Caulton left, on August 1, 1977. When details of the Caulton case came to light, the government moved quickly to avoid the concentration of power in the hands of one individual that had made such a scandal possible. From that day, virtually every duty Caulton had performed for the exchange also needed the additional approval of the British Columbia Securities Commission.

It turned out that Caulton had been in bed with promoters and had been paid to hand out listings. As an exchange employee from 1970 to 1977, he handled hundreds of transactions and got several hundred companies listed on the Vancouver Stock Exchange. He also maneuvered countless more transactions from mergers to reverse takeovers and the release of escrow shares to promoters.

Caulton was running a lucrative scam, getting free shares delivered to his Swiss bank account in return for regulatory favors. It was the same scam that had shaken the Montreal Stock Exchange back in the 1960s when it was discovered that an official had been receiving similar payoffs for years.

Untold millions have been bilked from the public in many countries as a result of Caulton's activities. No one will ever know the extent of his crime. The RCMP charged him with many counts of conspiracy and bribe taking in 1979 but he had already skipped back to his homeland, the United Kingdom, where he now lives in safety, with dozens of secrets. One promoter who paid off Caulton was convicted, but Caulton never stood trial and has so far successfully fended off extradition. Doust worked on the Caulton case for years, but finally the Canadian government called off extradition proceedings because legal costs were mounting, and there wasn't much hope of bringing him to justice. Charges against Caulton were stayed.

The case began with an anonymous tip-off to the RCMP detachment in Vancouver. The informant told the police that Caulton was on the take and had to be "juiced" in order for anything to get past his desk or his committee. The police began making quiet probes. Information was obtained from various promoters who had been in on the payoffs. Several became crown witnesses and their testimony formed the basis of Doust's case.

But to proceed with a case, the police needed to find the stock Caulton had received as payoffs. Fortunately, Caulton paid two visits to Vancouver after his resignation. Both times, police searched his baggage thoroughly. On Caulton's second visit, they found a photocopy of some of the Swiss bank records, indicating that he had an account, and some share certificates. Their most important discovery was a handwritten letter that linked him to the Swiss bank account.

Doust and the RCMP charged Caulton with ninety-four counts of bribe taking and conspiracy and requested that Caulton be extradited from the United Kingdom. But the British are fussy about what kind of evidence they will accept when it comes to shipping off one of their own to face criminal proceedings elsewhere.

"I sent my junior lawyer over to England, and I went over myself to meet with British authorities. We thought we had found a loophole," says Doust. The British said that the key evidence — a sworn statement from a Swiss banker about the delivery and sale of Vancouver stocks in Caulton's secret bank account there — had to be bona fide evidence, admissible in a Canadian or British court. The fact the statement had been taken in Switzerland rendered it unacceptable. So Doust's loophole was either to get the banker to come to

Canada or Britain to swear that the statement was true or to get the banker's statement admitted as evidence in a Canadian court.

"We decided to introduce his affidavit [the banker's statement] as evidence in the court case against the others. So we proceeded against the other accused. But the judge ruled the Swiss banker's affidavit was inadmissible on a technicality," says Doust. "That didn't work so the only thing left was to get the banker to swear his statement in England or Canada."

Doust went to Geneva to try to persuade the banker to come to Canada to testify. "I even tried to convince him just to fly to Heathrow, swear to the statement in the airport, and take the next plane back. That would have done it. We tried everything, but no way. He was concerned about banking policies. You can see why we get so frustrated."

During the trial, Doust uncovered what a neat little swindle Caulton had had going for himself. Swiss trading records show that he regularly received stock in Vancouver companies in return for favors. These favors consisted of spearheading approvals through the listings committee or rubber-stamping them himself, whenever possible. Payoffs in the form of stock certificates would be routinely delivered to the Swiss Volksbank in Geneva. Caulton would then wire the bank with instructions to sell. The sale was handled by Volksbank's agent in Canada, the Royal Bank in Montreal. The Royal Bank, in turn, used various trust companies and brokerage houses in Vancouver to conduct the actual share sale. Proceeds were transferred back to Caulton's Swiss bank account where he or his wife would withdraw money in cash.

Doust presented the court with Swiss bank documents, obtained by the RCMP, that showed deliveries of stock on the ledger, just around the time the committee approved whatever measure that particular company had requested. Sales would be noted in another column, days or weeks later, beside an entry noting what dollars were raised by the sale and were on deposit. For example, "May 13, 1975: letter from the Royal Bank opening the account and instructions to accept 5,000 Pacific Resources shares." This stock was sold weeks later for $8,500. On May 22, 1975, there's another entry, "16,830 New Pyramid shares delivered." These were sold later for $8,803.84.

Caulton made regular investments through this secret account. He also appears to have been given some bargains. The entry on December 23, 1975, shows the purchase of 10,000 units (shares and warrants) of a stock called Groundstar at a cost of $7,885.48, but six days later they were flipped for $16,697.22, a profit of $8,811.74. Stocks in a number of companies ended up in this Swiss bank account, among them were Tandem, Nu-Energy, Golden Granite, Nomad, Tacoma, Major, Super Scoop, Nevex, Global, Hitec, Seneca, Cherokee, Circle Builders, Colby, Thor, Kendal, and Secretariat. It was unknown whether any of these stocks were paid for or not.

There were several witnesses in the Caulton case. A British Columbia prospector named Roy Carlson and his partner Hans Buhr eventually testified for the crown. They bought and sold mining claims in remote regions, then peddled them to Vancouver shell companies in return for cash or shares or both. Between 1975 and 1977, however, Carlson was president of Nomad Mines Ltd. He and Buhr sold some claims to Golden Granite Mines Limited. During this time they associated with Dennis Johnstone, who made the necessary payoffs in stock certificates to Caulton in return for services rendered.

It was Carlson's understanding that the certificates would make things easier at the exchange in terms of gaining approvals for certain transactions, such as permission to issue 400,000 Nomad treasury shares to Golden Granite in order to pay for the claims. Caulton's payoff was 10,000 free shares. Carlson didn't really believe this would be necessary and decided to deliver personally the certificates to make sure they didn't go astray. He put them in an envelope and handed it to Caulton in Caulton's office in May 1977. Sure enough, the Volksbank ledger notes the entry, "10,000 shares of Golden Granite are delivered."

Harry Faulkner was the president of a Vancouver company called International Shasta Resources Ltd. In June 1976 the company had asked the listing committee to allow an underwriting. The company would sell 200,000 shares to three brokerage firms for forty-five cents a share. This stock was then to be resold to the public. While this was before the committee, Faulkner started to get calls from the owner of a local brokerage firm. The calls were unusual because this man was not involved in the underwriting proposal. The court received evidence that he was in cahoots with Caulton, and his job was to collect the payoffs and to get underwriting business out of it at the same time.

In June 1976 the brokerage owner requested 10,000 free shares to sponsor the request. Days later, he repeated his request, saying that the deal would be off if the shares weren't delivered, the court was told. He showed up in Faulkner's office and refused to tell him why the shares were required. He went on to warn Faulkner that if he told anyone about the request he would never get another deal through the exchange. He also told him to change corporate lawyers. Faulkner said he had never heard of such a thing. The man then pointed out that people at the exchange were not stupid enough to make just $18,000 a year working there and that they had been doing this for ten years and things weren't going to change.

"He went on to say that they were going to keep on deferring it [the underwriting at the listing committee] until such time as 'You get somebody working on it that knows what the fuck he's doing, like me,'" Faulkner repeated to the court.

Faulkner told his lawyer immediately and began recording these conversations. According to Faulkner's testimony, the brokerage owner said, "I want you to know that I'm working to help you get it through. I'll back off if you want me to, but if I do, you'll never get it through. It doesn't matter who's doing the underwriting, but without me it won't go through. I would suggest you bring ten thousand over to me. I'll only get a couple of it, and I have to look after the people over there. If the underwriting went through here, I would give them a piece of the commission."

When police got into Volksbank account number 7591425, they found the Shasta entries in the ledger. "June 30, 1976, enclose of 10,000 International Shasta shares; 50 per cent of proceeds to account." On July 7, 1976, the Shasta shares were sold for $3,556.21. The brokerage owner was charged, along with Caulton, Dennis Johnstone, and others, but was acquitted of any wrongdoing in 1986. Johnstone was convicted in 1986.

BLIND FOOLS AND THE AUDIT CASE

Doust recently became involved in one of the most far-reaching and frightening cases in Canada, a case involving Audit Resources of Edmonton. The case is a preview of the financial timebomb that awaits the Vancouver and Alberta stock exchanges unless they take strong measures to counter lax regulations that permit the activities of white-collar criminals.

In 1982 the Alberta government suggested that blind pools be permitted on the Alberta Stock Exchange. Blind pools are an entrepreneur's dream. They are also a crook's. Blind pools allow a company to raise money from the public even though it has no specific business plan and no assets. Investors are betting on the track record and expertise of the company's board of directors and on the likelihood that these people will take advantage of future business opportunities with the money raised. This allows entrepreneurs to obtain public money through a cheap, abbreviated listing process, take advantage of opportunities as they come along, and raise more money as needed. But because the company does not always have a specific purpose for the money raised, regulators and investors cannot check up on how the money is spent. This means that money can easily be wasted or simply stolen.

It is interesting to note that the only two states south of the border where gambling is legal and organized crime is commonplace — Nevada and New Jersey — also allow blind pools. Once Alberta joined that dubious list, the Yankee carpetbaggers sprang into action and came north in droves to join forces with their Canadian counterparts.

In 1982 the staff of the Alberta Securities Commission, citing U.S. scandals, raised concerns about blind pools. But in 1986 those concerns were overriden by the government-appointed commissioners; in an unusual move, Alberta's Securities Commission approved blind pools without even consulting the Alberta Stock Exchange, whose former president, Jim Milliken, was vehemently and outspokenly opposed to blind pools.

The change of attitude was due mostly to the lobbying of Bernard Davies, an Edmonton lawyer and former deputy director of the Alberta Securities Commission. Davies' offices were in the same building as First Commonwealth Securities, an Edmonton brokerage firm, and he was a friend of one of its owners, John Donaldson. Davies himself was no stranger to stock markets; he worked as a manager of a company owned by promoter Ann Mark, who got into trouble with British Columbia securities regulators in the late 1970s. Donaldson headed a stock brokerage firm which applied for a license in Montreal but was rejected by the Quebec Securities Commission because of alleged links to Irving Kott.

Davies lobbied hard in Alberta for the blind pools, as did Keith Alexander, the MLA for the White Mudd riding of Edmonton and a vice-president of Dominion Securities Ltd.,

Canada's largest brokerage firm and a member of all exchanges. Alexander was one of the authors of a white paper on Economic Development in Alberta which recommended blind pools, among other ideas. The white paper suggested listing only pools with 200 shareholders who lived in Alberta. This was supposed to safeguard the public because, the theory went, people would know the players involved. The Audit Resources affair showed that this was not the case, so the rules were revised in 1987: blind pools now require 300 shareholders, and there is no residency restriction.

Ever since blind pools were permitted in January 1987, the Alberta Exchange has been deluged with requests for permission to list new pools. An average of three new blind pools have applied for listing every day. "In 1987, the Alberta Stock Exchange turned away thirty companies because of the types of characters involved," says Vancouver-based RCMP Sergeant Rick Bowlby. Such pools attract unsavory players, and the screening process is not what it should be. Bowlby says several convicted swindlers already have companies on the exchange through indirect shareholdings, but others have undoubtedly slipped through.

Some 300 blind pools are now listed on the Alberta Stock Exchange and yet the province has not significantly increased its investigatory measures. "There are only three investigators for securities, insurance, and other financial matters in the whole province," says former president of the exchange Jim Milliken. "Can you believe that? No wonder the word's out. They're all headed for here. The system's going to self-destruct."

Not surprisingly, the very first Canadian blind pool (or "nickel lovely," as they are nicknamed in Alberta) ranks as one of Canada's biggest stock swindles. Called Audit Resources Inc., this blind pool caused the biggest bankruptcy of a brokerage firm in Canadian history; the laying of multiple charges of securities violations against brokers; the largest claim up to 1987 against the Canadian brokerage community's national contingency fund; tens of millions of dollars worth of paper losses for Canadian investors; criminal charges against nine individuals; and a lengthy investigation and trial, all of which cost taxpayers millions of dollars.

The story of Audit Resources begins even before blind pools were permitted in Alberta, with the launching of First Commonwealth Securities, the brokerage firm that handled the various transactions involved in the Audit scam. First Commonwealth was founded in the early 1980s by Robert McNeilly. Around 1981 McNeilly merged his brokerage firm with John Donaldson's First Alberta Securities. McNeilly and Donaldson became heavy political contributors to the provincial Tory party and were even photographed on the podium the night Don Getty became premier, their hands joined with the Gettys.

Undoubtedly, the duo's political connections didn't hurt in getting First Commonwealth a seat on the Alberta Stock Exchange in May 1985, which entitled it to trade directly for itself and its clients. The firm barely met the capital requirements for membership, $75,000 in free capital, or cash. As a result, during its short membership on the exchange, it was a constant worry to officials, who are responsible for ensuring that firms are properly financed and behave ethically.

For First Commonwealth, getting on the exchange was a coup. Before that it had been a broker-dealer, able to underwrite and sell shares but unable to execute trades on the floor of the exchange. (Broker-dealers have less prestige and make less money than brokers because they must hire brokers who are exchange members to make their trades for clients. This is called jitney trading.)

As a spanking new member, First Commonwealth wasted little time launching a stock promotion: Golden Star Resources Ltd. soared from forty cents to five dollars in just eight weeks during June and July 1985. It was the classic tout. It had no mine, no revenues, and no profits, but it had "great" prospects and blue-ribbon backers, including Don Getty, who became premier of Alberta shortly thereafter, and former Socred Premier Ernest Manning. In fact, the property was one of the assets of Getty's old company, Nortek Resources, which was bailed out by quasi-crown corporation, NOVA, An Alberta Corp.

I wrote a column about Golden Star that raised the suspicions of a regulator. He went to Alberta to check into the promotion. Even back then, First Commonwealth looked to most outsiders like a fishy financial proposition, but no one else in the press or regulatory agencies picked up on this.

The whole Golden Star promotion was silly, but the huge windfall got everybody in Alberta talking about First Commonwealth — from cabbies to schoolteachers. In essence, that reputation set up Albertans for what was to come. The publicity also attracted the attention of Floyd "Lee" Ogle from Greenwood, Arkansas, who had been cruising the sleazier edges of Vancouver's stock promotion community searching for contacts and opportunities to make big bucks. Unfortunately for Canada, he landed both.

Ogle eventually pleaded guilty on May 15, 1987 in the Provincial Court of British Columbia to conspiracy to defraud the public by artificially increasing the price of shares in Audit Resources.

The other accused have been acquitted. If Doust's appeal is successful, there will be a retrial. Doust's request for a new trial is to be heard in late 1988. If disallowed, Ogle will be a conspiracy of one, an interesting situation in light of the "information" he gave to the crown as to his role and that of others. It was entered into the court record on May 15, 1987, along with his plea of guilty. Doust paraphrased its contents to outline the scam and also described it in his opening remarks in the trial against the other accused.

The first phase of Ogle's plan was to get control of all the shares of a company and then get the company listed on a public stock exchange. The second phase involved wash or matched trades to raise prices artificially with a minimum of cash involved. The scam never got beyond the second phase but according to the usual pattern in other cases the third phase would have been to "blow off" shares to the public and get money for worthless shares. Ideally, this is done through an Amsterdam-style "European distribution." Telexes and correspondence working out such details were found in First Commonwealth's offices after police raided it months later. If Ogle had completed the third phase, he would have gotten away with the whole thing.

Lee Ogle's scheme began in the spring of 1986 with a plan to peddle a boatload of paper in a shell company called North Sun Resources, which was tied to several previous Ogle stock deals in the U.S. It was supposedly an over-the-counter stock trading in New York. The market maker was Capital Shares, with an office in Newport Beach, California, and a corporate charter from Nevada. It was a blind pool too. Ogle convinced McNeilly and Donaldson to get First Commonwealth to "make a market" in Canada, buying and selling North Sun's worthless shares. In no time flat, on the strength of the Golden Star success, First Commonwealth's enthusiastic sales force hiked the price to fourteen dollars per share. "That was the biggest single heist," admits Doust, "with Ogle getting maybe $2 million there, but we were too late to do anything about that one. Ogle dealt with Donaldson in Toronto to set this one up, and Donaldson got his reps to flog the paper. Ogle and an American promoter had all the North Sun stock. It was not trading over the counter. We're talking about $2 million worth of paper here. And to keep the scheme going, when people wanted to sell, and to prevent them from finding out they couldn't, they offered to swap North Sun paper for Audit stock."

Audit had been incorporated years before by McNeilly. It was a shell company with a charter, directors, and an unlimited number of authorized shares. It had no assets until Ogle came along in 1986 and bought it. Three proxies acted as purchasers and directors, but Ogle paid the bills. McNeilly got $31,000 in legal fees, and $500 went into the new company's treasury, making it the most expensive underwriting in history.

Financial statements for Audit were prepared, and First Commonwealth wrote a prospectus, which said that $31,500 was in the company kitty because 600,000 shares at five cents each had been sold to investors. Securities officials blessed the document and allowed the sale of two million more nickel shares, providing the original 600,000 sold were locked away and not sold for at least one year.

First Commonwealth said that its sale was a success and that all the shares were snapped up: 218 people bought 218,000 shares; it bought 82,000 for itself; and seventeen more individuals bought 1.7 million more. All this was untrue, Doust told the court. "The 1.7 million were sold to seventeen persons the accused were satisfied they could rely on to hold that stock and sell it at a time, at a price, and to a party that the accused dictated."

Most of the seventeen people didn't put up a cent, and they were paid seven cents a share in cash for lending their names to these purchases. One of these investors, Maxine Rath, who was Bernard Davies's secretary in Edmonton, was a friend of Donaldson's and she did not know until after the fact that she had bought 100,000 Audit shares for five cents and was about to get seven cents for them in cash. "Then he came up and paid her seven thousand dollars in cash," said Doust. In return, Donaldson asked her, along with the other sixteen initial shareholders, to sign a delivery slip acknowledging receipt of 100,000 shares which they had not ordered, did not pay for, and never saw.

Bernard Davies was also asked if he would put his name down for 100,000 shares, but he told Doust he was never informed that he had sold at seven cents. "They [Audit shares] were in the two-dollar range and I was out celebrating. I thought I was a rich man [$5,000 worth of nickel shares would have been worth $200,000] until I encountered Donaldson who explained to me that, completely without any instructions, my shares had been sold at $7,000." Despite the $193,000 discrepancy, Davies let it go. He thought it was a serious breach of faith, but for some reason he accepted the $7,000 in cash and signed the delivery slip, Doust told the court. Only one out of the original seventeen investors kept the 100,000 shares.

This was clearly a false underwriting, designed to create an illusion of popularity, activity, and price support. It did not raise a dime for company coffers, but Ogle was forced to put $100,000 in proceeds in the treasury anyway for appearance's sake. He soon scooped that out. To repatriate his money, Ogle invested the entire amount in another Donaldson underwriting, Tyner Mining, which traded on the Alberta Stock Exchange. At the urging of Donaldson as a Tyner director, the mining company postponed an issue of stock to the public and accepted instead a private placement of $100,000 from Audit.

But Tyner never saw the cash. The money was withdrawn in the form of a draft and sent to someone named Billy Jack Kersey in Reno, Nevada, payable, in turn, to someone else. "Nothing ever comes back to Audit. It paid out $100,000. Virtually its entire treasury. There is no evidence of investment, no return of any funds. The $100,000 is gone, at the instigation of McNeilly and Donaldson," says Doust.

The next step was to take the 1.6 million shares which had been bought and resold instantly and re-sell them to fifty more investors to give the appearance of continuing interest. "Most of them [these fifty people] paid nothing, got shares issued in their names, never saw the shares, signed the certificates off, never sold them, but in many instances were paid $50 or $100 for going to a brokerage house and endorsing a certificate to convert it to street form so they could be traded," says Doust. Those who found the nominees and did all the paperwork got $1,000 per name.

"Dan Meyer [a Vancouver broker] told me a client of his had asked him if he had any names to use for a shareholders list," says Monique Bourgeous, a Vancouver friend of Meyer. "Dan asked me if I would allow my name to be used. I consented. A week later, he called me on the phone and asked me to come to another brokerage firm [not Meyer's firm, which was Walwyn Stodgell Cochran Murray] to sign the stock certificate. I don't remember which firm, but someone at the office presented it to me. I didn't receive anything for this, and I didn't put any money up at all."

The shares all ended up in accounts controlled by Ogle, his associate, a U.S. promoter named Robert "Bozo" Lalich, or by Vancouver promoters Gary Bilodeau, Scott Rose, or Robert Palm, or Palm's brother and father. Shares were also sent to Ogle's associate Billy Jack Kersey in Nevada. On Friday, May 30, 1986, Audit began trading at twenty-five cents a share on the Alberta Stock Exchange, and prices hit $1.14 immediately. The strategy was to propel stock prices to five dollars apiece as quickly as possible through wash and matched trades. The five-dollar price level was critical because once prices were above that, the stock became "marginable." (Margining is a procedure whereby brokers lend clients up to 50 percent of the value of the shares they hold in account.) On the next trading day, Monday, June 2, the shares opened at $2.05 on a bid by Billy Jack Kersey, Ogle's Reno buddy. In the days that followed, buying pressure continued to lift the stock higher and higher.

But virtually all the buying was being done by First Commonwealth, and virtually all the selling was being done indirectly by Ogle. When shares hit seven dollars apiece, Ogle told his Vancouver pals each to take 20,000 shares (worth $140,000 at seven dollars a share) and deposit them in a new brokerage account in a new Vancouver brokerage firm.

This is how the scheme worked. Because the shares were worth seven dollars, or $140,000, Pal X would ask Broker X for a loan of up to 50 percent of the shares' value, or $70,000, with which to buy more. Pal X would then ask Broker X to buy him another 20,000 Audit shares. Meanwhile, Pal Y would deposit another 20,000 Audit shares worth $140,000 in a new account with Broker Y. Then Pal Y would instruct Broker Y to sell them, and they would be bought by Broker X. In that way, Pal X would buy shares without paying for them, and Pal Y would get a check from Broker Y for $140,000 for the sale. It was a sophisticated version of borrowing from Peter to pay Paul.

"Absolutely no money was put up, just two certificates for 20,000 each, which were worthless. The ring would get $140,000 in cash," says Doust. "It's a sophisticated way of buying stock on credit. When you own all the shares, you just pass the certificates around and take the money back." In essence, Ogle and his friends were withdrawing money from brokerage firms using their own cheap stock as collateral.

In the next three weeks, some $2,251,747 worth of checks from brokerages were handed over to Ogle's pals. The brokers who were doing most of the buying were Walwyn Stodgell's Dan Meyer and two more brokers at other Vancouver firms. Called layoff guys, they were trading Audit stock for the group.

The brokerage checks were converted into bank drafts, payable to the bearer and therefore untraceable, which were cashed in at a Canadian trust company in U.S. dollars. Most of that money disappeared south of the border. But occasionally, under pressure from Donaldson and McNeilly, Ogle would give cash to First Commonwealth, which was doing the lion's share of buying.

The scheme was running out of time and money. As it turned out, Ogle was in so much of a hurry that he inadvertently alerted officials about the stock and its activity. It was assumed that the group was about to begin blowing off stock to the public before bailing out. Ogle tried to motivate First Commonwealth's boiler-room boys with extra commissions in cash and Rolex watches (which naturally turned out to be fakes).

But attempts failed, and Audit prices began to fall as Ogle ran out of buying power to keep them up. The scam artists were also done in by their own treachery. Around July 16, 1986, Lalich decided to bail out and began selling off, or backdooring, the Audit shares he controlled.

Lalich called in sick that day and used a new broker to sell Audit stock. Backdooring made Audit prices fall faster because it increased the supply of available shares. That, in turn, meant that the Vancouver brokerage houses that were holding Audit stock as collateral stopped extending credit on Audit shares because prices began falling. Falling prices also meant that First Commonwealth was the only buyer. But the company had little money left and faced an audit by exchange accountants in two weeks.

On July 17, 1986, to counteract falling prices, Ogle decided to create some good publicity. He looked for a U.S. asset to buy, but before anything was bought he issued a press release announcing Audit's purchase of 50 percent of something called Trans Island Marine Salvage in Arizona. No purchase was completed, as the court later found out.

Then Ogle came up with another last-ditch effort. He lined up a loan from an individual to shore up First Commonwealth so it could continue to buy more Audit shares. Ogle's loan collateral was a $1-million (U.S.) certificate of deposit from Columbia Security and Transfer Ltd. in Fort Erie, Ontario, owned or operated by convicted tax evader Louis Mirando. The certificates were virtually illiquid, that is, difficult, if not impossible, to redeem.

The bogus press release was the end. Trans Island was a marine cable salvaging operation allegedly headquartered in landlocked Arizona. "We were told the company does not exist by Arizona authorities," said a spokesman for the

Alberta Stock Exchange. He added, with unbelievable understatement, "That raised serious questions with us."

On July 22, 1986, the Alberta Stock Exchange decided to shut down the stock the next day, and also First Commonwealth. Simultaneously, the RCMP were getting ready to move in on Ogle. They feared that Ogle would disappear south of the border with the victims' money, and it would be next to impossible to recover or extradite him for prosecution. Fears were heightened when, on Monday, July 21, trading records revealed that a combination of brokerage pressures by First Commonwealth's sales force and the bogus press release had translated into new public buying interest.

"That day McNeilly became concerned, as did the others, with the absence of title to any assets [in Arizona] and with the overextended position of First Commonwealth. They had failed to come through in obtaining proper legal title," says Doust. "What brought it all to a head was the fact they had not perfected any transaction to acquire an asset, even though they did issue a press release saying they had."

Meanwhile, Sergeant Rick Bowlby of the RCMP visited Doust's seventh-floor Howe Street office. Halfway through the meeting, a call came from RCMP headquarters. "We had no intention of arresting anyone at that stage of the game," said Doust. "We then became aware the Alberta Securities Commission was going to cease trade them. Then we were one hour into the briefing, and a call came from headquarters saying we may have a problem. The Alberta Securities Commission doesn't know what we're doing, and it has cease traded. I said, 'We must take Ogle now or not do it.' We got Ogle in the hotel room with $700,000 and McNeilly at the airport with $98,000."

Sergeant Bowlby described the arrests. "There was a briefcase under the bed [in Ogle's hotel room] which was locked, so we seized it, put him in custody, and took it to the prosecutor's office where we opened it. The money was bundled in hundreds and fifties in U.S. dollars. We charged him with being in the possession of the proceeds of crime. The night he was arrested, July 22, 1986, Donaldson and McNeilly were arrested. Lalich was the next day. We arrested Donaldson in Edmonton at his house at 3 a.m. There was no need to do that, but there was an error in communications. We could have gotten him the next morning. McNeilly was arrested at the airport on his way to Edmonton."

After the Vancouver arrests, Doust and Bowlby worked in Doust's office through the night preparing information for search warrants. First thing the next morning, Doust appeared in court for a bail hearing for Ogle and McNeilly in Vancouver, then he appeared before another judge later that afternoon to obtain search warrants for First Commonwealth's offices as well as for the homes and other offices of the accused. "I didn't leave my office until 8 p.m. the following night," recalls Doust.

Around 7 a.m. on July 23, the RCMP exercised their search warrants and entered First Commonwealth's Edmonton offices. Exchange officials had already seized the firm illegally and padlocked its doors. The exchange took that action after halting Audit share trades and suspending First Commonwealth as one of its members, giving it forty-eight hours to correct its capital deficiency. That deadline passed without satisfaction, so the firm was suspended for a further fifteen days and eventually bankrupted in September.

Following the arrests in July 1986, the RCMP laid stock-market manipulation charges of various kinds against Ogle, Donaldson, and McNeilly, as well as against U.S. promoter Robert Lalich and Hunter Brashier, both of California. They also charged Vancouver promoters Scott Rose, Gary Bilodeau, and Robert Palm and Vancouver broker Dan Meyer. Police claimed that, for the period between March 1, 1986, and July 22, 1986, the group used accounts and investors with various trading accounts in Vancouver and Edmonton; that it paid secret commissions to brokers to get them to sell Audit shares or ask clients to hold onto them; and that it wash traded or matched traded. Finally, Mounties charged Ogle and others with unlawful possession of the proceeds of crime between July 7, 1986, and July 22, 1986.

Two weeks after the arrests, Ogle made another mistake. He approached a Vancouver private eye and offered him $10,000 to break into the office of Len Doust and into RCMP headquarters to plant bugging devices and to destroy tapes and other evidentiary materials.

The private eye went straight to the RCMP with this information. He agreed to cooperate and met again with Ogle, this time wired with a body pack. On August 22, Ogle was arrested, this time for attempting to obstruct justice. "He was crazy. He wanted to hire women with AIDS and throw parties with cops to give them AIDS. He wanted to put money in cops' accounts," says Al Dilworth, a former chief investigator with the Superintendent of Brokers' office.

Ogle pleaded guilty weeks later to counseling to obstruct justice. During the sentencing, he brought in a relative from Arkansas to attest that he was a charitable sort who single-handedly supported a poor sister as well as his own family. At one point during the hearing, as Sergeant Bowlby passed by him in court, he drawled, "Please Mr. Bowlby, sir, let me go and I promise I won't do anything wrong again." But Judge D'Arcy McGee sentenced him to two years in jail, saying he showed a "determined effort" to frustrate the judicial process.

An interesting point about the Audit case is that the two sets of officialdom worked in isolation. "The RCMP didn't tell us anything because they weren't sure who they could trust at the Alberta Stock Exchange. The night before they did, they phoned and said they were moving in," says former exchange president Jim Milliken.

After the arrests, Donaldson and McNeilly convinced a provincial cabinet minister to put pressure on Jim Milliken to lift the suspension of their firm. He resisted. Once inside First Commonwealth, auditors confirmed Milliken's decision. Rummaging through documents, they found the questionable $1 million certificate of deposit from Fort Erie's Columbia Security posted as brokerage-firm collateral.

In September 1986 exchange authorities asked the Securities Commission to charge thirty-two First Commonwealth personnel with securities offenses. (A year later most were back on the street selling stock.) That same month, the Vancouver Stock Exchange halted trading in three more companies also connected with Bozo Lalich and Scott Rose: Nor-Con, Triactor, and Reba.

In the end, the Canadian brokerage community's emergency fund, called the national contingency fund, will probably pay out $3 million to the brokers who were taken by Ogle. Ironically, the brokers' own willingness to trust and lend money on new marginable stock perpetuated the scam. Ogle never specifically intended to victimize the brokers. However, the assumed third phase of the scam, distribution to the public, never took place, so the brokers were left with the worthless stock.

"The only reason why a company without any assets reached eight dollars a share [from five cents in two weeks] is because the accused acquired virtually all the stock themselves and traded it amongst themselves. They did their own buying and their own selling with the desirable effect being to move the price up, and Ogle sold all the way up. Probably got away with $7 million to $15 million. We'll never know," says Doust.

One year later, in August 1987, Ogle was deported to the United States after serving eleven months in a Canadian prison and after testifying. Hunter Brashier, whose father, authorities believe, was the brains behind the heist, cooperated with officials as an unindicted co-conspirator in return for having his charges stayed indefinitely. The Audit preliminary hearing lasted most of the summer of 1987.

In the spring of 1988, the judge ruled that many of the documents submitted by Doust were inadmissible. Doust and Bowlby withdrew their case and have since gone to the

Court of Appeal to get a ruling on the lower-court decisions regarding the admissibility of the evidence. They are hoping that the appeal court will rule that the judge's decisions were incorrect and will order a new trial in another lower court with another judge. The whole thing may not be resolved for years.

No matter what the outcome, Doust says the Audit case marks a new sophistication in manipulations in Canada. "In the old days you had to find a company, take it over, vend in worthless assets, warehouse these, and take your chances because you didn't own 20 to 30 percent of the shares. You also needed someone on the floor to help steer trades away from the public. Ogle showed how you can get in on the ground floor and own all the shares, using trading as an illusion to get prices up before the 'blow off.' That level of sophistication wasn't there before, and I'm sure it's going on all the time now."

Audit was also a good example of the lack of communication and poor methods of regulators and exchanges. Four weeks before the raids, New York authorities had begun making inquiries about North Sun. Nevertheless, Securities and Exchange Commission information on Ogle and Brashier and North Sun was not sought in time. Near the end, Alberta authorities requested information on Donaldson from the Quebec Securities Commission, but the file was missing.

It is easy to see how others have, and still are continuously pulling off these kinds of swindles. "For every Audit caught, there are another 100 out there," estimates Jim Milliken. "They are not even catching a small portion, and I don't think they ever will. They could if enough resources were deployed."

ALBERTA'S FOLLIES

As if Audit is not enough of a cautionary tale, several more cases involving the Alberta Stock Exchange underscore another problem concerning lax regulation. What follows are examples as to how manipulators can play one jurisdiction off against another within Canada.

For months Harvey Rubenstein drove his Jaguar from his luxurious lakefront condominium to RCMP headquarters in the shabby part of Toronto. Hookers and drunks populate the area. Rubenstein had to check in once a week to let the "horsemen" know he was still in the country. Since June 1986, the Mounties held his passport while his court appeal was being heard. But just to make sure he was still around, the court ordered him to pay a weekly visit to the RCMP and not to leave the province. Rubenstein is also wanted in the U.S. for securities violations and for allegedly running up huge margined accounts with Oregon brokers, one of which was pushed into bankruptcy.

On August 19, 1986, Rubenstein was sentenced to five years after pleading guilty to fraud and wash trading. A plea bargain agreement had been worked out that would have given Rubenstein's victims restitution of $138,000 in return for a suspended sentence for Rubenstein. He also agreed not to fight extradition to the U.S. But the provincial court judge, Darrell Draper, rejected the agreement as being too lenient. "If the accused is allowed to commit fraud and then pay a discounted amount, it would serve to encourage frauds at a time when large-scale frauds are all too common in Canada," said the judge, adding that there was no guarantee Rubenstein would be convicted in the U.S. even if extradited. Besides, he had prior convictions for fraud and grand theft.

Rubenstein tried to retract his guilty plea, but Draper refused to allow it. He appealed the sentence and won a reduction to two years. He requested leave to appeal that sentence to the Supreme Court of Canada but that was denied in February 1988.

Despite the restrictions, Rubenstein has remained busy. Short, bearded, and usually dressed in a track suit, Rubenstein is sometimes seen hanging around the viewing gallery of the Toronto Stock Exchange. He loves the market and it loves him. He continues to make deals, even while out on bail.

In the spring of 1986, another blind pool, Shabu Gold Mines Inc., sold 800,000 shares to the public at a nickel each. Shabu was listed in Alberta on February 19, 1987. Shortly afterward, it bought a number of mining claims from 69243 Ontario Ltd., owned by Jessie Taylor, Harvey's fiancé. As payment for the claims, Jessie was given 500,000 Shabu shares and also became a Shabu director and vice-president of public relations.

In Shabu's first thirteen weeks of trading, its 5.5 million shares soared from twenty-five cents to $12.75 each. It was a totally speculative company with several hundred Ontario mining claims and some cash as assets, and suddenly it became the Alberta Stock Exchange's most valuable company, with a market value of $78 million. Not surprisingly, it was shut down on April 2, 1987, by officials. The reason given was that the company had issued "false news relating to a private placement in the Bahamas that did not happen." But there were other concerns, and eventually the file was handed over to the RCMP.

Larry Wagar, a Calgary lawyer, became involved in Shabu and now regrets it. He said Rubenstein and many of his Toronto friends were heavy traders in Shabu shares. Rubenstein also took part in operations, attending the one board meeting held while Jessie was a director. As things turned out, her tenure was a mere day and a half leading up to March 31, when the stock reached its peak. Three days later, it was all over. There were no bids for the shares and they fell to two dollars. That's when the stock exchange moved in.

"We were all shocked at the price of the stock and were told there was heavy buying out of the U.S. because of the interest in the mining claims and because the right people were connected to the company," recalls Wagar. "We're pretty sure that Harvey's out of it completely now. We're trying to clean things up now, going through a bit of a reorganization, changing the name. Shabu got a bad name as a result of a couple of the guys involved."

Even though Shabu was shut down, life went on for Harvey and Jessie. They were married in May 1987. The entire Admiral Hotel on Toronto's waterfront, down the street from the couple's beautiful Queen's Quay apartment, was booked for out-of-town guests and twenty-five stretch limousines took the bridal party back and forth to the synagogue and a reception at Casa Loma.

And life continued for Shabu itself. Former listings vice-president Tom Callaghan became one of its directors and Shabu promptly went down to California and New York where it traded over the counter after December 1987 for around one dollar U.S. It is still suspended from trading in Alberta and still under investigation by the RCMP. In June 1988 it was cease-traded by U.S. stock regulators pending a probe.

Alberta also had a hand in getting Calgroup Graphics Corp. Ltd. listed, after it balked at disclosure requirements imposed by the Toronto Stock Exchange. The fact that Calgroup slipped between the cracks has become a very big headache for the Ontario Securities Commission, which has held extensive hearings into the mess.

When Calgroup went public in 1985, it published short biographical sketches of its officers in its prospectus. At the top of the list was its president, fifty-eight-year-old Donald Reid, whose biography begins with his childhood career as a vaudeville tap dancer. That was a nice touch, considering Calgroup inhabits the fringes of "showbiz" as a computer-animation company. Conspicuously absent, however, were some other fascinating biographical data about Mr. Reid, such as the fact that he spent time in prison in 1968 for his shabby role in the Atlantic Acceptance Corp. collapse and that he was a disbarred lawyer.

Back in 1983, Reid sought permission from the Toronto Stock Exchange to fold his computer company into a listed mining shell. To do that, certain disclosure documents had to be filed for public consumption. When Reid came up with his version, the exchange, quite rightly, insisted that his criminal past be included in any description of the company and its principals. Other jurisdictions, such as the United States and United Kingdom, legally require such disclosures.

Reid circumvented the Toronto Stock Exchange's decision by going to the lenient Alberta Stock Exchange, which did not require such disclosures. Within nine months of being listed in 1985, Calgroup stock leaped from $1.80 to $7.50 a share. The stock's huge jump, Reid's dubious record, and the fact that Ontario residents were buying shares caused the Ontario Securities Commission to step in. Even though Calgroup was listed elsewhere, it was still obliged to file financial statements and other documents in Ontario. The commission became concerned about bullish first-year financial forecasts of $12 million in pretax profits, especially when first quarter results showed a loss of $500,000.

An investigation was launched and hearings were held intermittently over fifteen months. Along the way, Reid wrote down $15 million worth of alleged film assets to a mere thirty-two dollars. Calgroup was a problem from the day Reid took it public and published incomplete disclosure documents. In 1986, as the squabble between the company and commission continued, its auditor Price Waterhouse quit, a highly unusual step for any auditor to take. Later Price Waterhouse said that there were no misrepresentations made to it during the preparation of financial statements. Reid sued the firm. Shares were allowed to trade again in December

1986 and fell to about $1.70 apiece. It was a shabby piece of work by the Alberta Stock Exchange.

Another example of Alberta's easygoing regulatory stance concerned an American broker called Joe Lanza.

In January 1986 the U.S. National Association of Securities Dealers concluded that "Primont Resources Ltd. was illegally manipulated from 19 cents to $11.50 on the Vancouver Stock Exchange in just four months in 1984." The group, a cooperative embracing brokers across the United States, fined Portland, Oregon, broker Joe Lanza and others $280,000, and Lanza was banned for life from buying or selling securities in the U.S.

When all hell broke loose south of the border, Lanza was involved in another Vancouver company that was also eventually delisted, Rich Lode Gold Corp. It provides another good example of how scammers play one jurisdiction off against another, in Canada as well as in the U.S., using the accommodating Alberta Stock Exchange, among others. In the fall of 1984, Rich Lode itself asked to be delisted from Vancouver because it felt harassed after three trading halts in two months. It had already applied for a listing on the Alberta Stock Exchange. It got its listing in August 1984, but by October its trading had been suspended, pending clarification of the sudden resignation of two of its four directors.

One of the directors had been high-flying Vancouver financier Bruce McDonald, who owns gold giant Noramco. He gave his reasons to the press, saying he left after learning that the board, in his absence, announced that shares would be sold at $3.50. He also said that Lanza, a broker and market maker, ran the company from Portland, an inappropriate situation because Rich Lode's board of directors, not Lanza, was supposed to be in charge.

Like McDonald, the Vancouver Stock Exchange had concerns about Rich Lode's $3.50 share issue. Officials felt it had not distributed enough shares to the public to determine a valid price. On August 22, 1984, Rich Lode was halted after shares hit $5.75 and cease traded August 31 after some carefully orchestrated, and misleading, press releases. The exchange dug in its heels and demanded that more shares be sold and that the company's management resign. Its president, commercial pilot William Bailie, resigned in September.

On April 9, 1984, Bailie had said the company continued to explore for gold near Nanaimo and was about to buy a good property for 50,000 of its shares. Later, he admitted that the property had been abandoned. On May 11, 1984, boasts claimed that the acquisition of Aero-Control Air Ltd. would add profits to Rich Lode's bottom line. Later, it was admitted that this was untrue, because Aero did not make profits. Bailie said on May 29, 1984, that Aero had reached an agreement in principle with Fort McMurray Regional Hospital to provide the hospital with an airplane and helicopter. Later, it was admitted that the contract was to go to tender. On June 11, 1984, Bailie said Aero-Control would maintain facilities for Augusta Aviation Corp. in Calgary at a handsome rent. Later, he claimed that the deal hinged on Aero paying $100,000 to acquire a lease on an unpaid-for aircraft owned by Augusta. On July 5, 1984, Bailie said the company had an agreement to acquire 10 percent in a Texas well. Later, he said that the company's right to participate was not definite.

As Rich Lode was feeling the pressure from Vancouver, it turned to Alberta for a listing, which it got in August 1984. Under U.S. laws, houses like Lanza's brokerage firm in Portland must have a minimum working capital balance at the end of each month or they cannot operate. If Rich Lode had not been trading on an exchange by August 31, Lanza would have been shut down because he owned a lot of Rich Lode shares, and capital invested in stocks that are suspended from trading cannot be included in the working-capital balance figures.

Lanza got his listing without a hitch, thanks to listings vice-president Tom Callaghan and his staff at the Alberta

Stock Exchange. The listing went through despite objections from Callaghan's Vancouver counterpart, lawyer Doug Garrod, who asked him to wait until "a number of serious disclosure problems" were worked out. Garrod even got Bullock to issue an August 31 cease-trade order to "add weight" to that request. But Callaghan proceeded to list the company that day, telling a Vancouver newspaper that the exchange hadn't mentioned inaccurate press releases or provided him with a good reason for refusing to list Rich Lode.

A FINANCIAL TIME BOMB

The Alberta Stock Exchange is a disaster waiting to happen. The very first blind pool was Audit, now enmeshed in court battles. Then along came Shabu. Blind pools are being listed at a frightening clip, and the provincial government has not devoted new resources to monitoring the activity. Even if the pools start off being operated legitimately, they can be easily taken over or controlled by illegitimate players.

What the brokerage community and other exchanges and the federal government must realize is that a financial system is only as strong as its weakest link. And Alberta is Canada's weakest link. As long as such laissez-faire, even reckless, regimes exist, scoundrels will play tough exchanges off against weak ones. Canada must crack down. The federal government must get involved. There is no other way of protecting the public.

Clearly, inept or nonexistent rules and regulators make life for crown attorneys and defense lawyers like Len Doust both troubled and profitable. As Doust puts it, "What really disturbs me is we are seeing a new sophistication to the scams and there is a money-laundering element to it. The way the Vancouver and Alberta markets are run is nothing short of criminal as far as I'm concerned, and don't let anyone tell you differently."

17/THE SCAPEGOATS

THE SAD SAGA OF ADRIAN DU PLESSIS AND HI PEG

As Audit Resources shares were feverishly trading on the Alberta Stock Exchange, similar trading was going on in Vancouver. Right in the middle of all of this was Adrian du Plessis, a floor trader with Toronto-based brokerage firm Walwyn Stodgell Cochrane Murray. His involvement eventually led to his dismissal by the firm, a new career in journalism, and a crusade against Howe Street and all it stands for.

The traders on the floor in Vancouver used to call Adrian "Bowling Shoes" or "Brunswick" (after the automatic pin-collecting machines in bowling alleys). Quiet, scrawny, and bespectacled, and sporting a punker's hairdo, Adrian got the nickname because he likes to wear pink, kelly green, or turquoise oxfords. He has never been "one of the boys," neither in dress nor in manner. Soft-spoken and clean-living, he wouldn't join the rowdies for an after-work drink in the bar at the Four Seasons Hotel where floor traders hang out. But something else distinguished Adrian from the rest of the pack. Honesty and courage.

It wasn't always that way. Adrian looked the other way in the heady days of 1983 and 1984 when he made a bundle as a Vancouver floor trader. "I made $100,000 or so in the market and took off with my girlfriend to Africa," says du Plessis. "I came back from that trip with different values. I don't know why." He got a job with Walwyn Stodgell as a floor trader in October 1985.

Eight months later he ruined his brokerage career by leaving the floor of the Vancouver Stock Exchange, going to a pay phone, and blowing the whistle on what he thought was a serious breach of exchange rules. He was eventually fired by Walwyn for "refusing to follow instructions." But Adrian sued for wrongful dismissal because he says he had been asked to break exchange rules and he had refused. His story is a fascinating look into the shadowy world of trading in Vancouver where, it would seem, anything goes.

Adrian left high school in 1980 and, on the advice of his girlfriend, who worked at Canarim Investments, applied for a job at the Vancouver Stock Exchange. He started as a board marker, one of dozens of novices who occupy the catwalk overlooking the trading floor and chalk up price changes on a long board listing Vancouver's 2,400 stocks. Within six months, he landed a job as phone clerk at Canarim. There he met John Woods, Canarim's senior floor trader. "Woodsy took a liking to me and sponsored me to take the securities exam," recalls Adrian. "In late 1981, I passed the exam and became a floor pro trader."

Pro traders execute buy and sell orders for clients but also are in partnership with their brokerage firms, trading for their firm's own account. They play the swings of stock prices, up or down. Rules allow this, but pro trades can only be executed after the public's orders have been filled. Traders vie for such jobs because most firms split trading profits with pros fifty-fifty, even though the firm puts up all the cash.

Adrian left Canarim in May 1983 to work for a smaller firm, Wolverton & Co., as a pro trader, because it offered a more generous profit-sharing scheme, 60 percent for the trader and 40 percent for the brokerage firm. After making

$100,000 in profits for himself, he took a year off to travel in Africa and Europe and returned to join another smallish firm, Heywood Securities.

In October 1985, he joined Walwyn Stodgell as a floor trader. His troubles began on May 22, 1986. Walwyn had given birth, as an underwriter, to a new company called Hi Peg Resources, set up to explore for minerals. The company's price was a mere forty cents for one common share and one warrant. As with any new company, it was listed after it had 200 shareholders. Many of these people had paid pennies for their shares and warrants and would be interested in cashing in their chips for a profit once the stock hit the board. Hi Peg's promoter was Bozo Lalich and Lalich's personal broker was Dan Meyer. In May 1986 Adrian was assigned to conduct Walwyn trades in Hi Peg, simply because he handled all Walwyn trading in companies whose names began with the letters D to H.

"The day before trading began, I was called by Meyer and told to buy all the warrants of Hi Peg offered for sale and to keep others away. I was told there would be two others [brokers buying warrants or shares] with us, [Continental] Carlisle and Westcoast [Securities]. I was told they might do big crosses [trades of large blocks of stock in a company], but not to let in any outside buyers," says Adrian.

Such an order contravenes exchange rules, because pro traders are not allowed to prearrange trades, or match them, and they are not allowed to deny the public first crack at buying or selling shares. Traders cannot themselves buy or sell before the public gets its chance.

"The first day, I was given orders to give 50,000 to Carlisle and to buy 50,000 and to ignore other trading. This continued as a pattern. The trades were matched, and there were high sales every day. The first day's trading in Hi Peg, the first big block order came from the trading desk and was phoned. This time I was told to accept trades directly. I was ordered to sell 50,000 shares to Carlisle or Westcoast."

On May 21, 1987, Dan Meyer called Adrian and instructed him to take orders directly from him by telephone, contrary to company policy. Trades are supposed to be placed by brokers through a trading desk where a written order is filled out in triplicate and then sent down to the trading floor. Floor rules require that traders then go on the trading floor and offer the shares for sale "in open outcry" to anyone who wishes to buy them, keeping in mind that clients get first crack.

During this time, Marcia Kirk was on Walwyn's trading desk, and she says Meyer was phoning Adrian asking him to buy or sell stock without a written order. "That's something we're really strict about. This is because the broker can come back and say I didn't want to buy that, and the firm can get stuck with having to pay for the stock. Meyer did that a few times to Adrian."

It appeared to Adrian that Meyer was breaking company rules, and not very subtly. As Adrian tells the story, "The first day I got an order to sell 50,000 to Continental-Carlisle from Meyer. He said go there and do what we're supposed to do. Meyer tells me Carlisle is going to take the order for sure. But ten minutes goes by and no order. This is getting outrageous, so I thought to heck with that and I went to my position on the floor and screamed out the offer for the shares as I'm supposed to do. The pro traders started to come out, sniffing around, detecting a manipulation and price hike. Two guys asked for stock, and I had to give it to them. I could not deny them according to the rules. Meyer was furious and asked me what happened and I told him two other guys bought some.

"He said, 'Leave them out of it,' and I said, 'You're not going to run a rigged deal through me,' and he hung up," said Adrian. Walwyn's office manager, Carl Busby, then called. "Busby called me right away and starts off nice day and stuff and then he says, 'I hear there are some problems.' I was hot and bothered, and I said Meyer was breaking the rules and Busby said, 'Take Meyer's orders and I'll take responsibility.'"

Meyer started calling Adrian to place trades from different phones for some unknown reason. Marcia Kirk thought the firm's telephones were tapped, and perhaps Meyer suspected the same thing. Adrian complained about Meyer to his boss, Walwyn's senior trader, Brad Holmes. "Carlisle's senior trader was embarrassed by the lack of timing, but he didn't talk to Busby. He spoke to Brad Holmes. He told him to watch these guys [the promoters]. Brad said to me, 'Do what you can live with and just keep calling the trades out.'"

On opening day, trading started at thirty-five cents. By the time the bell sounded the end of trading that week units hit eighty cents. Adrian felt the promoters were painting the tape. "They would enter buy orders at a price slightly higher so the close was up each day. By Friday, Meyer says, 'Buy all you can. Offer it at seventy-eight or seventy-nine cents to buy and fill and bid us eighty cents.' The pattern was the same. Every morning there were big trades, then it would sit until about one o'clock or one-fifteen and there would be big orders to close higher."

That weekend, Meyer complained about Adrian to his boss Brad Holmes at the firm's softball game. "Brad said, 'Meyer's raising a lot of shit,'" Adrian remembers, "and at the weekend ball game said he was upset about crooked floor traders." Adrian balked at filling oral orders despite Busby's assurances. At the beginning of the second week, he insisted that all orders had to go through the trading desk and had to be in writing, as per rules. "I told Busby it was too blatant, I did not want to talk about it, and I wanted a record of the trades. I said I would not execute an order until it was in writing."

Other pro traders began to notice the pattern of hiking share prices at the beginning and end of each day. They wanted a piece of the action and began to pick off shares whenever Adrian announced them for sale. Meyer got increasingly angry. "Meyer still kept calling twenty or thirty times a day, and he started trading heavily, 200,000 shares a day," says Adrian.

"By the end of the second week, the ninth or tenth trading day, shares were up to $1.40. Then it suddenly went quiet and trading stopped. I figured I had toilet-trained them. I talked to Marcia and said, 'Great! No more calls.' She said, 'You know why? Bozo is the promoter of Audit Resources on the Alberta Exchange and he's in the office directing orders through Meyer.' She said he got Audit from twenty-five cents to $1.40 in one day."

Adrian found that the heat was off for a few days. The next week, Meyer began nagging him again. Adrian excused himself from the floor and went to a pay phone in a nearby building and anonymously tipped off exchange authorities, telling them that something seemed amiss with Hi Peg. The next day, on June 13, 1987, the exchange requested Hi Peg's trading sheets from Walwyn. "On Friday, June 20, Brad invited me for a drink at the Four Seasons bar. I said, 'What's up?' And he says, 'I don't know how to do this. But it was you or me and you lost.' I said to him, 'I love the market. I'm not crooked, I'm naive.' I grilled Brad about Hi Peg, he seemed uncomfortable, and said he was really sorry to do it. I went back to the trading floor and Woodsy was there. He asked me what was going on and I said, 'I'm fired. I didn't trade enough. I didn't do their lousy deal.'"

On June 23, 1987, Adrian went to see Walwyn manager Carl Busby to ask what was going on. Adrian sued for wrongful dismissal shortly thereafter. Walwyn's statement of defense says Adrian was fired for being late despite warnings; for exceeding trading limits in the trading account despite warnings; for spending excessive time off the trading floor despite warnings; and for failing to perform his duties competently.

A few days after Adrian spoke to Busby, both Busby and Meyer resigned when trading in Hi Peg and Audit was halted and criminal charges involving Audit were laid against Lalich, Ogle, Donaldson, and McNeilly. All were acquitted in spring 1988 and the Crown is appealing this in fall 1988 and asking for a retrial. No charges were ever laid concerning Hi Peg.

JOURNALISTS' CRUSADE

The Black Friday scandal in 1984, caused by the collapse of Beauford Resources and its sister companies, focused my attention onto the Vancouver Stock Exchange. It was an astonishing story and I devoured the scant details that appeared in newspapers in eastern Canada. Then I met and interviewed Rupert Bullock in 1985, during his attempt to clean things up, and I realized then that such scandals were not unusual. What finally convinced me that Vancouver was a veritable sewer of skulduggery was the delisting in December 1986 of International Tillex, the Vancouver Stock Exchange's most valuable single stock. Suddenly, some $172 million in paper value vanished into thin air and a police probe was launched.

My investigations made me decide to write this book about sophisticated financial crimes. I went to Vancouver to do more research and ended up writing a snide article in the *Financial Post* in April 1987 about Vancouver's "sleaze index." This was my description of the informal list of known stock-market manipulators whose activities have an enormous following because they can make people rich. The article was also a summary of some of the more spectacular recent scandals. I indicated my concern about the number of Americans listing companies on the exchange and about my interview with Alan Dilworth in which he told me that his department was 50 percent understaffed.

My article also pointed out how some investors actually looked for sleazy deals by hunting through insider trading reports, where they could recognize the names of proxies who front companies for crooks. They did this to cash in on the manipulation on its way up. In Vancouver, I'm told, there are four-dollar promoters and eight-dollar ones, meaning that some can manipulate stock up to four dollars a share each and others are capable of taking it to much greater heights.

I also pointed out how the game had changed, from peddling paper in companies with questionable mining claims to peddling paper in companies with questionable high-tech prospects. Called "high tekkies" in the trade, such outfits had more sex appeal than mining companies enjoyed in Vancouver, especially after Bullock instituted his mining evaluation committee, which ended most of the mining company swindles.

After that article, I got a call from Adrian du Plessis. We talked for an hour and agreed that the exchange was a disgrace and needed to be either reformed or shut down. That conversation led to a partnership, which involved sharing information, and to a number of exposés and revelations that have helped policymakers look at what they have wrought.

Various other journalists have taken on the Vancouver Stock Exchange, but many of the best ones have retired from the fight. One of the first to attack the Howe Street establishment was a diminutive, soft-spoken business writer named Der Hoi Yin. Married to an experienced and successful stock broker, Hoi Yin penned the first columns that questioned the market's morality. During 1984 and 1985, she wrote a widely read financial column in the *Vancouver Sun* three times a week, which made her many enemies on Howe Street. As a result, she was the object of many rumors, including one that she had a trading account with Peter Brown's Canarim and had become extremely wealthy.

Rumors that she was cashing in on information before it appeared in her column led Superintendent Rupert Bullock to open an investigation into her trading practices and those of her husband. The exchange also did its own investigation. But neither found any evidence of wrongdoing.

Shortly thereafter, Canarim's Peter Brown told a black-tie audience of several hundred people in Vancouver what he thought of Hoi Yin and her journalistic skills. The publisher of the *Vancouver Sun* happened to be in the audience and he became absolutely furious. He got a copy of the tapes made of the proceedings, produced a transcript, and called the paper's libel lawyer. The *Sun* threatened to sue Brown for libel unless he retracted his remarks and apologized. Brown capitulated and wrote a letter of apology which was printed on a half page of the *Sun*.

Der Hoi Yin left the newspaper in 1986 and accepted a job with the CBC's "The National" as its economic reporter. She and her family now live in Toronto. "It's not an episode in my life I like to talk much about. Professional stress is one thing, but personal stress another."

After Hoi Yin left, things were quiet on the Vancouver journalism front until Adrian blew the whistle on the Hi Peg affair. But that was to be only the start of his troubles. By 1987 he was working for John Woods, co-owner of *Stockwatch*, the Hansard of Howe Street. Woods hired him to edit press releases and write the occasional commentary on the market. *Stockwatch* is published every week and contains the boiled-down version of every press release and decision affecting Vancouver's 2,400 companies. But Peter Brown's Canarim owns 48 percent of it.

When Adrian began writing exposés about market nonsense for British Columbia magazines, and feeding local journalists information, the trouble really started. Frustrated by the lack of action from the exchange and the SOB's office, Adrian occasionally fed information to the provincial Opposition, by sending it to Moe Sihota, the New Democrat's financial critic in B.C.

Sihota caught the attention of the press and other politicians. He kept hammering away to embarrass the Socreds, Peter Brown, and the other Howe Street traders. The target of his abuse, British Columbia Finance Minister Mel Couvelier, somehow found out about du Plessis's cooperation and called Vancouver Stock Exchange president Don Hudson to complain. That April, the stock exchange offered Adrian a job as an investigator. He turned it down. Brown complained to John Woods about Adrian's activities. In June, Adrian was unceremoniously dumped from *Stockwatch*.

ADRIAN AND THE RABBI

One of Adrian's major battles has been against a speculative company called Technigen Platinum, run by former Winnipeg rabbi Lawrence Nesis. *Stockwatch* published an unflattering account of the company's creative writing techniques in the April 11, 1987, issue, just around the time the company's stock was reaching its peak price. Nesis sued Adrian and *Stockwatch* over the article, citing alleged inaccuracies. Someone even hired a Vancouver private detective, former Mountie Pat Westphal, to follow Adrian around.

On May 22, 1987, Adrian du Plessis was sued for libel, again for an article on Technigen he had written in *Western Report* magazine. After June 20 he was no longer with *Stockwatch*. (In the fall both lawsuits were dropped. *Western Report* apologized without Adrian's consent and the other suit against *Stockwatch* was simply scrapped.)

What was all the furor about?

Technigen Platinum Corp. was listed on July 30, 1986, at $1.50 a share. The company owns Joytec, creator of the GS 2020, a video machine with a white golf ball attached. When a player hits the ball, the computer is supposed to register the strength and direction of the stroke and simulate it on screen. But far more creative than this technology were Technigen's series of carefully phrased press releases and investment letters, which helped to boost stock prices in months from $1.50 to $16. In April 1987 shares hit their peak, despite the fact that not one sale of a $23,000 simulator had been rung up.

Technigen's driving force is Lawrence Nesis, a former New York lawyer who became a rabbi in Winnipeg. He left his calling, for reasons unknown, to become a tax-shelter specialist. It was rumored that the market maker for his Technigen stock was Bobby Slichter, and much of the buying power and promotion push came from California.

I wrote a piece in the fall of 1987 in *Maclean's* magazine, criticizing the exchange because it allowed Technigen to flout the rules of full, true, and plain disclosure, designed to ensure that present and future investors know what insiders know. I pointed to Technigen as a good example of how such rules were disregarded with impunity.

On November 4, 1986, Technigen announced it would buy 100 percent of Joytec (the Saskatchewan-based inventor and manufacturer of the golf simulator). It said the machine was "scheduled to start rolling off the production line for delivery to the world market early in 1987." Technigen shares hit $4.15 that day. In January 1987 a promotional letter sent to brokers and others claimed that "sales are now proceeding worldwide and Joytec is presently in negotiations with four of the top ten Japanese trading companies including Marubeni of Tokyo, which had 1986 sales in excess of $50 billion!" Technigen estimated that Joytec would produce 4,000 machines worth $113 million in the first full year of production.

On January 29, 1987, Technigen announced that a Lloydminster, Saskatchewan, businessman named Larry Christie would buy 139 machines "within two years" and on February 17 Technigen announced an agreement with Marubeni; the Japanese company would market the simulator on an exclusive basis in Japan after a period of evaluation. The stock hit $8.875 a share. Despite such boasts, on February 20 seven of Joytec's thirty-two employees were given layoff notices, including its much-vaunted production manager, Bob Bugden. However, these employees were asked to stay on for another week, until February 27. On February 26 Premier Grant Devine visited the plant. The layoffs were never announced by Technigen. Joytec issued a press release in Saskatoon about the layoffs, but Technigen did not.

On March 16, 1987, Technigen announced that Marubeni had "recently won the exclusive distribution rights. With sales orders backlogging rapidly, delivery of the simulator worldwide is scheduled for the fall of 1987." On April 1 it announced a $116-million sale to Corporacion Relacio S.A. of Switzerland, secured by a $1 million letter of credit. The stock hit $11.25, then $12.87, then $16 by April 3. On April 9, 1987, Premier Devine led a Saskatchewan trade mission to Japan and met with Marubeni and other firms to promote the machine and other products. On April 21 local newspapers questioned the boasts and pointed out inaccuracies and omissions. Share prices fell to $12.25, and the Vancouver Stock Exchange halted trading and asked the company to answer the questions that had been raised.

Trading resumed two days later. "Our questions have been satisfied. They issued a release. We are satisfied so long as it is clarified and there have been other public exposés giving additional information," said Alfred Woo, vice-president of listings for the exchange. But the so-called exposés were written up in a local paper, whereas most of the investors lived outside the city of Vancouver, outside British Columbia, and even outside Canada.

(In any case, not all the questions were answered. Maybe they never will be. Technigen neglected to say that Marubeni was never firmly committed to buy the machines, but had only signed a letter of intent.)

Without skipping a beat, Nesis announced a $72-million sales deal in June with Computech (Canada) Inc. of Mississauga, a computer sales and service company. Computech was to buy 4,000 GS 2020s over three years "from availability" and put up $500,000 in irrevocable letters of credit forty days before the first shipment. Following the announcement, shares went up again to about seven dollars after falling to as little as four dollars each after the trading halt.

The same press release announced revisions to the Corporacion Relacio deal. The Swiss company would let Computech market machines in eastern Canada and the northeastern U.S.; in return, it could reduce its letter of credit from $1 million to $500,000 by September 30, 1987. Lastly, the release said, "Data-Dee Services Inc., a private company based in Toronto, had been instrumental in the Computech deal and would get 100,000 free Technigen shares over a period of time as payment. At seven dollars a share, that tallied a tidy $700,000. But Technigen said a month later that Data-Dee's fees were worth more than twice that, or $1.5 million.

By November 1987 Nesis was crowing about signing up Marubeni officially, and an article by the *Globe and Mail* Tokyo correspondent said, "Nesis is a happy man. He had just defied the naysayers; he had just finished negotiating a deal with Marubeni for the distribution and licencing of his golf machine." True, Nesis had a written agreement with Marubeni, but it was merely to study the simulator's software before deciding whether or not to buy the rights. This was significantly different from Nesis's press releases in the past, which boasted that thousands of machines would "roll off production lines" in Canada to serve the Far East. In fact, if the software worked, Marubeni planned to make the machine itself and give Joytec a small royalty. In a U.S. document due to be filed in January 1988, which was leaked from the Vancouver Stock Exchange, Technigen itself estimated that the entire value of the Marubeni deal might be only $200,000 in 1988 or hardly enough to pay salaries in Saskatoon. Then in June 1988 Technigen announced that it had agreed to pay $350,000 to Marubeni to get Sony Corp. to look at the technology.

"We think there is good potential. Therefore, we would

like to assist and help Joytec Ltd. Of course, some people in the press do not like the performance or press releases made by Joytec or Technigen. Responsibility to protect investors is up to President Nesis, and we advise him to make very fair press releases all the time, not misguide or mislead the potential investors. That's what I would like to say," said Marubeni's Tokyo spokesman, T. Imaizumi in November 1987.

Technigen also failed to inform the public that Corporacion Relacio, described as a Swiss company, was in fact a Panama shell company with only $13,000 worth of capital, well below its $116-million sales commitment. Moreover, the Corporacion's irrevocable letter of credit was deposited in the name of David Charles Stuart, of Maple, Ontario, a convicted swindler whose activities are known to police and securities officials in several provinces.

Adrian discovered that, back in 1970, British Columbia had imposed a permanent trading ban on Stuart, but his file, and countless other records, were destroyed by officials in 1978 because of a lack of space for storage.

Stuart's trading ban became an issue in October 1987, when Technigen announced that Corporacion Relacio's obligation to post a $1-million letter of credit would be lifted because it had agreed to buy $1 million worth of Technigen shares in Stuart's name, with Stuart as agent. This led to a hearing by the British Columbia Securities Commission to determine whether to let Stuart buy the shares as an agent. In January 1988 his purchase was allowed, mainly because the Corporacion was not buying a very big stake of Technigen. This was a short-sighted decision because there were no restrictions imposed on what Stuart could own. Surely, if he is considered unsuitable as controlling shareholder, he is even less of a suitable prospect as an owner.

Technigen spokesman Gary MacDonald said the company was not concerned about Stuart's past and pointed to some misunderstanding about the original $116 million sales deal. "I'm not an apologist for Mr. Stuart's life. The offense was years ago. The press release containing that figure [$116 million] was taken overall out of context. It was a distribution contract containing provisions and sales quotients. Perhaps it was inaccurate to describe it as sales."

The public was never told everything about the Computech deal either. Press releases portraying Data-Dee as an independent Toronto company were incomplete. It is a wholly owned subsidiary of Computech. It means that the $1.5 million to be paid to Data-Dee was not a finders' fee but went indirectly to Computech, a form of signing bonus in return for agreeing to promote and attempting to sell the machines.

By the spring of 1988, Technigen's boasts about full-scale production had not come true. The Saskatoon facility had laid off more engineering personnel and was not producing hundreds of machines. CBC's "Fifth Estate" did a short documentary on the company, reinforcing what I had said in my *Maclean's* article. Company officials went permanently underground, refusing any interviews. Then, in April 1988, one key employee left Joytec and told many people that little, if anything, was going on at the plant. Money to pay employees was running out. Meanwhile, Nesis and another officer had moved into huge houses and were living the high life. Nesis bought a place on exclusive Point Grey Road, and Joytec's Larry Machula lived in a big house in Saskatoon and drove a Ferrari. Such expensive toys were not paid for by corporate profits because there weren't any. In June 1987, some 375,000 Technigen shares were released from escrow, each worth ten dollars at the time on paper. Nesis owned 355,000 of these, for which he had paid one cent each.

Technigen was yet another depressing example of business practices in Vancouver, where regulators are unable to check up on creative writing techniques or on the crowd of questionable characters behind the hype. But regulators continue to allow an inadequately informed public to buy shares, in the absence of "full, true, and plain disclosure." By the summer of

1988, Technigen's marvelous plans to launch full-scale production in Saskatoon still hadn't come to fruition and probably never will.

Adrian and I were outraged. Technigen still had nothing to show for all its self-generated publicity. No major production, no actual sales, and a greatly reduced workforce in Saskatoon. Government grants, tax write-offs, and shareholders' money were all for naught.

THE GAMETEK GAME

Another Lawrence Nesis promotion was the boosting of share prices for a company called Gametek, which manufactured a coin-operated mechanical game called the Grappler. Nesis worked to bring Gametek to the attention of many blue-ribbon shareholders, including Vancouver's wealthy Belzbergs through their First City Financial Corp.

During the first seven months of 1987, Nesis worked his magic and Gametek shares went from forty cents to three dollars. In the summer of 1987, prices bounced up and down from forty cents to two dollars, until August 6 when the Belzberg's First City bought one million Gametek shares from the company directly for a mere fifty-five cents a share. Naturally, Gametek share prices tumbled and the Vancouver Stock Exchange stepped in, insisting that the price be hiked. On August 29, without admitting it was due to regulatory pressure, Gametek announced a new deal worth eighty-nine cents a share, or 60 percent more than the price paid by the Belzbergs. The exchange was on the right track, but it didn't go far enough. It was blatantly unfair for Gametek's board to make a side bet, at bargain-basement prices, for shares that had cost members of the public nearly four times more two weeks before the deal.

As with Technigen, Nesis had a field day with press releases. In the spring of 1987, Gametek made the following announcement: "The Company has an arrangement with the B.C. Lions Society for Crippled Children where they will assist the company in the distribution of the game in B.C. and will, to the extent possible, collaborate with other Lions organizations throughout the world in soliciting their help on behalf of the company."

On August 20, 1987, Gametek said: "The distribution agreement with the B.C. Lions Society will be mutually terminated on September 15, 1987, since the Society has indicated it is unable to react quickly to the distribution of the Grappler." The arrangement was never replaced anyway, so what was the rush?

I took a look at Gametek's latest press releases, certain that they would maintain the tradition of hyperbole. Nesis had left by then but I was right about the releases. A January 1988 Gametek press release seemed seriously misleading, according to information I was able to obtain. I wrote a story about its coin-operated machine, the Grappler, arm-wrestling's answer to Pac Man; players feed it coins to pit themselves against the gigantic arm. The story embarrassed the company.

On January 26, 1988, Gametek issued a press release stating: "Gametek is pleased to announce an agreement with Deith Leisure PLC to form a joint venture company which will own and operate Gametek's Grappler arm-wrestling game in the United Kingdom. Gametek will have a 50 percent interest in the new venture." As stated in the release, Deith is a respected distributor of pool tables and other games. Its founder, Bob Deith, still runs things, and he confirmed the agreement, adding that he very much likes the Grappler. So far so good.

Gametek's release continued: "Deith Leisure will make all of its existing 60,000 distribution outlets in the U.K. available for potential installation of the Grappler. Included in these 60,000 outlets are a large number of pubs which are the primary market for the Grappler." The statement that Deith will "make available all of its existing 60,000 distribution outlets" is misleading. Deith has various machines and pool tables in thousands of locations, none of which belong to Deith itself. It cannot "make available" what does not belong to it.

But here is the clincher: "Deith estimates that through its 60,000 outlets in the U.K. at least 5,000 games will be placed under this program during the first year of operation. In addition, the Grappler will be marketed in the U.K. and elsewhere in Europe to other game distributors to whom Deith Leisure currently distributes. At least $8 million after all manufacturing and operating costs" will accrue to Gametek. The way I read that, some 5,000 Grapplers were to be sold in Britain and more on the continent.

Here's what Bob Deith said in a taped interview: "We're still going through a testing program. Subject to the income of the game being consistent and the breweries' acceptance [the breweries own the pubs], I wouldn't have thought more than 1,500 to 2,000 for the U.K. market. It's early days to be too firm with the numbers yet." Deith's estimate of 1,500 to 2,000 is quite different from Gametek's press release figures of 5,000 sales in the first year. That misleading statement also makes mincemeat of Gametek's estimate that it will reap "at least" $8 million after costs. Deith says he had no firm figures on revenues because he had no idea whether machines would be sold or leased or how much revenue they would get as people used them.

I called Gametek to confront them with this. The vice-president of marketing, Sandy Brown, was surprised by Deith's remarks. "The 5,000 is his number, not ours. I find it unusual or odd. In a letter of agreement in point form, he says projections are for 5,000 to 10,000 over 1988 and 1989, and it is signed by Bob Deith. We have nothing to hide." Finance vice-president Ted Myrah said that the sales projections had been sent from Britain on January 21, 1988, and that the press release was issued just five days later to comply with timely disclosure rules at the exchange. "If there had been any movement in the stock and the exchange discovered we had the agreement without announcing it, we would've been hammered."

None of this explained why Deith would put something in writing, then change his mind so dramatically, if, in fact, this was the case. What did it mean to the $8 million projections? Why did Gametek issue such a bullish press release when Deith said it was too early to be firm with numbers? The whole affair was suspect, but even after I had pointed out the inconsistencies, there was no reaction from the Vancouver Stock Exchange. Not even a press release requesting clarification was ordered by the exchange.

On June 29, 1988, Gametek trading was halted after it was reported that the company had been sued for $940,000 by the Belzbergs to cover losses and also by certain users who claimed that they had broken their arms by trying to wrestle with the Grappler. When trading was halted, Gametek was trading at ten cents a share.

CHOPP GOES THE WEASEL

ChoPP Computers Corp. Inc. produced another scandalous series of events. It was promoted by two friends of Lawrence Nesis, Don and Josephine Hutton. ChoPP became the most expensive stock in Vancouver in 1987. In thirteen months it went from seventeen cents a share to the equivalent of $125 a share. There was absolutely no reason for the stock to be trading so high. The company had no assets, only promises. Controversy began to dog it, and regulators started to look more closely at it. Then suddenly in 1987, the Huttons, who were promoting it, voluntarily delisted it, removing in one fell swoop $120 million in paper value.

Like a growing number of Vancouver companies, ChoPP came out of California. Its promoter, Don Hutton, was born in Swan River, Manitoba, in 1930. He became a chartered accountant but left that profession in 1968 after a run-in with the Institute of Chartered Accountants for British Columbia over some questionable bookkeeping entries. He turned his hand to stock market promotions where he has been highly successful, apart from a failure in 1973 which led him to declare personal bankruptcy. He moved to Vancouver in 1980 and later to California.

ChoPP's claim to fame and fortune was that it had a deal to produce the world's greatest super-computer, a high-speed, high-tech creation similar to the kind that giants like IBM are also developing. "Not one box was ever produced," commented Al Dilworth. ChoPP's announced merger with another U.S. computer company helped run the stock up to $120 by December 1985. It was lifted even higher with some celebrity name-dropping, as promoters announced with great fanfare that Michael Jackson's brother Randy Jackson was going to invest $2 million in ChoPP. Weeks later, that deal was called off without explanation.

Four months later, in June 1986, strange things began happening. A mysterious company located in St. Vincent, British West Indies, started circulating newsletters questioning ChoPP's prospects. The company, Durant Livermore Cutten and Bliss, was an investment counseling firm, and it told its clients to sell short ChoPP shares. (One of the firm's founders, Mr. Livermore, was a notorious Wall Street swindler who eventually shot himself in a hotel in 1940.)

ChoPP president Don Hutton became upset and sent a letter to shareholders claiming that he was the victim of a "poison pen letter campaign" and that Durant Livermore was itself shorting the stock. ChoPP asked for a trading halt to stop the downward slide which reached forty-two dollars a share, then delisted the stock. Probes in Canada and the U.S. had been launched, but they stopped after the delisting. In 1987 ChoPP got a listing on NASDAQ and hit a high of nearly three dollars a share. By April 1988 it had been evicted from its La Jolla, California, offices for being US$18,000 in arrears in rent. The company's listing had also been dropped from NASDAQ the month before because it did not meet the net worth test, and it had pruned down staff from thirty-two to two.

Like New Cinch and Technigen, ChoPP was another high flyer that turned out to be a dud. A few local editorials ranted and raved, but by the end Canada had been taken for a ride once again. ChoPP lost nearly $6 million between its inception in January 29, 1979, and July 31, 1987, when it published its last financial statements. Where did all the money go? Where did the $120-a-share value go? Why was it allowed to happen? The last word was that, in April 1988, ChoPP's California engineering staff was hired by a company named Metaflow Technologies, Inc., which was about to be taken over by Vancouver Stock Exchange-listed Elan Industries Inc. Brokers in Vancouver were being told that the engineers had brought with them a great new technology. Adrian du Plessis and I thought that phrase had a familiar ring to it.

THE ARCHBISHOP AND I

In October 1987 Adrian and I met in my room at the Four Seasons Hotel in Vancouver to compare notes and discuss some research projects he had undertaken for me. By this time, I was paying Adrian a weekly retainer and money over and above one day's work on an hourly basis. I had asked him to look at Axiom International Development Corp., which had a Chinese hotel deal going, and had jumped suspiciously after an announcement about the biggest single private placement that year on the exchange, some $42 million worth. The volatility of its stock price — from pennies to three dollars in a few months — had been raised by Moe Sihota in the legislature in Victoria. But Sihota didn't know the half of it.

Axiom is similar to many Vancouver companies, a shell whose control, name, and goals are always in a state of flux and whose clutch of offshore assets is impossible to verify. Axiom's head office is in Vancouver; its executive office is near Dallas. Its president is in Hong Kong, and its principal asset is 10 percent of a Beijing hotel project. On June 19, 1987, Axiom announced a takeover agreement to swap eighteen million treasury shares for cash from Jaweed Aziz, a Pakistani citizen who has offices in Houston and the Philippines. Aziz was made chairman of Axiom's board. A month later, he changed the terms of his offer from cash to certificates of deposit.

Adrian told me that a private placement (a large block purchase of $42 million worth of treasury shares) was coming from Columbia Security and Transfer, somewhere in Ontario. That was a company operated by Louis Mirando, a convicted tax evader who had been arrested for money laundering in the U.S. the summer before and had been under police surveillance ever since. Columbia's name had also come up in the Audit case, and its certificates of deposit were thought to be illiquid. Smelling a scam, I decided to look into the company. It turned into one of the most bizarre stories I have ever researched.

I talked to a source of mine inside the SOB's office to tip him off about Mirando's record and the fact that the Ontario Securities Commission had a great deal of information on him. The commission had scotched an attempt to use one of Mirando's certificates of deposit to prop up First Commonwealth in Edmonton before it collapsed, and then the cops came in. Five days later, after I returned to Toronto, Axiom issued a terse press release saying that the $42-million private placement deal had been called off after some "meetings with RCMP" officials. It also announced that its chairman, Jaweed Aziz, who held the certificates of deposit, was no longer with the company.

I became increasingly suspicious, especially because RCMP sources told me they hadn't even talked to Axiom. I decided to call the company. Its president, Dingban Wang, was in Hong Kong, so I called the head office in Texas and talked with corporate secretary Brad Long. Trying to sound friendly and helpful, I told Long how badly I felt for the company, that they must have been victims, sucked into such a questionable deal. Long fell for it, agreed that it was unfortunate, but said that the certificates of deposit had been guaranteed by the Greek Orthodox Church and that he had letters confirming this. I couldn't believe my ears.

I asked him for copies of the letters, suspecting that the whole thing was phony. The letters arrived two weeks later, and I began making phone calls. Nothing checked out. Axiom's management said it had made one phone call to double-check letters of reference before it issued press releases about its $42 million deal. It seemed an inadequate amount of checking to do, considering the size of the deal.

The written guarantees included letters dated September 1987 from a New Jersey parish. "I, Archbishop Makarios, spiritual leader of North and South America," read one of the letters, "highly recommend any involvement of the churches [in New Jersey] concerning certificates of deposit issued by Colombia [sic] Security and Transfer of Fort Erie, Canada and owned by Jaweed Aziz, Consultant of the College of Defence, Metro Manila, Philippines." Unfortunately, the archbishop is not recognized by the official Greek Orthodox Church. "The individual has no connection with any church we would consider even half legitimate," said a spokesman.

The archbishop's letterhead was strange. On top, in bold print, were the words "Greek Orthodox Church, Archdiocese of North and South America." The letter was signed by the "spiritual head," Archbishop Makarios. First of all, Archbishop Makarios had been the prime minister of Cyprus and had died years before. Second, the church's letterhead address was Ellis Avenue in the Bronx. This seemed to me to be a residential street address near a hotbed of drug-dealing activity. Third, the phone number was not printed but merely typewritten on the side.

I had my research associate, Nancy Thomson, call New York information and, sure enough, the phone number was not right, and the address of the Greek Orthodox Church administrative offices was in a high-rent office tower in mid-town Manhattan. We called and the spiritual leader was a different archbishop. No one had ever heard of the Greek Orthodox Archdiocese on Ellis Avenue. I hired a private detective to drive past Ellis. He called the next day and reported that it was a modest two-storey dwelling. He told me that he had rummaged through its garbage can and discovered that the owner was a retired furrier named Gus Poulos. He had also found out that the telephone number was not registered in the archbishop's name.

I called Poulos, and he confirmed that these were not the offices of the Greek Orthodox Church, which was capable of guaranteeing $42 million worth of certificates, but that some peculiar splinter group was using his house as a mail drop. "I was getting the archbishop's mail, but he has left. I don't get his mail no more. I think he's somewhere in Yonkers," he said. When I called the archbishop's phone number, a voice answered and said, "Hello," and confirmed to me that he was Archbishop Makarios. When I challenged his church credentials he said, "I independent." He said his diocese included churches in Mexico, Detroit, Toronto, New Jersey, and the Bronx.

When I asked him about the $42-million certificates of deposit guarantees, he said he couldn't answer questions because his English was so poor. He suggested I call back a couple of hours later and get one of his priests to answer questions. I did call and the priest said he knew nothing about anything. I also called Peter Kostakos, the priest in charge of the three New Jersey parishes which had allegedly guaranteed the certificates, as well as John Savvides, described in a letter as "chairman of the parish." Kostakos referred me to Savvides and said he knew nothing. "I'm the ecclesiastic department, John is the financial department. I never heard of these certificates."

Savvides said he had copies of the certificates of deposit and explained that the parish knew Aziz and had another reason to help him out by guaranteeing the certificates. "Aziz controls the certificates. I know Mr. Mirando and I know Aziz. If they succeed to build projects and are successful, then the church got to get some profit, I guess."

I asked him how to get hold of Jaweed Aziz and he said he would get back to me. Ten minutes later, Aziz himself called from Houston. Thirty-eight-year-old Aziz had given Axiom letters of reference that described him as a consultant to the College of Defence, Metro Manila, Philippines. (When I called the college several days later, this information was contradicted by the college's commandant, G.H. Lansangan Jr., who said he knew Aziz as a "freelance consultant on the Middle East who lives in the Philippines sometimes. He doesn't work here and never has.")

Aziz described himself to me as a businessman and Pakistani citizen. He said he had been a Muslim originally but had joined Archbishop Makarios's church and contributes to it. He said he had involved the church by guaranteeing to bring its religious beliefs to China. "I donate to the church, and basically the church wants we should introduce the religion of the church in China. I was thinking if Axiom has really a contract I could get more contracts and then permission to build a small church there."

Aziz said he could not understand Axiom's problem. He claimed that the certificates were good and cashable anywhere in the world. He also claimed that Firestone Development, a U.S. public company, had accepted the certificates in a share swap worth US$13 million. "Besides, there is the guarantee from the churches."

It was all a joke to my mind. Savvides and Kostakos said they had about 300 parish members and no church building of their own. They were renting at the time. It was impossible to believe that they could justifiably guarantee $42 million worth of certificates. I wrote a story in the *Financial Post* in December 1987 relating all of this information, then attacked regulators for not checking out what was going on. I also went after the company for not doing its homework.

After my story appeared, Axiom stock plummeted to cents. Readers sent me letters applauding the exposé. Even so, the exchange and the Superintendent of Brokers never called the company on the carpet over the bizarre events. No clarification was requested and the company was allowed to conduct business as usual. Then I got two letters — from exchange listings vice-president Alfred Woo and exchange president Don Hudson. They were furious about my story and said that the Vancouver Stock Exchange had been delivered a bum rap. They claimed to have scuttled the private placement and said that in this case they had done a good job as regulators. They wanted to know why I didn't print that.

I wrote Hudson and Woo back and also did another column in February 1988, as a follow-up to the Axiom affair. I did not mention the exchange's role in all of this because Woo had not returned a phone call I had made to him during the course of researching the original story. Besides, the exchange's story did not jibe with what Axiom had told me, nor with the information contained in the press release issued to the public. Axiom said the questionable nature of the people behind Aziz was all discovered accidentally and confirmed by the Mounties.

The exchange's letter to me, however, claimed that the exchange had been questioning the validity of Aziz's purchase all along. "Indeed, the exchange's listing department effectively killed the deal by refusing to accept the certificates of deposit as payment for issuance of Axiom's treasury shares," Woo wrote.

I wrote Hudson a letter back and also wrote another column, calling the exchange's role in the Axiom affair into question. Why didn't it look into the company's management in light of the fact that the company didn't do its homework? Why hadn't the exchange forced Axiom to clarify the messy situation after my initial column?

Although regulators out west didn't twig to the significance of all of this, some individuals down south did something about it. The Securities and Exchange Commission started looking at Firestone Development, which had allegedly accepted Mirando's money, and found that Mirando's Columbia Security is Firestone's transfer agent. Firestone is being monitored south of the border. In addition, I got a letter from the real Greek Orthodox Church to which I had sent a copy of my original article. The spokesman said that the church was "troubled" to see the name of Peter Kostakos in my column. "Our archdiocese has a priest by that name who has no parish assignment at the present time, nor does he hold any position of any kind within our archdiocese. He's listed among our inactive clergy," wrote Bishop Isaiah of Aspendos, chancellor of the church. Church policy dictates that Kostakos cannot remain ordained with the recognized church if he remains a member of Makarios's sect.

About the only thing my story did was to make the stock plummet, alert American regulators to a potentially shady deal, and set in motion the excommunication of a priest. I didn't shake the exchange into realizing what a sham and a potential fraud this was. Although the church and the Americans took note, back in the wild and woolly west the Vancouver Stock Exchange continued to shoot the messengers with the nerve to bring bad news.

Although Adrian and I can take pride in the fact that we have exposed a number of shady transactions, we and others like us have done little good. The media, rather than the swindlers, continued to bear the brunt of criticism. Worse yet, I started to notice, beginning around March 1988, that our efforts and those of others were actually backfiring. That month, several convicted swindlers and manipulators, who were being monitored by intelligence experts in the RCMP and in various regulatory agencies, got bolder and even advertised in prominent Canadian financial newspapers that they had become directors of public companies. It wasn't hard to figure out why. As negative publicity pummeled Vancouver, it excluded Alberta. That meant many scams and scoundrels changed venue. As such ridiculous situations as Gametek's inflated figures or Archbishop Makarios's nonsense fell on deaf regulatory ears, it became obvious to crooks that anything was possible.

Little wonder many observers have given up, sold out, or left town. It does not seem to matter what the past or reputation of a person is: anyone is allowed to list, promote, or invest in companies in partnership with an unwitting public. Investor protection in western Canadian stock exchanges is a myth. More unfortunately, it is a swindler's dream come true. The only solution is to bring in the federal government to lift the standard of regulation up to the highest, not the lowest, common denominator. The western policymakers are committed to laissez-faire markets, making them unknowing accessories to some of the biggest white-collar frauds in Canadian history.

III

The Money Launderers

18/THE BORDER

Bill Stringer guards the busiest border point in North America, the Peace River Bridge between Fort Erie, Ontario, and Buffalo, New York. He is in charge of an elite group of American border police, called the Contraband Enforcement Team, Customs Service, of the U.S. Department of the Treasury. The members of this highly trained police force, who wear guns in holsters and have more power than their municipal counterparts, can suspend civil rights, interrogate individuals for hours if they are suspicious, and seize private property without due process if it is contraband or if it is a vehicle used to smuggle goods.

We meet in a dilapidated office with Stringer and two members of his team to talk about the problems of trying to stem the constant flow of illicit drugs and other contraband across the border. Outside the dirty windows, the traffic is constant as trucks, buses and cars stop to talk to unarmed border officials in kiosks. Some 25,000 vehicles stream past here every day, a volume which is a smuggler's dream.

"The best time to get through is during rush hour or when people are coming out of the Fort Erie racetrack. It's bumper-to-bumper for an hour, there are literally thousands of cars in five or six lanes, and we simply don't have the horses to pull suspicious ones over. So we let them through in both directions," says Stringer.

The team's tasks are usually tedious, but sometimes they can be dangerous. In 1982 in Blaine, Washington, a border guard was shot at point-blank range by an American fugitive who was merely asked to step out of his car. Stringer's group does not work the border booths, but focuses on undercover and intelligence operations and is called in when drugs might be involved. Today a car has been pulled over to the side. In addition to going over the car's interior with a fine-tooth comb, one of Stringer's team members brings over a specially trained dog from a nearby kennel to sniff out drugs. His handler, who wears a towel in the back of his belt, takes the dog in and around the vehicle. Dogs are exceedingly accurate and if drugs are smelled, they simply freeze in their tracks. In this case the dog detects nothing and is led away by his handler for his reward. The handler takes the towel out of his belt, lets the dog grab one end, and plays tug-of-war for a few minutes.

Without a doubt, Canada is a gigantic loophole through which billions of dollars worth of drugs and dirty money pass annually. Canada is a smuggler's and money launderer's mecca. The narcotics business generates an incredible $150 billion a year in cash transactions. Though teams like Stringer's on both sides of the border scoop millions of dollars in contraband each year, much seeps through, particularly laundered money, which is the lifeblood of the drug business.

Both sides employ enormous resources to catch culprits. There is an army of 10,000 customs inspectors in Canada, some 5,000 at border crossings alone. The U.S. deploys at least that many on its northern border and even more along the Mexican border and Florida coasts.

Even so, the border has a number of unmanned crossing points. Small aircraft and boats can land in the U.S. at tiny airports or marinas that rely on the honor system when it comes to customs declarations. There is no radar tracking the flights of small, low-level aircraft. Canada is too vast to patrol. For instance, there are at least a hundred hidden coves off our east coast and hundreds of islands off our west coast, but only five drug patrol boats available to monitor activity.

"We don't even know where all the airports or landing strips in Canada are. Let's face it, you can land an airplane filled with drugs on a highway or lake in some isolated area up north," says Jim Johnston, Canada's director of customs investigations and interdiction. "You can load heroin onto a radio-controlled aircraft one-quarter of a mile from the border and fly it across without physically touching it. This is a huge country with a lot of land and no surveillance at the border. But nothing can be done politically. The issue is you cannot disrupt the marketplace. This is the world's biggest trading relationship and to arm the border would slow everything down."

Drugs can be brought in in large quantities this way, but indications are that smaller amounts of drugs are simply sent through the mail. Dogs work the postal facility but do not sniff all pieces of mail. Only suspicious-looking parcels from drug-producing countries like Colombia or Turkey are routinely investigated. And, of course, dirty money is undetectable if sent through the mail.

Canada is a major transshipment country for narcotics, particularly heroin, speed, and marijuana. Some drugs, notably cocaine, come from the U.S. to Canada, but the flow is overwhelmingly from north to south. RCMP assistant commissioner Rod Stamler estimates that about $10 billion of narcotics a year is smuggled across the U.S.-Canadian border. He says nearly 90 percent of all heroin consumed in the U.S. comes via the revived French Connection (Middle East-Marseilles-Montreal) or via Toronto and Vancouver. If Stamler's figures are correct, the drug business here ranks as the country's fifth-largest enterprise, in terms of revenue. Similarly, according to estimates, in the U.S. the drug business ranks as one of the biggest industries, worth $150 billion a year. "One kilo of heroin costs $6,000 and is worth $10 million on the street," says Stamler. "The money and profits are exorbitant. There is simply nothing like it."

A U.S.-Canada free trade treaty will open up things even more, as customs staff and tariffs gradually melt away by the end of the century. This will only make smuggling easier.

Although getting the product to market is easy, the Americans are determined to make the laundering of drug profits considerably more difficult. Big-time drug rings are literally drowning in cash, which must be laundered to disguise its origin. So much cash is generated that it cannot all be spent without making police or tax officials suspicious. Most street-level deals are conducted in twenty-dollar bills, and the sheer physical bulk of all that cash presents logistical problems. A suitcase full of twenty-dollar bills weighs about a hundred pounds and holds only about $1 million. Most of this cash can be reinvested in buying more drugs, but every year organized crime must launder billions of dollars to turn it into clean cash which can be invested or spent.

Laundering is the act of erasing the source of money and is done for a number of different reasons. Criminals need to hide the proceeds of crimes or kickbacks. Even legitimate people need to launder flight capital, when they flee corrupt or declining countries in contravention of foreign currency restrictions. For others, flight capital must be hidden from tax officials, ex-wives, or business partners. Flight capital streamed into Amsterdam's boiler rooms from countries with currency controls or oppressive taxes.

The Americans have been trying to crack down on money laundering for two main reasons. First, Washington is losing billions of dollars in tax revenues to the underground economy which is not paying taxes; and second, it is also losing the battle against drug trafficking. Only by grabbing drug proceeds can the government mortally wound traffickers. Elliott Ness was never able to nab Al Capone for bootlegging, murder, or extortion, but he finally locked him up and threw away the key when accountants caught Capone laundering the proceeds of his crimes to evade taxes.

One of the principal weapons in this battle are U.S. currency controls; any cash transaction of more than $10,000 must be reported. This includes such transactions as depositing cash into a bank, taking it across the border, and giving it to a stock broker or lawyer. The original owner of the money must fill in an extensive form outlining the source of the funds, and a copy of this form is sent to tax officials to ensure that the money is declared for income tax purposes. Currency controls don't catch crooks, but they do cost them time and money and leave a paper trail for investigators to follow.

Because Canada has no such controls, it is God's gift to money launderers. Anyone can bring cash across the border, get it into our banking system, and transfer it to some sleazy tax haven in the Caribbean where branches of Canadian banks are ubiquitous. This is less risky than trying to smuggle it directly to the islands. The money can then be repatriated through a variety of clever means, which vary from using unregulated stock markets such as Vancouver or Alberta to using boiler rooms or many other businesses.

THE MEXICAN STAND-OFF

A border incident in the spring of 1987 shows just how inadequate Canadian laws are. Four Mexicans in a car with Mexican plates arrived at the Canadian border crossing at Bellingham, Washington. They were asked to pull over for an inspection. The customs officers wanted to check whether they were smuggling in drugs or anything else and also whether they were fugitives or potentially illegal aliens, who get into the country for a visit and never leave. An immigration official was summoned to interview the men, while their passport numbers were checked for warrants or other information on a central computer shared between the two countries. The passports were clean, but police were summoned anyway after the customs officer noticed that the back tires on the car didn't match the front ones. Suspecting that drugs had been hidden inside, the officers removed the tires and found $2 million in American bills jammed in the hubcaps and in a false bottom strapped to the gasoline tank.

In most other countries in the world, such an attempt to smuggle in cash would be illegal. Not in Canada. Although its manner of transport was highly suspicious, under Canadian laws the hidden cash did not constitute contraband. Cash cannot be smuggled into Canada because there is no duty on it. It was obviously being brought in to launder, but money laundering is not an offense in Canada per se. The only applicable offense is "to possess the proceeds of crime knowingly," and that is usually impossible to prove.

The Mexicans had not broken any laws, but they were denied entry into Canada. Suspicions were aroused when the Mexicans could not provide a good explanation for carrying so much cash and not declaring it. The police decided that the easiest way to get rid of them was to have immigration officials refuse them entry. American customs officials were informed that the Mexicans were being sent back through the U.S. border checkpoint, and they got ready to nab them. Sneaking cash into Canada may be legal, but sneaking cash out of the U.S. is not. The requirement that all transactions of $10,000 or more must be reported applies to tourists or traveling business people, as well as to citizens and residents. It makes money laundering considerably more difficult and expensive.

Not surprisingly, the four Mexicans had not filled in a form. The Americans confiscated the cash and the car, threw all four in jail, and deported them. "The joke is, if they had brought their cash in a suitcase or briefcase and declared it, they would have gotten in," says Michael Crichton, manager of intelligence for Revenue Canada Customs and Excise in southwestern Ontario. It goes on every single day of every single week.

The Mexicans failed to get into Canada only because they were visitors, but any Canadian citizen or landed immigrant can set up a money-laundering scheme with impunity. Many already have. Here's how the most primitive method works. Fill a car trunk with $2 million in cash and drive from the U.S. into Canada. The only border checkpoint you must cross is Canadian. This means that the reporting requirement in the U.S. can be avoided completely. At the border a Canadian official will ask, "Have you anything to declare?" Still no problem. You merely reply, "Yes. I have $2 million in cash in my trunk."

"Pull over," he'll say. So you pull over for an inspection, open the trunk, and wait for questions. You tell the official that you inherited some of the cash and won the rest at various casinos or racetracks. The customs official takes note of the cash, license-plate number, and your name and address. But he will not ask whether the money has been declared south of the border. That is not Canada's problem. Even if you admit that is the case, you and your money cannot be sent back to the United States. That would constitute an extradition. Extradition is a time-consuming process which occurs only after the U.S. has laid charges, obtained an extradition order from a court, then formally applied in Canada for deportation of the accused. To escort a citizen across the border without an extradition order would constitute kidnaping. In any case, the failure to report a cash transaction is not an extraditable offense under the Canada-U.S. Extradition Treaty. Even though conviction nets you a fine and short prison sentence, it is not a particularly important crime.

In Canada the only laundering crime is being in the possession of the proceeds of crime knowingly or having cash and not declaring it for tax purposes. But even if the inspector suspects that either or both is the case, you can get away with it. Even if the inspector takes note of your name and the amount of money, under our laws, customs transactions are sacred. Information cannot be given to police except under certain conditions.

"If people declare goods or cash, there is a confidentiality rule. We may hold onto their name, but we cannot give out that information carte blanche unless it's an ongoing investigation. We must be very careful, and we approve each case on an individual basis," says Michael Crichton. "There are no lists circulated between enforcement agencies, and there is no central data bank."

The information cannot be shared with Revenue Canada, nor does Revenue Canada share any information about suspected tax evaders or investigations with either police or customs officials. See how simple it is? You have now brought the money in.

Another strategy is simply to drive through and not declare the cash. Chances are you will not be inspected; and even if you are, there is no tariff on cash so that it cannot technically be smuggled. The means of transporting undeclared cash can be seized by customs officials, but you can keep the cash. "You cannot smuggle money because, technically, there is no duty on it," says Crichton. "We could, for instance, take the car the money was in, or the purse, if it was undeclared, then found. But we would have to give you back your money."

19/How Money Laundering Works

Money laundering is called smurfing in drug circles, after those shapeless, doughy cartoon characters. Inspiration for this expression came from the widespread practice of employing frumpy, elderly women with shopping bags full of cash to deposit drug proceeds in dozens of bank accounts. A smurf simply goes from bank to bank depositing cash. Once in the banking system, funds can be electronically wired anywhere in the world for safekeeping.

Obviously, a constant flow of a large amount of cash deposited by one individual into one account at one bank or trust company raises suspicions, but smurfs make multiple deposits daily at hundreds of branches in different names. "On a good day, working in teams, they can do thirty, even forty transactions at $5,000 to $7,000 a shot," says Gerard Kenna, a former FBI agent who trains U.S. bankers to spot money laundering. The secret is using a smurf who looks innocent. An FBI report in 1982 documented how a ring of twenty elderly women each made three deposits of US$8,000 per week in six different banks; and within fifty-two weeks, they had laundered $150 million. Smurfing fees range between 7 and 15 percent of the total amount laundered.

SMURFING FOR FUN AND PROFIT

Prominent real estate developer Paul Durish has a strange trophy hanging in his Hillsburgh, Ontario, recreation room. It is a Swiss chocolate bag which once contained $42,000 in Canadian cash. Back in early 1987, a man Durish barely knew arrived at his doorstep and asked him to deposit the money in his own account and withdraw it in the form of a banker's draft, minus a fee.

"I took it down to my Toronto-Dominion Bank branch, deposited the cash, and kept 7 per cent [$2,940]. Then I gave him a check for the balance. The bank didn't bat an eyelash, put it through their money counting machine in no time. In fact, he had $42,060, so I just kept the extra $60 to pay for my time, and that brought my fee up to $3,000," says Durish. "I didn't know him very well, and I didn't ask him why he wanted me to do this. I didn't ask him where he got the money. It was the easiest $3,000 I've ever made in my life."

Durish did absolutely nothing illegal. He declared the fee as income for tax purposes and framed the bag as a joke. The story illustrates how simple it is for an established customer to make a huge cash deposit in a bank with no questions asked. In the U.S., both Durish and the person whose name appeared on the bank draft would have had to fill out government forms.

As Durish showed, money laundering is easy, highly profitable, and legal. Of course, a large-scale drug operation cannot rely on such hit-and-miss favors to launder huge volumes of funds. But it can still be done. A researcher and I decided to see how easy it was to get rid of, for instance, US$20,000 in twenty-dollar bills.

We opened new accounts with all five major Canadian chartered banks in 1988 on the strength of a driver's license and one credit card. We asked counter clerks whether we could deposit $20,000 in U.S. cash with them, then have it transferred to an offshore bank immediately. No problem, they all said. However, clerks at the Bank of Nova Scotia and the Royal Bank were suspicious. The Royal Bank clerk warned my researcher that a number of cash deposits would lead to an internal investigation, saying, "We don't want any money laundering here. We'll just close your account out as soon as we suspect anything."

Even if an account is closed after one or more of these transactions, banks are afraid to breach confidentiality rules and rarely share information with outsiders, such as police, customs, or tax officials. They certainly don't share such information with other banks. This allows launderers to move from one bank to another. Even if they exhaust the supply of banks, they can start all over again with a new identity on a fake driver's license and credit cards. But such obstacles become too costly. There are far easier ways to deposit cash into the banking system.

THE PIZZA CONNECTION

"Walk-in laundering is for the rank amateurs," says RCMP's Rod Stamler. "What you do to get away with it is to set up restaurants as fronts. If you are not greedy and you're willing to pay some taxes, you declare artificial profits, pay taxes and your money is laundered. For this, freelancers charge 25 percent. But some drug dealers do their own laundering."

Businesses that traditionally generate large amounts of cash can deposit large amounts of cash into banks without raising suspicions. That is why organized criminals are often proprietors of restaurants, nightclubs, casinos, racetracks, resorts, currency exchanges, wrecking yards, bingo halls, and cash-rich retail outlets like pizza parlors.

One case involving a significant Canadian component was called the Pizza Connection case because it operated through a chain of pizzerias in the U.S., which served as Mafia outlets in the early 1980s. The pizzerias were manned mostly by illegal aliens from Sicily who had been smuggled to the U.S. via Canada. These hired hands received, packaged, and distributed drugs, then collected and delivered the money every night in a pizza carrying case to a central vault. The Pizza Connection trial in New York City began in January 1986, lasted most of the year, and resulted in multiple convictions. In the 130-page indictment, the U.S. government also alluded to a 1983 attempt to launder huge amounts through certain Montreal boutiques.

Most of the pizzeria money found its way, via couriers and suitcases, to banks in Bermuda. "The money came in here years ago [in the 1970s and early 1980s] when Bermuda banks still accepted cash out of suitcases," explains the Canadian-born Attorney General of Bermuda, Saul Froomkin. "We cooperated fully with the DEA [U.S. Drug Enforcement Agency]. From here, a lot of the money went to the U.K. or Italy where it was invested in legitimate businesses. We also changed our rules as a result. Now this government feels there is no justification for accepting large cash deposits."

The Pizza Connection launderers also used Wall Street. Some $4.9 million in cash was deposited at Merrill Lynch, Pierce, Fenner & Smith Inc. and another $15.6 million at E.F. Hutton & Co. to buy blue-chip stocks.

A similar case in March 1987 involved Gary Eder, a forty-one-year-old salesman at Wall Street's Paine Webber Inc., who was convicted of participating in a money-laundering scheme. The indictment alleged that Eder laundered at least $700,000 in client's money, in amounts of $70,000 at a time, divided into smaller amounts to avoid filing government currency-transaction reports. The money was sprinkled around in various accounts on different days.

THE MOOSE PASTURE METHOD

Another successful way to launder millions at a time is to use wash trading, matched trading, or other stock market fraud techniques. Wash trading is ideal for money laundering because a drug dealer can buy one million shares of Moose Pasture Inc. for a dollar each from a broker or promoter, in cash and under the table. The broker or promoter then has to get rid of the cash. The drug dealer is not registered as the owner of the stock. The official owner will be a phony offshore corporation owned by the dealer. Such a purchase is known as a private placement and sometimes also as an exempt buy, which means that it is exempt from a regulation that states that stock purchasers of large blocks must hold onto stock for one year before selling it. Exchanges allow big-volume buyers to sell immediately after they have bought.

The phony offshore corporation then sells the shares to another phony offshore company or to a phony Canadian outfit controlled by the drug dealer. The entire transaction is fiction but is registered at the exchange as fact.

The wash trading continues, as shares are traded among various phony organizations or conspirators at ever-increasing prices. Eventually, when the price is right, the swindlers all sell their shares to the public at huge profits. If the phony Canadian corporations are the final sellers of the stock at huge profits, they declare the capital gains as income for tax purposes, and then the money is laundered. If the phony offshore corporation ends up selling the shares to the public, it pays a Canadian withholding tax of 15 percent to Ottawa, and then the money can be shipped back overseas. Nice and neat.

Amsterdam's Canadian-operated boiler rooms were also very adept at laundering flight capital in Sweden, Israel, Austria, and dozens of other countries. They sent couriers to these countries to swap cash for stock certificates or receipts entitling them to stocks. But the boiler room boys sometimes double-crossed their co-conspirators by failing to send along the stock, by giving them shares in worthless companies, or by handing over counterfeit certificates.

MORE WAYS TO LAUNDER

By far the fastest way to launder huge amounts of money is to fly a courier with cash, or a bulk shipment, to corrupt Caribbean or Central American banks for deposit. Then the money can be repatriated as a loan. That is still occasionally done, but a crackdown by the U.S., the bulkiness of a large amount of money, and increased surveillance at airports have made that increasingly difficult. Airport officials spot suspicious parcels every day of the week. For example, customs agents nabbed Maria Lilia Rojas in 1983 with $1.6 million stuffed into six Monopoly boxes. In 1986 $7 million in cash was seized from a private Colombian jet plane in Texas. It's probably easier to simply hide money in a car, boat, or plane and take it to Canada.

But there are many other, more imaginative ways to launder funds. A favored money-laundering transaction is to exchange cash for gold bullion. This can be done with no questions asked in Toronto and around the world. The gold can then be smuggled elsewhere to avoid detection or taxes and cashed in when needed. My researcher and I approached the Bank of Nova Scotia's retail gold department, for instance, which said it would sell up to $5,000 worth of bullion for cash on any given day. But if they sold any more than that to one person, they required a certified check, bank draft, or money order — but that could also be untraceable.

When we asked gold giant Deak Perrera, a currency-and-gold exchange, the Toronto spokesman said it would take virtually any amount of cash and would even act as a currency exchange. So instead of buying gold at Deak, we could deposit our $20,000 in cash, convert it to another currency, and Deak would wire it to any bank around the world. Before doing so, however, he said, that Deak required two pieces of identification and, if the cash was being transmitted offshore to a corporation, it would need a document proving that the sender had signing authority on the offshore account.

(It is interesting to note that Deak Perrera's predecessor company, Deak & Co., filed bankruptcy in the early 1980s when big customers withdrew their deposits after Washington's Commission on Organized Crime linked the company to money launderers. The founder-owner of Deak & Co., Nicholas Deak, was murdered gangland-style in his office shortly thereafter.)

The problem with turning cash into gold is that, though bullion is more compact and more easily hidden than cash, it is still risky to move around and must be kept in a safety deposit vault or safe. It is much simpler to do money laundering through currency exchanges. We telephoned Friedberg & Co. Ltd. and Bendix Foreign Exchange of Canada in Toronto where both managers said they would be more than happy to convert $20,000 Canadian cash into U.S. funds, then ship it anywhere. All they needed was the account number and address of the offshore bank. There was no mention of the need for identification.

We also decided to test brokerage houses and telephoned the blue-ribbon Bay Street firm Midland Doherty Ltd. We asked the salesman if it was possible to open an account and buy stock with cash, sometimes as much as US$20,000 a week or more. He told us to wait while he checked then came on the line and said, "No problem." Likewise, we checked with a broker-dealer (a brokerage firm without an exchange seat that sells unlisted stocks) called Trend Capital Securities Ltd. in Toronto. We asked its spokesman if we could buy Toronto Stock Exchange-listed stocks like Bell Canada with, say, $20,000 in cash. Trend's salesman said there would be a fairly high commission because the trade would have to be jitneyed or done through a broker like Midland Doherty, which has trading privileges. But, with that proviso, he called it all a great idea. "Just one thing, though," he said without skipping a beat, "bring the cash down before lunchtime, so it can be deposited into the bank right away."

We also found Canada's foreign-owned, or Schedule B, banks accommodating. Most of these banks have no branches set up to deal with small customers. They are mostly involved in large-scale lending operations with major corporations or in the purchase of government or corporate securities. However, several of these banks were more than willing to accept our cash-deposit business for transfer offshore. The Bank of Hong Kong, for instance, said a $20,000 cash deposit and transfer offshore was no problem, and asked us to bring it in early enough so it could be counted that day and a day's interest earned on it.

Calls to trust companies and credit unions confirmed that there are no ceilings on cash deposits. In fact, credit unions are ideal money-laundering vehicles. In Ontario, for instance, twelve people can make a joint application to open and operate a credit union. If the application is approved, the union becomes a full-fledged, government-insured, deposit-taking institution. Theoretically, the Crooks Credit Union could take enormous amounts of cash from fictitious individuals and companies, then lend it back to them, or allow it to be withdrawn in the form of bank drafts payable to bearers, or even transfer it into the banking system for transmission abroad. Instant money laundering.

THE CARIBBEAN BANKERS

Every day in a hotel on Grand Cayman Island near the Royal Bank of Canada's main branch, money-laundering seminars are held free of charge. Interested participants are told how to open up offshore accounts and what the rules are in various jurisdictions, and then they're served rum punch.

Historically, Canadians have had many dealings with the Caribbean, from the coastal trade in salt fish between the Maritimes and the islands to the postwar development of tourism, as well as gambling and tax havens in the Caribbean. In the Bahamas, for instance, four Canadian banks, the Royal Bank, the Bank of Montreal, Scotiabank, and the Canadian Imperial Bank of Commerce, account for 80 percent of local banking. The Royal Bank is the Bahamian government's official bank, and the Scotiabank is Prime Minister Lynden Pindling's. Former Argus chairman E.P. Taylor and Lou Chesler, both of Toronto, pioneered real estate developments there. Chesler got the first casino license in the Bahamas. Just twenty years ago, Canadians developed the mosquito-infested Cayman Islands. Now that tiny British colony is a dirty-money capital, with 20,000 residents, 18,000 corporations, and 500 banks with $143 billion in assets, more than all of the major banks in New England.

This cozy arrangement between Canadian banks and businessmen and Caribbean transactions was interrupted in the late 1970s by the Americans, who pursued the Bank of Nova Scotia in a celebrated legal case with an aggressive Miami grand jury. Two more cases against Scotiabank and the Royal Bank of Canada followed, establishing the legal precedent that any foreign bank operating in the U.S. was subject to American laws and courts, regardless of where in the world it operated. Ottawa protested through diplomatic channels and even sent a lawyer to argue against such "extraterritoriality" before the U.S. Supreme Court. But to no avail. The precedent still stands, piercing for the first time the sleazy offshore secrecy laws that have protected so many crooks for so long.

The Bank of Nova Scotia case involved a probe into the activities of known narcotics trafficker Frank Brady, who had been caught in front of television cameras with a planeload of marijuana at his ranch in Florida. He was later released on a technicality. The jury discovered in 1983 from an informant that Brady's money was mostly on deposit at the Bank of

Nova Scotia in Nassau, and it ordered the bank to hand over Brady's financial records. The bank refused, saying that to release information would violate Bahamian bank-secrecy laws and also that the U.S. had no jurisdiction over foreign banks operating offshore. The grand jury found that unacceptable, and on March 1, 1983, Scotiabank documents in Nassau and the Cayman Islands were subpoenaed.

The bank asked U.S. courts to quash the order but was refused. The bank was given until May 31, 1983, to produce the records, but it did not do so. U.S. government lawyers asked courts to rule the bank in contempt of court, and on October 10, 1983, the bank was given one week to come up with documents or face a $25,000-a-day fine until it complied. Ten days later the bank came up with one solitary document, saying that it was all that could be found. The court disagreed and gave it more time to come up with the information. By mid-November 1983, the governments of the Bahamas and the Cayman Islands bowed to pressure from the U.S. government (which threatened to cut off aid to the islands) and from the bank (which threatened to shut down operations). The bank handed over the information after getting immunity from prosecution for violating bank secrecy laws.

The bank documents helped obtain guilty pleas from Brady's wife and several of his henchmen. The court eventually ordered Scotiabank to pay $2.5 million in fines, noting that laws "should not be used as a blanket device to encourage or foster criminal activities." It was not the first time, nor the last time, that U.S. courts took on Canadian banks and offshore secrecy havens.

In 1981 a jury in Fort Lauderdale tried to get from the Bank of Nova Scotia the Bahamian bank records of Robert "The Dance Man" Twist, of Florida. Twist had deposited US$950,500 in the bank's branch after bringing fifty bales of marijuana in to Fort Lauderdale. On the same day he deposited the money, he wrote a check on his account there for the same amount to buy a Lear jet.

Rather than take on an offshore haven, the jury subpoenaed Scotiabank's Florida office for Twist's records. A year later, the bank was fined $500 a day for contempt when it refused to release documents. When the fine was increased to $25,000 a day a year later, the bank handed over the records unceremoniously in a cardboard box. Subsequent testimony showed that Twist had laundered millions of dollars through his Canadian bank in Nassau by bringing in suitcases of cash through a rear door and then counting it along with the bank staff. Twist was eventually convicted, and the affair cost the bank $100,000 in fines.

Twist said during his court trial that tax officials overstepped when they went after his Scotiabank records. "I think it was illegal," he said. The fine the bank was forced to pay he described as "nothing more than bribery."

Things got worse in December 1984, when a Bahamian Royal Commission into the drug business revealed in its report many more ugly dealings by Canadian banks with American drug runners. Testimony and documents told the story of Bruce Griffin, alias Peewee, a drug dealer from Florida who loved fast cars, fast women, and fast horses. In 1979 he deposited $22 million in cash in just four months at the main branch of the Bank of Nova Scotia in downtown Nassau. One single deposit was $7 million. The FBI estimated that Griffin reaped a staggering $100 million annually from smuggling between 1975 and 1981 and put his money into accounts opened by forty corporations in the Bahamas. The money was then sent to another company with an account in a Scotiabank branch in the Cayman Islands, then it went to Scotiabank's New York City office, and finally it was handed out as loans to Griffin's various American corporations involved in horse breeding, car racing, and the real estate business.

Huge deposits were such a common practice in the Bahamas that in 1983 the tiny Royal Bank branch in Bimini, the only bank on the island, reported U.S. currency deposits of $12.29 million, 50 percent higher than the entire balance of payments for the Bahamas for that year. Bimini's population is only 2,000, and most of them are unemployed fishermen, so the only plausible explanation for such a high level of deposits is smuggling. There were also rumors of corruption among government officials there.

Montreal *Gazette* reporter William Marsden, in a fascinating series of articles on money laundering in 1986, tells a story of money laundering on Paradise Island: "Miami lawyers Burton Levy and Leonard Levenstein helped launder money for Florida drug smugglers and had a 'friendly' Scotiabank manager on Paradise Island named David McPhail. Ellen Plough of the Florida Law Enforcement Agency said McPhail placed their deposits into a trust account, then wired the money to the Netherlands Antilles, where it was put into company accounts. This made it impossible to trace who made the original deposit. Plough said when she tried to trace bank records, Scotiabank couldn't find many of the documents, and a statement Levenstein gave Florida police said McPhail was 'tipped' $1,200 to $1,800 every time they made a large cash deposit. When he was transferred to another branch in Freeport, his smugglers moved with him, Plough said. He left the bank to run a jewelry business and has since returned to Canada."

American legal hardball has translated into two diplomatic initiatives designed to stop Caribbean smuggling and laundering. First, in 1985, Washington announced its Caribbean Basin Initiative, a package of trade concessions and aid in return for agreements from governments to cooperate in combating drug smuggling. A number of nations have signed and agreed to participate in Operation Bat radar surveillance to stem smugglers.

Second, in 1986, the Cayman colonial government, Britain, and the U.S. signed a treaty to eliminate the island colony's bank secrecy law as an obstacle to U.S. criminal investigations, a move spurred by the Bank of Nova Scotia case. Not surprisingly, money-laundering activity has moved elsewhere, notably to Central American countries like Panama and Costa Rica. But the Cayman agreement is being used as a model to convince others to sign.

Bermuda cleaned up its own act following embarrassing revelations about the Pizza Connection case. It was another embarrassment for Canadian banks with their extensive offshore operations. Evidence was that in November 1980 Salvatore Amendolito deposited hundreds of thousands of dollars in Bermuda and also, for instance, $233,387.20 in small bills in a Bank of Nova Scotia in Nassau, Bahamas. His next deposit was $329,983.12 in money orders, travelers' checks, and cashiers' checks, each one less than $10,000 in value. This was only a small fraction of the millions of "narco" dollars laundered through Canadian banks, according to Amendolito, who became a key Pizza Connection witness.

Bermuda banks no longer accept cash, partly because of the efforts of outspoken Attorney General of Bermuda, Saul Froomkin. An expert on money laundering who conducts seminars around the world for bankers and police, Froomkin says islands such as Anguilla, St. Vincent, and the Caymans, and Central American countries like Panama still accept huge cash deposits with no questions asked. "Any bank or anyone knows something's wrong with someone carrying around large amounts of cash. No one in his right mind walks around with huge amounts of cash," says Froomkin. "No law says banks or anyone else must accept this business, even from a customer. The only obligation to a customer is regarding the funds already lodged in the bank. In Bermuda, banks no longer accept large sums of currency.

"There is absolutely no legitimate reason for secret banking other than raising revenue. Suddenly in the past fifteen to twenty years, there is a proliferation of offshore banks and secrecy laws protecting their customers after hundreds of years of not needing this. Why? So governments can raise money easily, sell licenses for $1,000, charge annual fees, and close their eyes. Other countries look the other way and let the raping and looting go on as long as it's in another jurisdiction. The Americans are taking a hard stand, facing multi-trillion dollar deficits. The drug business is rampant, and people are evading taxes. It's a massive fraud against the government."

Cambridge professor and chief Commonwealth fraud officer Barry Rider concurs. "Without a doubt the Caribbean is the principal money-laundering area in the world, but the principal end deposit areas are Liechtenstein, Luxembourg, London, Switzerland, the U.S., and Canada. Allowing forfeiture [seizure of illegal profits] in Caribbean countries or other money-laundering countries is pointless because there are often no assets there. They are transferred out immediately to end-deposit countries and they won't respond to forfeiture orders from developing countries."

Once secrecy laws are instituted, organized crime groups move in, taking over the business life, and corrupting the political and judicial life of small countries, says Rider. "We have indications that at least three Commonwealth countries are, for all intents and purposes, owned and run by organized crime groups."

A GOVERNMENT RESPONSIBILITY

Money laundering and drug smuggling are big issues in the U.S. and have garnered a great deal of media coverage. In 1985 a Boston scandal resulted in a crackdown on banks across the country. The First National Bank of Boston, America's sixteenth largest bank, waived the cash-reporting requirement for its client Genarro Angiulo because he was a customer in good standing and had many cash-generating businesses, restaurants, and hotels. For seven years, Angiulo or his associates arrived with paper bags full of cash. Some 163 bags containing $2.2 million were brought in between 1980 and 1983 alone.

Then it was discovered that Angiulo headed an organized crime family in Boston. An investigation uncovered US$1.22 billion in unreported overseas transactions, which the bank had carried out for him. The bank pleaded guilty in February 1985 to failing to report the transactions and was fined $500,000. Ever since, the country's 13,000 banks have been subjected to tougher scrutiny. Two other banks in Boston, the Bank of New England and the Shawmut Bank of Boston, also admitted to failure to report transactions. They admitted that substantial cash shipments abroad had gone unreported. The 13,000-member American Bankers' Association, the industry's trade group, revealed that forty-five big banks were seeking criminal immunity from the Treasury department in exchange for full disclosure. The U.S. Congress is considering a mandatory ten-year jail sentence for bank employees who do not comply with the requirement and may reduce reporting levels to US$3,000. Such pressure south of the border means that even more money will be shipped northward.

Oddly enough, all the press attention in the U.S. on the crackdown on laundering has completely ignored Canada's important role. The Boston *Globe* did a series on money laundering in 1986 but did not point a finger at Canada. The article included a map showing how billions of dollars in surplus cash deposits were reported in banks located in the ten largest cities in the southern half of the continental U.S., whereas there were no cash reserves reported in the northern half, where most of the drug transactions take place. The writer of the article therefore concluded that the south was laundering the money.

But the article failed to look farther northward. Bank of Canada figures for 1983 to 1987 show that cash deposits of U.S. and Canadian currency in Canadian banks, trust companies, and credit unions in Toronto, Montreal, and Vancouver in certain denominations were increasing much faster than were overall deposits or money supplies. Tourists? Not likely. As the Americans crack down on money-laundering activities in cities like Detroit, Boston, New York, and Chicago, the money is coming north to Canada. The absence of any anti-money-laundering laws means we live in the financial equivalent of the Prohibition, when Canadian bootleggers operated with impunity north of the border providing criminal services to their American partners.

Ignorance about Canada's huge role in all of this money-laundering activity also exists on this side of the border. The first case in Canada that resulted in new amendments to stem money laundering involved the disgraceful case of Luis Pinto. Pinto had been a valued customer of the Royal Bank of Canada's affiliate in Colombia. He was a prominent businessman and an elected member of that country's Senate. Pinto was arrested by the FBI in 1983 for his role in a massive scheme to launder profits from cocaine smuggled into the United States. While cooperating with U.S. officials, he divulged a great deal about his operations, including the fact that he had salted away some $726,000 in the Royal Bank's main branch in Montreal under the names of his Spanish in-laws. Canadian drug enforcement officials fought the Royal Bank in court for the money, under provisions in the Criminal Code that allow the seizure of the proceeds from crime. But the attempt failed. "We couldn't use any process to acquire possession, and the money was transferred back to Spain," says RCMP Assistant Commissioner Rod Stamler.

Pinto was murdered in August 1985 in a motel outside St. Petersburg, Florida, by hired Cuban assassins. His case provided the best example to date of the fact that, although the Mounties always get their man, when it comes to drug prosecutions, they rarely get his money. Indeed, the Pinto story clearly showed the inability of Canadian authorities to seize bank accounts, even when it is illegal to possess the proceeds of crime knowingly. The Royal Bank's lawyers argued that bank deposits were not tangible assets but rather the bank's IOU to the depositor. The courts ruled against the Mounties and the funds stayed in the bank.

Pinto was jailed and fined in the United States, and the U.S. Treasury Department tried to collect the fines by filing suit in Canada against Pinto's in-laws, in whose names the money was still held. After Pinto's death, his in-laws and U.S. Treasury officials settled out of court, leaving Canadian officials out in the cold.

The Pinto case led to the drawing up of Bill C-61, a proposal designed to crack down on organized crime and the drug trade by allowing Canadian police to seize the proceeds of crime. Introduced by Justice Minister Ray Hnatyshyn in 1987, the bill was still grinding its way through Parliament in 1988. It was studied by a legislative committee of the House of Commons, where opposition was mounted from civil rights organizations, defense lawyers, and some bankers on the grounds that it abused civil and economic rights.

The bill's opponents are wrong. Not only is the legal reform long overdue, but it does not go far enough toward helping trace, freeze, and seize illegally amassed money on deposit in Canadian financial institutions.

The RCMP and police worldwide have been fighting a losing battle against the world's biggest and most lucrative business, drug trafficking. And police have become frustrated because Canadian laws attacked the branches, and not the roots, of the problem. Murderers are relieved of their weapons, and it is a criminal offense to be in possession of burglar tools. Similarly, laws and courts must disarm drug traffickers by seizing the tools of their trade, namely fast boats, aircraft, and refineries. Such items can be legally seized, but they can be easily replaced, unless laws also deprive traffickers of their most important weapons: cash and the financial assets that are the lifeblood of the drug business.

In essence, Bill C-61 allows government authorities to seize bank accounts, cars, boats, or other assets purchased with money that has come from the drug trade or from fraud, prostitution, murder, robbery, or extortion. It gives police greater powers to investigate financial activity or to freeze assets until the sources of revenue are identified. It will also make it possible for police to obtain highly confidential tax records from Revenue Canada, under strict controls, if such information is needed in a drug probe.

Bankers say that problems are referred to the security departments of the banks and that suspicious transactions or customers are reported to police. Some banks say publicly that they require affidavits from customers who are making cash deposits of more than $10,000, but no customer is forced to do so. As my research has found, none of the banks actually insists upon affidavits. Thus far, Canadian banks have successfully lobbied against the type of reporting rules or currency controls the U.S. has instituted, even though these rules are effective in frustrating laundering and assisting in its detection.

"The Royal Bank processes 250 million transactions a month in its computers and that represents only 25 percent of the banking business in Canada," says Royal Bank spokesman and counsel Jack Burnett. "As you can see we must find in that haystack the needles without grinding the whole system to a halt."

Civil rights watchdogs also worry about such sweeping powers, but those fears are misguided because the bill requires that police first get permission to search or seize from a court — the traditional safeguard against overzealous police officers. Others say that courts should not have that much power. But every day courts deny bail to accused persons and on occasion freeze assets that are in dispute in a lawsuit until litigation is concluded. Such powers are already entrenched in our justice system.

Bill C-61 does not go far enough. It should require banks, other financial institutions, currency exchanges, accountants, and lawyers to keep records of all large transactions and to report to police all suspicious transactions. Reporting requirements like those in practice in the States must be adopted to leave a paper trail for law enforcement officials trying to track down ill-gotten gains. Such reporting requirements were to have been included in the provisions of C-61, but unfortunately Canada's powerful banking lobby rejected them, arguing that such measures were too expensive and impractical.

Bill C-61 will give people or banks immunity from civil litigation when they report transactions (if they are sued for breaches of confidentiality). But any decision to divulge information is left up to the individual — a naive proposal considering that bank employees, lawyers, and accountants may be accomplices in money-laundering schemes. Justice Minister Hnatyshyn told the House of Commons that he has been assured by the country's financial institutions that they will cooperate by voluntarily reporting suspicious transactions.

There can be no compromise when it comes to the drug trade. Society must make choices, and in this case an individual's right to financial privacy does not outweigh the cost inflicted on society by illegal drugs. Banks and other financial institutions should report all large, suspicious transactions, passing along the expense of recording transactions to their customers. This is a small price to pay to purge the Pintos from our system. As with the professionals who must report suspected child abuse, money handlers must be forced to help disarm drug traffickers.

20/FLIGHT CAPITAL

Although money laundering is primarily associated with the drug trade, the practice is not confined to the criminal classes. Wealthy businessmen sneak money out of their inhospitable or unstable countries, bleeding the undeveloped world dry of precious capital, an estimated $75 billion so far. Closer to home, American tax collectors estimate they lose $9 billion in tax a year from tax evasion. Even major U.S. corporations are involved in laundering money to pay bribes or kickbacks, or to evade taxes or customs, as the following cases illustrate.

The world's best-known money-laundering scandal involved the notorious IOS, Investors' Overseas Services, run through Canadian companies by New York hustler Bernie Cornfeld. This scam, which eventually involved 50,000 victims in countries around the world and a sales force of 5,000, sucked flight capital into a high-flying mutual fund. Cornfeld's cash couriers took hundreds of millions of dollars out of countries in contravention of currency controls and other laws, all in the name of bringing capitalism to the proletariat. A former Trotskyite, Cornfeld eluded the law for years, thanks to the lack of Canadian regulations in the mutual fund business (Cornfeld astutely moved his head office to Halifax toward the end). But it was all about money laundering, businessmen handing over cash to IOS to hide it from tax men, ex-wives, present wives, future wives, business partners, or police. In fact, the joke around the office when Cornfeld bought his first fancy airplane was that he would shortly launch Capital Flight Airlines.

Cornfeld established his first mutual fund in Luxembourg in 1962. He started by tapping U.S. servicemen in Germany, then he latched on to employees of U.S. multinational firms living abroad. With those clients, IOS branched out into dozens of mutual funds and operations in most countries around the world. By the late 1960s, IOS was the most important blackmarket currency exporter. According to one estimate, it had $20 to $30 million illegal sales in Italy alone. In cash.

This money was funneled into mutual funds, investment trusts, insurance companies, real estate outfits, banks, and even a few publishing companies. Because offices were outside the U.S., Washington could not, and never did, go after Cornfeld.

IOS's investors, besides sneaking money out of their countries, felt they were making an investment in the type of good life that Cornfeld himself so lavishly displayed. He hung around with *Playboy* founder Hugh Hefner and the leggy beauties who occupied his two castles, three townhouses, and various apartments.

IOS eventually went public, starting in Toronto. This venture was spectacularly successful. Shares were listed at $12.50 and ended up at $75 by the end of the first day's trading. Cornfeld relocated the head office to Canada, but two years after that, in 1968, the outfit was found to be insolvent. Negative publicity triggered a run by worldwide unit holders who wanted their money, with redemptions running at $8 million daily. Cornfeld stepped down, and a new chairman met the annual meeting in 1968, held at Toronto's Royal York Hotel. Cornfeld did not attend and was dropped as a director.

Eventually, Cornfeld was done in by an even bigger swindler, the equally notorious Robert Vesco, who is still at large after being charged in 1972 with looting $224 million from the IOS mutual funds. Son of a Detroit used car salesman, Vesco plundered what was left of IOS's assets. Cornfeld went to jail in Switzerland over the fiasco; Vesco has been living as a fugitive ever since. Like the Amsterdam boiler-room boys, Cornfeld and his company capitalized on amassing flight capital from a cheating world.

AIR TICKETS

Most people do not realize that IATA, the International Airline Transport Association, which links the world's airlines, is also one of the world's biggest financial institutions. It acts as a clearing house for all of the swaps and other transactions conducted daily between hundreds of airlines. Police on several continents believe that a well-organized ring of Canadians originally from Kenya and of East Indian origin, has been successfully orchestrating airline ticket scams through IATA. Such scams threaten the financial stability of airlines and even nations.

IATA is located in Geneva. Every day it matches up transactions, much like a bank. If a traveler buys a ticket with Airline A but changes to an Airline B flight, Airline A's ticket will be accepted as payment by Airline B. No money changes hands, but a settlement will be reached weeks later at IATA. Airline A sends along the money it received from the traveler who took Airline B's flight instead. The money is remitted to Airline B by IATA at that point.

The system has one serious flaw. It is based on trust in a world filled with untrustworthy characters. Banks have known this for decades, although some still get duped. For instance, a bank will accept any check drawn from an account at another bank as a deposit. But the deposit, or even part of it, cannot be transferred or withdrawn until the check is cleared, which means when the money is actually received in the new account. This is not the case with the airline business, and it's becoming a multibillion-dollar worry.

Back in 1983 one well-organized ring of Canadians laundered an estimated $27 million out of Nigeria in eight weeks before authorities caught up to them. Another scam, involving a Toronto travel agent, resulted in one of the world's first fraud charges for laundering money via airline tickets.

This is how the scam worked. A Nigerian businessman who wanted to get his money out of his country or hide it for some reason bought $2-million worth of tickets on Nigerian Airways flights from an unscrupulous, money-laundering travel agent. (While that sounds like a lot of tickets, consider the fact that a first-class fare one way between London, England, and Sydney, Australia, is $4,900.)

Governments require financial institutions and even travel agents to prevent one currency from being converted into another without a record. In this case, the businessman's airline tickets were only redeemable in nyera, the local currency. This was stipulated on the face of the tickets. The Nigerian agent sent the tickets to an accomplice in Toronto. That agent then swapped the $2 million worth of Nigerian Airways tickets, at a slight discount, for "miscellaneous change orders," known in the business as MCOs. These are like gift certificates, or letters of credit, recognized by all airlines. They can be held in inventory, used as currency to buy any other tickets, or sold just as they are for a discount.

The proceeds, just slightly less than $2 million, were put into two bank accounts: some $1.5 million was in the name of the Nigerian businessman, which could be kept in Canada or electronically transferred to any country of his choice. The rest of the money, nearly $500,000, was kept by the agents.

Because the Nigerian Airways tickets were only redeemable in nyera, the MCOs were also only redeemable in nyera, so the Toronto agent simply removed the attachment that spelled out that restriction. Then he sent the entire batch of

MCOs, in small denominations, to a London travel wholesaler, who cashed them in for batches of tickets from Quantas, Australia's national airline. The Toronto agent received $1.8 million for his nearly $2 million worth of MCOs, a discount of $200,000 which reduced the agent's money-laundering fees to $300,000.

The Quantas tickets, in turn, were sold to Australian travel agencies. As passengers finished their flights, Quantas turned in the MCOs it received as payment for its tickets to the IATA clearing house only to discover that they could only be cashed in for nyera, as originally stipulated. Quantas got nothing for its MCOs. According to Dennis Phipps, "Such airline ticket fraud is costing the industry the most money of any crime, even stolen tickets. That's because tickets are easier to negotiate than bank notes. There are also thefts of blank tickets kept by travel agents, several thousands at a time. These are then moved to another part of the world. Laundering organizations are actively involved in this."

Some agents simply reissue restricted tickets for clean ones, purposely dropping restrictions found on originals, and fencing them for half price. "It could be months or years before IATA catches up to this," says John Buckley, Toronto spokesman for Consumer and Corporate Affairs.

In a separate case in January 1988, a ring of ticket launderers south of the border was broken up by investigations launched in the U.S., U.K., and Canada. It began in mid-1987, when 2,278 in blank airline tickets were stolen in a bust-out at a Las Vegas travel agency. (A bust-out, as opposed to a break-in, happens when thieves hide inside a company until it closes business for the day. They steal items, then break or bust out.) In the Las Vegas incident, airline officials calculated the losses as high as $5 million. A Toronto travel agent was charged with conspiracy to commit fraud.

Sometimes crooks buy a financially troubled travel agency for a very low price simply to make off with its ticket stock. Then tickets are forged and sold at legitimate travel agencies or in unlicensed discount operations at half the going rate. "The industry is unwilling to discuss the extent of losses, but an IATA confidential survey among thirty-nine member airlines said its clearinghouse transactions which ended up as losses totalled $12 million. If you apply that to 331 airlines in total, the loss figure is $2 billion annually," says Phipps, now a security consultant in London. "As for stolen or missing tickets, there are some 800,000 out there now. About 60 percent are ever used, and the average loss per ticket is $4,000. That adds up to $23 billion a year. And it's happening and starting to affect the stability of national currencies."

21/THE PRICE OF DOING BUSINESS

SEX AND MRS. FOROFOR GRAPES

Canada is more dependent upon trade than any other industrialized nation on earth. And there is crime and corruption galore in the rough-and-tumble world of imports and exports. Commonplace are kickbacks, payoffs, and bribes, which the Mexicans call "mordida," or small bites. In the United States, these are euphemistically referred to by the corporations that must pay them as sensitive payments. Whatever the label, such payments are constant and require money laundering to hide them from tax officials, corporate bosses, and central bankers.

Caught in the middle of this dilemma was Canadian Kenneth Perry, who peddled Canadian sulfur around the world. Some say he was entangled in doing a good job for bad people, but others say he nearly pulled off the supreme scam. Whatever the conclusion, the Perry affair provides a delicious smorgasbord of money-laundering techniques.

Between 1973 and 1977, Perry was president of Cansulex Ltd., a sulfur-trading group owned by giants such as Mobil Oil Canada, Dome Petroleum, Chevron Standard, and others. Sulfur is a by-product of processing natural gas and is used in everything from gunpowder and matches to antibacterial drugs. Canada has mountains of the stuff, and Cansulex sells it to dozens of countries.

By most accounts, Perry was a super-salesman. A lawyer from Manitoba, he had globe-trotted for Denison Mines, Rio Algom, and the secretive Mannix coal and construction barons of Alberta. As Cansulex president, he traveled eight months out of the year, always first class, visiting customers in thirty-two different countries. And his results were spectacular. Cansulex's sales jumped from $28 million in 1973 to $77 million by 1977.

But a chance conversation over cocktails at a Copenhagen conference caused his downfall. There, Cansulex vice-president Donald Tanner ran into a South African customer who told him that the sulfur was top quality and deliveries always on time. But he told Tanner that the price was getting a little steep at $34 a ton. Tanner knew that Cansulex only received $31.50 a ton from its South African sales, so when he came back to Vancouver, Tanner initiated an audit into Perry's affairs.

Shortly after taking over the reins, Perry had talked Cansulex's board into setting up an offshore trading company to protect its South African sales from politically motivated economic sanctions. Cansulex would sell its sulfur to the Bermuda trading company which would, in turn, sell it directly to South Africa. That way, argued Perry, the business was insulated from political problems because Cansulex could argue that its customer was Bermuda. Perry also began to sell sulfur destined for other countries to Bermuda, if those sales involved sensitive payments.

Perry was hauled before his board to answer questions. He explained that the difference in price was to pay off the South African intermediary who facilitated the deals and handled some of the shipping details, but who wanted to keep his money outside his country to get around its currency controls. What Perry could not explain away was the fact that he owned the Bermuda company and that there was no money to speak of left in it. The members of the board did not buy his excuses and were convinced that Perry was skimming the money for his own personal use. Though they had no evidence, the board fired Perry immediately and contacted RCMP Sergeant Ron Harvey.

Sergeant Harvey soon discovered Perry's Achilles heel. The six-foot, seven-inch man was a sexual athlete and had indulged in love affairs with many women who had worked for him. Harvey guessed that such a man would tend to confide in his women employees even if there was no sexual relationship. Harvey began working down the list of ex-employees who could help finger Perry on fraud. He hit paydirt in August 1978 when he telephoned Hilary Wiffen, who lived in England in a Yorkshire village. She said she had some information for him, and he took the next plane there.

"We met in a country pub and had a pint of beer each. We small talked for awhile about Canada and stuff, then she reached into her purse and pulled out a tatty piece of paper folded in half. She pushed it across the table toward me and it read 'Mrs. Forofor Grapes.' That was the name of the secret Swiss bank account where Perry salted his dough away."

Sergeant Harvey flew immediately to Geneva, Switzerland, and obtained search warrants from Swiss authorities on the strength of Wiffen's evidence. And sure enough, "Mrs. Forofor Grapes" was in Perry's name and contained $1.3 million. Another of Perry's ex-secretaries, Doreen Wolfe, explained the account's bizarre name: "My apartment number was 404. Grapes was a fruit we often ate."

Wiffen said Perry had often asked her to go to Bermuda to withdraw a large amount of cash and fly to Switzerland to deposit it in Mrs. Forofor Grapes. Harvey discovered that many sales were being shifted through Bermuda and that there were probably other bank accounts in Perry's name. But these were impossible to find.

In September, a month after Harvey found the evidence he needed, Cansulex sued Perry for the proceeds and sued as well the Bermuda accountants, lawyers, and banks involved in the offshore trading company for turning a blind eye to the funneling of money to Switzerland. Cansulex also made a $1-million claim to The Insurance Co. of North America in Toronto on a bond it had taken out as a form of insurance as protection against dishonest employees. All these lawsuits had to be kept on ice, however, when Sergeant Harvey laid charges of criminal fraud against Perry in October 1977.

The trial, held in 1981, was a fascinating glimpse into money laundering on a worldwide scale. Perry admitted to the court that he had been taking secret commissions or kickbacks and facilitating income tax evasion and the circumvention of securities regulations, currency controls, and commodity price ceilings in several countries where he sold sulfur.

He also admitted to depositing $1.3 million in Mrs. Forofor Grapes without the knowledge of Cansulex's board in order to protect them from prosecution. He said $1 million of this was held in trust for two individuals — Dennis Pottinger and Charles Hun Assyd — who had arranged sales of sulfur to South Africa and Morocco. The other $300,000 was "a consulting fee on some coal properties in northeast B.C.," paid in cash to him by a large Canadian mining company and deposited in Switzerland to avoid Canadian income taxes.

Perry said he had met Pottinger by chance in 1975 in the lobby of the posh Charleton Hotel in Johannesburg. The two retired to a bar and negotiated a deal whereby Perry would pay Pottinger a commission for assisting with sulfur sales to South Africa. But Pottinger wanted his commissions deposited secretly outside South Africa to circumvent that country's foreign-currency controls. Such an arrangement was also income tax evasion.

Perry told the court that Assyd was an agent for a Moroccan firm and that he had agreed to bill Assyd's firm a higher price than Cansulex would receive and deposit the difference in a Swiss bank account for Assyd. That arrangement broke several laws: it breached currency restrictions, defrauded Assyd's company, and evaded income taxes in Morocco.

Other arrangements included a shifty maneuver involving a French multinational and its Brazilian subsidiary, designed to circumvent tax and currency controls and commodity price ceiling laws, as well as involving payoffs to a relative of an Oriental shipping magnate in return for getting Cansulex cargos in and out of several Far Eastern harbors quickly. These kickbacks were directed into a San Francisco bank account, deposited in cash by Perry personally.

Perry said he was trustee for these funds, which is why accounts into which they spilled were all in his name. That was fine, except that Perry had made a number of withdrawals from Mrs. Forofor Grapes over the years, including a large one to pay off the mortgage on his Vancouver house. If the money was for others why was he dipping into it? No problem, said Perry. Pottinger went into hiding after the legal actions were launched, said Perry, "If it got worse, he said he'd come forward and I could use whatever funds were in there for legal expenses and also living expenses."

Such arrangements were kept from Cansulex, Perry said, to protect the oil companies which owned pieces of Cansulex. "This was because it had become very, very clear at that time to anybody in the international business that, if you were going to engage in sensitive payment arrangements, you'd make sure that nothing appeared in the books of the company," Perry told the court.

Perry may have been alluding to cases such as that in which the Lockheed Aircraft Corp. was fined $647,000 in 1976 for making $30 million worth of secret commission payments without recording them as such on its books. Also, the entire board of directors of Gulf Oil Corp. lost their jobs in the 1970s under similar circumstances. Perry told his fraud trial that, because most of the companies participating in Cansulex were American-owned, the so-called sensitive payments at issue should have been disclosed to the U.S. Securities and Exchange Commission. This would have blown Pottinger's cover and, at the very least, resulted in embarrassing questions, Perry said. Thus, he said, the Swiss bank account method was set up. "Cansulex didn't ask me directly [about my arrangements] at a board meeting because they didn't want to know," Perry testified. "They knew enough about how international business conditions were at that time to know what was going on."

Perry told the court that he took great pains to hide what he was doing. Whenever he was away, his office door in Vancouver was locked, testified another former secretary, Gilian Nixon. She also said Perry used her address as a mailing address whenever his travels took him to Bermuda. She always prepared two different travel itineraries. The one she kept at home was real, and she used it to reach him; the other was fiction and strictly for office use.

At the trial, Perry's brilliant barrister, Calgary lawyer Chris Evans, argued before the jury that, unless they felt that Pottinger, Assyd, and others never existed anywhere in the world and were completely a figment of Perry's imagination, Perry was innocent of fraud charges. Perry backed this up. "I was playing by rules which I could not win. The ever-narrowing ledge on which I was walking, with a soaring rock wall of increasing sales and profits on one side and a raging torrent of ever-rising standards of business conduct on the other, had to diminish to where a foothold was no longer possible," Perry told the court.

Jurors bought this line of reasoning and acquitted Perry in April 1981. He returned to Vancouver where he continued to scour the world doing deals. A year later, the civil lawsuits were settled out of court for undisclosed terms, after threats by Perry that he would demonstrate that these were (and are) standard practices by putting at least twenty-eight oil company executives on the stand. Three years later, Perry died of a heart attack and was buried, along with the truth. Was he simply an efficient executive caught between a rock and a hard place or a world-class criminal?

Perry never confessed, but a Christmas card he sent to me following the publication of a full-length feature about these cases, gave some hints, even though his message was characteristically cryptic. My story, which appeared in the *Toronto*

Star and was syndicated across Canada, was carefully balanced, never taking sides for or against Perry and Cansulex. Inside his card he wrote: "The Christmas Season is a time of 'argumentum ad misericordiam' and 'locus paenitentiae.' This card is sent to you in the spirit of Christmas. Signed K.G. Perry."

"Argumentum ad misericordium" is the Latin version of the inscription on my namesake's temple, the Goddess Diana of mythology. "Argumentum" means argument, evidence, proof, or appeal and the expression means an appeal for mercy or an argument designed to call forth a merciful judgment. "Locus" means place and "paenitentiae" means repentance, hence a place (or opportunity) for repentance. Kenneth G. Perry, without a doubt, was as clever (and cryptic) a contrepreneur as Canada has ever produced.

MARITIME MONEY LAUNDERING

For Quebec's dredging companies it was salad days during the construction of the St. Lawrence Seaway between 1955 and 1959. There was too much work around to bid on every contract. But after that huge project finished, idle equipment, layoffs, and poor profits were the norm, as companies competed aggressively for pieces of a considerably smaller pie.

In 1966 the two biggest firms agreed to fix bids on government contracts in Quebec. That illegal cartel spread to every other dredging firm and region in the country, costing taxpayers millions more than necessary for the work because payoffs were funneled to firms and public officials alike.

Government contracts have always been a dirty business, but the companies sank to rock bottom after 1966. Before 1966, for instance, Harold McNamara, founder of Quebec dredging giant McNamara Corp., would make out a check to himself for $25,000, cash it, and give the proceeds to the campaign fund raiser for a Liberal minister of public works to get a favorable ruling on tender bidding. After 1966, the dredging companies used a more sophisticated system. McNamara and his arch-rivals, the company owned by the well-connected Simard family of Montreal joined forces. McNamara Corp., owned by British construction giant Bovis Corp., agreed to prearrange bidding with Simard-owned Marine Industries Ltd.

The pie was divided up so that the considerably larger Marine Industries was entitled to 70 percent of all future Quebec business; McNamara Corp. got the rest. In return, McNamara Corp. would have Ontario all to itself, unless a contract was huge, in which case Marine would be cut in for some of the profits. According to the arrangement, either they would bid together and one would agree to bid higher than the other or one would agree not to bid at all.

Two years later, the agreement was amended to give McNamara Corp. 70 percent of Ontario and Marine the rest; the new agreement would also include McNamara's traditional bidding partner in Ontario, Construction Aggregates Co. Inc. of Chicago and its Hamilton subsidiary. McNamara and Construction Aggregates also agreed to give kickbacks of 1.5 percent of their business to a Marine Industries vice-president, Louis deRome.

Naturally, money-laundering schemes had to be devised to hide Louis deRome's kickbacks from Revenue Canada, as well as from his employer. The first payment of $64,000 in early 1969 was allocated to the "deRome Retirement Fund" by a phony invoice scam. A fake company in Panama billed McNamara for the amount, for work allegedly done in Nicaragua, a difficult place to double-check. McNamara issued a check, and it was deposited into a Long Island bank account set up in trust for deRome.

The conspiracy widened in 1969, when a huge federal land-reclamation project came up for bidding in Quebec City. Secret arrangements were made, and McNamara agreed to bid higher than Marine Industries in return for a subcontract equal to 30 percent of the dredging work. But Harold McNamara, who had founded and still ran the firm, had to pay off other companies that wanted to bid. He agreed to pay Canadian Dredge & Dock Ltd. about $150,000 to bid high. Then a British Columbia firm, Sceptre Dredging Ltd., began sniffing around the project. It too was bought off for $150,000 and agreed not to bid at all. Not surprisingly, Marine Industries won the day by bidding $7,950,000, even though this was significantly higher than Sceptre's untendered bid of $6.9 million.

Sceptre's intrusion led to a nation-wide deal, and the companies met twice to hammer out an arrangement, finally agreeing at a meeting in Vancouver's posh Capilano Golf and Country Club to split the country at the Alberta/Saskatchewan border. The parties agreed to stay out of one another's turf. Their representatives would meet on a regular basis to discuss upcoming bids and payoffs. Horace "Joe" Rindress, vice-president of the Simard company J.P. Porter, was appointed to mediate deals and to keep score sheets: records of who paid payoffs to whom, which were destroyed after the deals were settled. Needless to say, score sheets are not official corporate documents. Marine Industries was run by Simard family members but had been sold a few years earlier to a provincial Crown corporation, Société de financement du Québec. J.P. Porter was controlled and run by the family.

The corporate gangsters continued merrily on until they met their match in Hamilton, Ontario, where they had to extend payoffs to a government-appointed official and master money launderer. In 1970 Stelco invited tenders from McNamara Corp., J.P. Porter, and Canadian Dredge & Dock to reclaim some land from Hamilton harbor. McNamara Corp. won the contract on a bid of $1.97 million in June, and Porter was to share in its profits as part of the secret, illegal deal. But a month later, the scam artists were outscammed. Rindress got a call from the Hamilton Harbour Commission and was informed that it might not approve the floating of pipes across the harbor, a procedure necessary to complete the task cheaply. Rindress called commission chairman Ken Elliott and was told permission was available for "a price" of $15,000, payable to Elliott. The payoff was made.

To launder the payment Elliott and his sidekick Reg Fisher concocted a number of schemes, but in this case the $15,000 payoff was made through two under-invoicing and over-invoicing scams. Elliott produced a fake invoice for $13,500 for electrical contracting work that never took place and sent it to the J.P. Porter Co. Rindress backdated a purchase order for this bogus work and paid it by check to Elliott's associate, Reg Fisher. The check was deposited in Fisher's company account and weeks later Fisher withdrew the amount in the form of a manager's check made out to another bank. This was then cashed and deposited into Fisher's personal bank account, presumably to be paid to Elliott minus a small fee for his trouble. The rest of the payoff was made through a simple transaction of under-invoicing. Porter Co. sold a piece of equipment worth $2,000 to Elliott for $400, a net benefit of $1,500, which was the rest of the payoff.

Elliott was born in Hamilton in 1933. He was the foul-mouthed son of a well-connected father who owned a shipping business. Elliott dropped out of high school to work in the family business but sold his half to a brother in 1961 and bought a Dairy Queen franchise. He had been a Hamilton harbor commissioner for years.

Reg Fisher, a cultured retired banker, was born in 1913 in Winchester, Ontario. He was fired by the Bank of Montreal in the 1950s for alleged conflict of interest involving a customer, but he successfully sued for wrongful dismissal. He went on to become a trust company manager, and in 1969 he retired and ran a part-time tax and financial consulting business. He kept the books for Elliott's Dairy Queen and much, much more.

Elliott obviously liked doing business with Rindress, and in 1971 he talked about a new dredging project. He said he wanted J.P. Porter to get the deal, "providing Rindress would agree to 'kickback' fifteen cents per cubic yard dredged to Elliott personally," according to crown prosecutor Rod McLeod in a statement made at the trial. "Elliott said the bids would be by invitation only and the commissioners could invite McNamara and Canadian Dredge to bid against J.P. Porter. Rindress told Elliott he could make arrangements with the two to bid higher, thus ensuring his company got the contract."

Rindress was concerned about being able to get $150,000 out of Porter to pay off Elliott. But Elliott said that for a fee equivalent to 20 percent of the amount, he would handle the money-laundering side because he had a "proven system to launder funds out of the company," McLeod said. Rindress arranged to pay off $200,000 to Canadian Dredge for its high bid. That meant that of the $1 million contract more than one-third was going toward payoffs.

Elliott then agreed to help Rindress launder $125,000 of his $200,000 payoff to Canadian Dredge, in return for a 20 percent fee, or roughly $32,000. He had his dummy Swiss company, International Marine, invoice a joint venture project being run by J.P. Porter for US$156,312. Evidence at the trial showed the check was issued and deposited in a Florida bank account opened for International Marine by former Ontario Provincial Police officer Harry Atkins, a self-employed private detective at the time. Bank documents described International Marine as a sole proprietorship with operations in the Bahamas. Atkins was then instructed to withdraw a cash deposit of $125,000. The rest of the money stayed in the account as Elliott's laundering fee and was withdrawn later and placed in safety deposit boxes.

Naturally, such large cash withdrawals required an explanation, and Atkins told the Florida bank manager that he needed to make large cash withdrawals weekly to meet payroll commitments in the Bahamas. Atkins withdrew $48,000, $39,000, and $43,000, for a total of $130,000, from the account, keeping $4,000 for his costs and fees. He then flew to Toronto and, with Elliott in tow, handed over $126,000 in cash to Rindress at the Royal York Hotel. Rindress, in turn, handed it over to a Canadian Dredge executive.

Meanwhile, Elliott's son Wayne rented several safety deposit boxes at the same Florida bank under his parents' names, R.E. and D.J. Elliott. On a regular basis, Elliott's wife, Daisy, made large cash withdrawals, and placed the cash in the safety deposit boxes there and elsewhere. Elliott would travel down regularly to his Hollywood, Florida, condo to withdraw his ill-gotten gains.

The bid rigging got more outrageous as time wore on, despite the fact that participants knew the police were snooping around. A Toronto harbor project, which should have cost around $4 million, was inflated by payoffs to $7.17 million. McNamara Corp. was the lucky winner, and it even had the gall to bill the government for "cost overruns," bringing the total tab to $7.7 million. For these and other deals, Elliott and Reg Fisher continued to play money launderers through some clever schemes they devised.

Evidence showed one scam involved a wrecking yard. On July 26, 1972, Elliott asked Marvin Frank, the owner of A.J. Frank and Son in Hamilton, to send J.P. Porter Co. a phony invoice totalling $21,337.80 for the phony sale of 3,498 feet of twenty-inch pipe. Elliott said the money was payoff to Rindress, and the invoice would be paid with no questions asked. The check was deposited into A.J. Frank and Son's bank account. Marvin Frank then set up a phony invoice scheme with Morris Lax, president of Morris Lax Scrap Metal, which billed Frank and Son for pipe it never received. Frank and Son issued Lax a check for $21,214.20; Lax cashed it and paid the cash back to Frank and Son. Days later, Frank and Son gave the money to Ken Elliott, who kept it for himself.

"Scrap yards are ideal for money laundering," says Rod Stamler of the RCMP. "Revenue Canada got involved in this and went to the yard. Nothing had ever moved in or out of there for years. Stuff was just rusting. It was all for show. There was a major Revenue Canada investigation into tax evasion."

All of this proceeded, as authorities grew increasingly suspicious, until 1973, when a deal took place that revealed to officials the tip of a money-laundering iceberg. Montreal's Hall Shipping Corp. had arranged to sell a rust bucket of a boat sitting in Montreal harbor to one of the Simard companies, J.P. Porter Co. Ltd., for $25,000. Then Porter's vice-president, Horace Rindress, suddenly introduced Reg Fisher as the buyer. A deal was struck, but Hall later heard that Fisher had flipped the boat the next day to J.P. Porter for $75,000. Somewhat miffed, the company questioned why anyone would pay three times more for a boat than it was worth, especially when the fair price had been within his grasp.

Prompted by public allegations of corruption in Hamilton, the RCMP undertook a lengthy investigation. Commercial crime officer Rod Stamler approached Hall to get the relevant documents. The police discovered that Elliott was to be paid off by getting the ship for $25,000, then flipping it for $75,000 to Porter and others. Fisher was the front man and thereby earned $2,000; he parked the money in his personal account, withdrew it as bank drafts payable to himself, then cashed it in at another bank. The rest of the $48,000 cash was paid to Elliott.

The resulting court case contained many hints of the way contracts were awarded in those days. In one case, McLeod told the court that in February 1972 another Simard-controlled company, Richelieu Dredging Corp. Inc., had pre-arranged to win a St. Lawrence River dredging contract. Richelieu's president was Rindress, and he arranged payoff terms with Syd Cooper, president of C.A. Pitts in Toronto, as well as with Canadian Dredge & Dock and McNamara Corp. After a great deal of haggling, the group became frustrated when the project was put on hold by the federal government because of spending constraints.

Crown prosecutor Rod McLeod told the court: "By late July 1972, Rindress met with Jean Simard, director of J.P. Porter [Marine vice-president and a member of Quebec's prominent Simard family which controlled Porter, Marine, and Richelieu] and advised him of the situation. On August 21, 1972, Treasury Board [in Ottawa] approved the awarding of the contract to the lowest bidder — Richelieu Dredging."

Rindress made a deal with police and agreed to incriminate Elliott and others by carrying a body pack and recording conversations. Some illuminating conversations were held in a submarine in South Carolina, which Elliott had just bought for scrap. They took place while investigations were under way, but before charges were laid and they exposed the cockiness and rationalizations behind the actions of so many contrepreneurs.

In one telling conversation, Elliott advises Rindress on how to stonewall Stamler and other investigators. "I've gone through this for two years. You only had it for the last six months, but it's been on my ass for two years. I just made up my mind six months ago, fuck it. What can they really do? I've been all through it. The worst I can do is wind up with a fine for conflict of interest so they can criticize me in court and in the newspapers. Fuck it. As far as the political payoffs — they can kiss my ass. That's all he's [Rod Stamler] after is political payoffs. But you, Joe, you were acting on behalf of them, [the Simards]. It was their fuckin' company. It's their responsibility."

In the end, Fisher and Elliott went to jail, and most others entered guilty pleas and were fined or jailed. Multimillionaire contractor Syd Cooper went to jail after coming to court every day in a chauffeur-driven limousine, as did wealthy Harold McNamara, who netted a five-year sentence. In addition, most companies were fined millions. Well-connected Jean Simard (Robert Bourassa's brother-in-law) was convicted, but a retrial was ordered by an appeal court. The crown decided not to pursue the matter.

When Elliott had spent some time in jail after the trial, he alleged that two fellow Hamilton harbor commissioners, including John Munro's campaign manager, Joseph Lanza, were beneficiaries of the payoffs, but the matter was not pursued in the courts because prosecutors did not believe him. But the sideswipe by Elliott became a hot election issue during 1975 and Munro voluntarily handed over his personal and constituency financial records to Stamler.

22/Drug Money

THEY GROW MORE THAN GRAPES IN NIAGARA

Bordertown lawyer Gary Hendin lost a promising career when he turned to the lucrative business of laundering money. Bright and ambitious, he had worked his way through law school by the relatively early age of twenty-three, he and his wife then settled into a quiet law practice in equally quiet St. Catharines, a small town located between Hamilton and Fort Erie, in the heart of the grape-growing region. He began work with a small firm, then struck out on his own, eventually employing nine secretaries and two bookkeepers. He belonged to many local organizations and charities, nearly captured a nomination for the Liberal Party in the area, and was a member of the local police force's gun club.

In about 1980, he was approached by "organized crime figures," and several laundering schemes were concocted. He incorporated M & M Currency Exchange, and every two weeks or so, the criminals sent their money to his law office via couriers. Hendin personally took the cash, often delivered in paper bags or gym bags or attaché cases and usually in $20 bills, into his office library. He would put the cash through his $6,000 money-counting machine and sometimes walked to the Bank of Nova Scotia's main branch in St. Catharines with the cash in a suitcase. On seventeen occasions, he deposited a total of $252,900 by sending a teenager to the bank on a bicycle. The money was then picked up by drug dealers, and couriers flew the money to Florida, where it was used to buy more cocaine to bring to Canada. Leftover cash was deposited, by courier, in the bank accounts of shell companies on the Cayman Islands. Other drug proceeds were kept in Canadian cash for living expenses or to buy marijuana in Toronto. Some was laundered through Hendin's real estate schemes in Canada to give the drug dealers legitimate local income and assets.

Hendin set up and was president of two investment companies called Cencan and Joshua. Between July 1979 and October 1983, the Bank of Montreal advanced Joshua and Cencan some $1.2 million in loans. Amazingly, Hendin triple-hatted in these transactions, acting as solicitor and president for Cencan as well as solicitor for the bank branch and for Cencan's clients who borrowed mortgage money from the firm. The bank loaned money to Cencan, which, in turn, placed it in higher-interest mortgages. Hendin defrauded the bank, however, by lending money to certain clients and then, when it was allegedly repaid, not returning the money to the bank as agreed under the terms of the loan. In some cases, the money was never repaid, but he forged affidavits saying that the loans were paid up, thus removing mortgages from the property land titles.

In another transaction, Hendin pretended to lend $324,802 for a property purchase to a company involved with an organized crime figure. The loan was recorded as a mortgage on the property, and Hendin later gave the company a partial discharge, despite the fact that no money changed hands. The imaginary loan was a means of laundering $324,802 worth of dirty money and getting it into the hands of the organized crime figure legitimately; the pretend payoff created a legitimate asset on the books of Hendin's companies, which were owned in part by the crime figures too. Such schemes ended with Hendin's arrest and Cencan's bankruptcy. The Bank of Montreal was out $1.2 million because Cencan's liens against properties had been removed and no money was left.

Hendin admitted he was recruited by unnamed organized criminals to launder drug money and pleaded guilty in May 1985 to laundering $12 million over three years through clever real estate and currency exchange transactions. He also pleaded guilty to defrauding the Bank of Montreal.

Hendin's fun with figures came to the attention of Revenue Canada auditors. Audits led to several counts of income tax evasion involving millions of dollars. Hendin was not involved directly in the importation or distribution of narcotics, but acted as a highly reputable front and launderer for these operations. The judge blessed a joint prosecution-defense deal which included a five-year sentence and a $1.2 million fine, equivalent to 25 percent of Revenue Canada's claim. "The court must also be concerned towards a solicitor who, as an officer of the court, would not only defraud a client [this bank], but who would throw his efforts into aiding the underworld in carrying out a scheme, in which it did untold harm to an untold number of persons." Hendin was disbarred a year after the case.

It was one of the few sentences for money laundering ever handed down in Canada and the only time a defendant has made a deal with the crown and agreed to the relatively stiff sentence of five years. Hendin also agreed to sign a statement of facts, setting out the details of his crime. But conspicuously absent, and probably the reason why he so readily took a big fall, are the identities of the organized crime figures for whom he laundered money. All he did was admit that he laundered funds.

Hendin's statement shows how easily washing is done in Canada. He is a textbook smurf. The going rate for such smurfing is about 7 percent on the types of volumes he was handling, which would have netted him a cool $840,000 in just three years. Hendin's lawyer suggested his money laundering fees were only 3 percent, or $360,000. His actual fees remain a mystery, as does the true total of funds he may have laundered for these mobsters. Nonetheless, Hendin was pleading poverty by the time he was sent to prison, partly because the charges against him and his disbarment deprived him of the ability to make a living.

Considering the size of his crime, Hendin got off lightly. He could have received seven years for assisting in drug trafficking, five for evasion, five more for money laundering, plus fines. But the judge took into consideration the fact it was a first offense and that Hendin had already suffered a great deal. He had lost his thriving legal practice, he had been socially snubbed, and he was finished business-wise. It was a sad ending for a young man who had everything going for him: business success, brains, and a nice family. It was also ironic considering that his Russian immigrant father, Gary Hendin Sr., a prominent Kingston, Ontario, businessman, performed many community services in that prison town, including a stint as the "first Jewish president of the John Howard Society," an organization which helps convicts.

"The offender is thirty-six years of age, married, and the father of two children," said the judge who sentenced him. "He graduated from law school at a very young age. He comes from a family with a very strong background, and he has, undoubtedly, brought shame and embarrassment, not only to himself, but to his entire family. He has destroyed his own life as a barrister and solicitor by being disbarred as a result of these charges. He, apparently, had great ability, which resulted, according to his counsel, and which I accept, in a thriving, financially successful law practice. He is also said to have taken active part in a number of community endeavors. One can only conclude that his desire for life in the fast lane, as his lawyer put it, after being involved in some manner with the underworld, so brought him to take part in the illegal activities."

The crown prosecutor was not inclined to be so merciful. "The scope of his crime, the method that he used, the total rejection of the law in which he was trained, indicate that rehabilitation is going to be a long process and, therefore, again, calls for the maximum period of incarceration that's available. I can provide Your Honor with no precedent of this sentence. As far as I am aware, this is the first time in Canada that an individual has agreed to the maximum period of incarceration under the Income Tax Act."

SERGEANT PRESTON

Young, good-looking Stephen Pakozdy had all the toys until Christmas 1983 when he wrapped up as a Christmas present $145,000 cash in a shoebox. That's when an airport security guard with an eagle eye spotted the suspicious package and asked him to open it. When all that cash was found inside, airport officials immediately summoned Sergeant Robert Preston, head of Edmonton's anti-drug-profiteering unit. What followed was the unraveling of a sizable drug empire in western Canada, created by a very clever laundering scam involving a sleepy Edmonton storefront operation called Pine Village Quilts.

It also illustrates the wisdom of units like Preston's. "The only thing they ever got Al Capone on was income tax evasion. Same with this guy. We never found an ounce of drugs on him or near him. He was smart, but we followed the money trail," says Preston. "The airport call was the beginning. It was a routine check, at that point he was unknown to us as a drug dealer. He said he had problems with the tax department, that he had emptied the till of his business, and that he was taking it to a broker in Toronto to buy some mutual funds and other investments. That gave us enough reason to confiscate the cash, and I started a joint investigation with Revenue Canada. The money, we found out later, was actually going to Toronto to buy marijuana."

For the next two years, Preston and another investigator spent most of their time tailing Pakozdy and following up other leads. They found out that Pakozdy's lifestyle was nothing short of lavish. Only twenty-eight years of age at the time, he had graduated from an Ontario university and was the son of a physician who died when he was a youngster. He and his wife Susan owned a four-acre estate outside Edmonton, complete with a pond, paddocks, and a beautifully furnished log cabin. They owned matching Porsches as well as an Audi and he bought her fur coats, expensive jewelry, and exotic holidays to the Caribbean and elsewhere.

Preston discovered that Pakozdy spent $6,700 in two years traveling back and forth to Ontario and another $18,000 in 1982 and 1983 traveling. That was a great deal of cash-register skimming, especially considering the fact that Pakozdy's only apparent income came from Pine Village Quilts, a listless little shop on an Edmonton sidestreet, which was sometimes open only four days a week because business was so slow. Nevertheless, Preston discovered that some days Pakozdy deposited $5,000 in cash into Pine Village's bank account, despite estimated daily sales of a mere $200. The deposits were used to support high living, but countless thousands more was cashed in to buy gold bullion, which is easily hidden, easily liquidated, and completely anonymous.

Such large sums of cash were actually being generated from drug sales run out of Pakozdy's Edmonton warehouse, where a delivery man, a warehouseman, and a bookkeeper ran operations. All three were paid cash under the table but had no idea what was in the parcels they accepted, stored, and delivered. None of the three were charged and all cooperated as witnesses. Police did not discover the warehouse's existence until raids were made on Pakozdy's home, store, and his bookkeeper's home, where the phone number was found scribbled on a notepad.

Ironically, admits Preston, if Pakozdy had stopped dealing in drugs immediately after his money was seized at the airport, he would have faced just income tax evasion charges. "We would never have gotten him, but he figured he'd never get caught. He was arrogant," recalls Preston. "At the airport he said to me, 'Hey, want to buy a Porsche? I've got one for sale, but you cops can't afford that stuff.' He was cocky."

By June 1985 Preston had enough evidence to move in with search and arrest warrants. But it was only an analysis of Pakozdy's suspicious lifestyle that made charges against him stick. In 1979 he was worth $12,300, but by 1983 he had $353,000 in assets. After he was arrested, Preston said Pakozdy's clandestine books showed $500,000 in unexplained income acquired in little more than one year. This was disbursed into stock market investments and gold transactions. According to his drug ledgers, he had sold $200,000 worth of marijuana from the U.S., Vancouver, and Toronto in just four months.

He ran a very slick operation, never doing any of the dirty work himself. His man in the warehouse fielded everything from pick-ups to deliveries to placing orders with drug suppliers. Pakozdy had a custom-built, three-quarter ton truck complete with a false seat to stash the contraband on trips to Ontario or Vancouver. Out west, British Columbia shipments came in from California by air to Pender Island. Planes would buzz the bay, drop their payloads and yachts would scoop the bobbing bundles out of the drink. They would take them to the mainland, where trucks awaited the marijuana or hashish for shipment to the interior. Such shipments would be broken into smaller parcels and delivered, on demand, through Pakozdy's sizable network of street-level drug dealers. Naturally, all transactions were in cash and proceeds were delivered directly to his bookkeeper, a 50-year-old woman who worked out of her home, along with her husband who was in the furniture repair business. When police burst into her place, they found a ledger in a small gray leather pouch on a sofa.

The ledger itemized transactions from costs to accounts receivable. Pages were destroyed as bills were paid. For instance, one entry reads "27 November 1984 to June 8, 1985: projected net profits $53,606; profit per pound, accounts receivable, total sales $394,288." Another entry: "Bad stuff, rebate $25."

Shortly afterward, charges were laid, and Pakozdy bolted, jumping bail with Susan. For the next six months the two lived as fugitives in California, leaving their lawyer a note addressed to Preston which said, "I'm not running from justice but because I know you want to bankrupt me."

Preston was entitled to do just that under changes made to the Narcotics Control Act in Canada in 1982, which paved the way for units like his, designed to hunt down drug dealers by following their money trail, and to take away all their expensive possessions. "These guys are not afraid of jail, but they are afraid of being broke. He was greedy and well connected to the business community and enjoyed status until the charges showed he was a crook."

Finally, the couple returned to Canada voluntarily and surrendered for a deal in 1986. Pakozdy agreed to plead guilty if Susan was spared. Her charges were stayed by the court the day he pleaded guilty. Pakozdy never divulged information on his drug network.

He got four years for trafficking and two more years for money laundering, plus two and one half years more for tax evasion and jumping bail, to be served simultaneously. With good behavior, he'll be back on the street in 1988. However, the court seized all his assets, says Preston. "They sold his truck, stripped his house of furniture, artwork, everything, sold off jewelry, cars, furs, and the bank foreclosed on the log house estate. We made money on this one. It seems that drug enforcement may eventually pay its own way. This is more fun than any other job I have held in the force . . . taking the toys away from these drug traffickers."

CATCHING UP TO DRUG SMUGGLERS

RCMP white-collar crime chief Rod Stamler has been pushing, along with the other Mountie brass, for better laws to fight money-laundering. There is little question that that must happen. At the very least, Canada must institute the type of reporting requirements that exist in the U.S. The rules should even be tougher, applying to any cash transactions of $2,500 or more. Failure to file such reports should net a lengthy prison sentence to discourage banks, credit unions, and their customers from salting away criminal profits in Canadian deposit-taking institutions, where deposits are kept for a matter of seconds until they can be transferred offshore. Similarly, our brokerage houses, credit unions, currency exchanges, and other institutions must be made to accept the types of ceilings and supervision the biggest Canadian banks have attempted to undertake.

But such measures only attack the branches, not the roots, of the problem. The massive narcotics trade is the root cause, and in the absence of new laws, there is probably little that can be done about the degree of drug smuggling that has made laundering such a multibillion-dollar growth industry. New laws are needed in the U.S. and Canada to crack down on the consumption of narcotics. Right now, on both sides of the border, traffickers get lengthy prison sentences, while drug consumers get off lightly with small fines.

The lawmakers do not realize that the current jurisprudence situation flies in the face of the type of simple economic principles that affect the price of any commodity, namely supply and demand. Tough sentences against traffickers decrease the supply of the drug; lenient ones for usage enhance demand. The result is that the commodities, which are in this case narcotics, fetch extraordinary prices. If users were severely punished, demand, and prices, would drop. That would discourage many crooks because risks would be higher and rewards lower.

"Napoleon once said the only way to stop smuggling was to station his troops along a border every ten feet, but that would leave the country vulnerable to attack," says American border policeman Bill Stringer. "You cannot seal a border. Down in Mexico we put a high, electrified wire fence and land mines. President Nixon constructed a $150-million fence. And still they get through. At one point near El Paso, there's a concrete bank and fence at the border. One Mexican actually made a fortune cutting through the fence for a fee to enable illegal aliens to work in the U.S. They would commute every day and by night go back home to Mexico. He charged a toll fee for the holes he cut in the border."

Anything short of tougher drug sentences will mean that the Stamlers and the Stringers will constantly be frustrated in their crusade to ensure a drug-free North America. The border is becoming even more open, and the smugglers and money launderers are getting smarter by the minute. International law enforcement agencies cannot meet the challenge because they are without sufficient resources, much less sufficient jurisdictional power. As a result, swindlers scurry from one country to the next, conscious of which borders act as barriers against investigations, criminal charges, and lawsuits. Canadians are among the best at these techniques, partly because the citizenship signifies extraordinary mobility among nations and also because Canada harbors fugitives because it lacks extradition, tax, and other treaties with most countries (apart from the United States). Such treaties facilitate legal cooperation and help bring culprits to justice.

Such legislative or diplomatic shortcomings are little understood either within or without Canada. Without changes, the Amsterdams and wash trading scams on the Vancouver and Alberta stock exchanges will flourish and spread, laundering money, undermining some economies, corrupting certain regulators, and bilking thousands of investors and companies out of money. It is a nation's disgrace.

EPILOGUE

After I finished the manuscript of this book, the leaders of the seven largest economies met at the G-7 Economic Summit in June 1988 in Toronto and endorsed a strongly-worded communiqué calling for a crackdown on drug trafficking and money laundering. It seemed out of place to most at this annual financial gathering of world leaders. Some commentators thought it was strictly U.S. political grandstanding, since drug usage is epidemic and one of that country's most serious sociological problems. But few realize that drug trafficking and concomitant money laundering are economic issues of enormous importance. This book illustrates how the free enterprise system itself is in peril because of the sophistication of contrepreneurs and their cunning use of secrecy and tax havens, banks, stock markets, brokerage firms, and laissez-faire or corrupt regimes.

Through sheer ignorance, Canada is a haven for money launderers and stock market swindlers from around the world. Canadian born and bred boiler-room boys launder huge volumes of money for mobsters and defraud stock-market investors, sometimes as a sideline. This book documents how in the case of the highly organized Amsterdam swindle a relatively small number of perpetrators can bilk the world out of billions of dollars worth of savings, ruining along the way the reputation of stock exchanges like Vancouver or of companies like DeVoe-Holbein Canada Inc.

As Amsterdam illustrates, justice fails when it comes to

international frauds. So the beat goes on. During a three-month period in early 1988, I wrote several more stories in the *Financial Post* about boiler-room activities involving more stocks on the Montreal, Toronto, Vancouver, and Alberta stock exchanges. For instance, in March 1988 I wrote about four companies being pushed by a Spanish stock promotion outfit run by a fugitive from U.S. fraud charges who lives part-time in Toronto. The companies knew nothing about this and were upset about it. The incidences of boiler-room touting are so numerous that I could devote my full-time effort to writing about such activities, but I have other assignments.

By late 1987 and early 1988, a dozen more Canadian-operated boiler rooms operated in Dublin, Gibraltar, Lugano (Switzerland), Cyprus, Spain, and Costa Rica. In late 1987, Cypriot police had shut down two boiler rooms run by Canadians, while in late spring 1988, Irish police were holding discussions with the Dutch to determine what to do about several Canadian boiler rooms in Dublin. The Securities and Exchange Commission made civil allegations of fraud in 1988 against Vancouver promoter Leonard Zrnic and other Canadians in relation to a promotion outfit in Costa Rica selling mutual funds. Then in spring 1988 a trial date was set to hear 1986 civil allegations of fraud against Zrnic and other Canadians concerning the sale of shares in Golden Bear Resources Ltd., a Vancouver Stock Exchange stock which was delisted.

Meanwhile, here at home Canadian stock market regulators continued to operate in a vacuum. That is why fresh scandals surfaced during 1987 and 1988, replays of the same old scams. In June 1988 another scandal loomed when a Singapore merchant bank launched a lawsuit against two of the Vancouver Stock Exchange's most active promoters, Eugenio (Eugene) and Francesco (Frank) Sirianni, and a listed company. The bank alleged that the Siriannis bribed a bank manager to sell US$700,000 of debentures and to get up to

US$1 million in sweetheart loans. Details as to the size of the bribe, or whether it was actually received, are not included in the statement of claim.

The lawsuit was filed in the Supreme Court of British Columbia and a statement of defense by the Siriannis was also filed. "Each of them denies each and every allegation of fact contained in the statement of claim. The defendants submit that the action against them be dismissed with costs," read the statement of defense by the Siriannis.

Controversies are nothing new to Eugene Sirianni. He is an Australian promoter who is listed as the owner of Vancouver-listed F.C. Financial Corp. F.C. in turn owns F.S.L. Financial Strategy Ltd., and together they have at various times owned or managed pieces of such dubious Vancouver companies as Echo Mountain Resources and Golden Tech Resources Ltd. Golden Tech has been under investigation by the Royal Canadian Mounted Police for some months and Echo Mountain has been under investigation by the Superintendent of Brokers' office.

The statement of claim made juicy reading and was filed on behalf of Republic National Bank of New York (Singapore) Ltd. against both Siriannis, F.C. Financial, and F.S.L. "In or about January 1987 the defendants, acting in a common plan and scheme and each as agent for the others, promised to reward Edward Zulaica, who was the plaintiff's manager and vice-president of the plaintiff, if he would fraudulently and corruptly cause the plaintiff to enter into certain transactions for the benefit and advantage of the defendants and each of them, and contrary to the best interests and to the disadvantage of the plaintiff."

"In expectation of the bribe," Zulaica in October 1987 extended US$500,000 lines of credit to the Siriannis with Vancouver stocks as collateral. They each borrowed $347,916 and gave the bank shares in F.C. Financial Corp., Golden Lion Resources, Lifequest International Inc., and Wizan Production, according to the bank's statement of claim. The bank said there was "fraudulent misrepresentations as to the nature and value of the security." In February 1987 the Siriannis also allegedly sold US$700,000 worth of debentures to the bank saying they were capable of resale and redemption "knowing the said representation to be false or without belief in its truth or recklessly or without regard to its truth."

The bank also accused them of manipulating stock market prices "fraudulently creating a market in said security by purchases on their own behalf or through their agents to artificially inflate its market price." The bank asked for damages and costs. Sirianni said that he and his brother were counter-suing Republic Bank for trading losses, because the bank sold some of their shares pledged as security after they tumbled in price following the October 1987 stock market crash. He said that the bank went after them as a gesture of "sour grapes" over the fact that it had invested in the stock and lost its shirt. He denied all allegations.

Meanwhile, during the spring and summer of 1988, several scandals broke in Alberta. The exchange delisted Jen-Tek Enterprises and Explorations Inc. because of the company's "peculiar" situation after share prices soared. Jen-Tek was touting an impending takeover of a Toronto pharmaceutical company under the guidance of a promoter whose family has had run-ins with police. Weeks before, Alberta had also discovered that a notorious Toronto criminal was behind another one of its companies, and an investigation was launched.

It was simply more of the same. Politicians and regulators simply scratch their heads, unaware that there is not only a proliferation of problems but loopholes galore making the activities of contrepreneurs virtually legal. To be fair to these policymakers, however, I had no idea until I undertook this research how pervasive the problems were. I also had no idea that there were links to organized crime or the laundering of drug profits. Besides boiler rooms, money laundering can be undertaken through massive private placements. And my research revealed that a handful of mysterious Swiss and Caribbean banks had made private placements in hundreds of speculative companies of dubious value listed on the Vancouver and Alberta stock exchanges. Some of the banks had been linked to organized crime in the past, but their current ownership was unknown. So was the identity of their depositor-customers who were putting up the money for the private placements.

Such massive holdings from mysterious entities pose many important policy questions. Why can't we force disclosure of the beneficial owner of anything in Canada? Regulators and tax officials should know the identities of all beneficial owners so they can supervise their activities. What if investigations or charges determine that laws are being broken? Without knowing the identities of beneficial owners, police and prosecutors and regulators are up a creek without a legal paddle — whether it is a matter of bringing culprits to justice or of collecting unpaid taxes.

Extra measures are necessary. Regulators applaud exposés like mine, as long as I don't take a swing at their actions. Some feel that exposés are a deterrent to crooks and an important caution for the public. But in fact they are the opposite. Adverse publicity shows how little is, or can be, done by regulators or police. Exposés do not deter, but actually spur the bad guys on. "I've never had so much business since all that bad publicity," bragged convicted swindler Charles Stuart to acquaintances after his name was dragged through the mud in the media for misdeeds in British Columbia.

Extraordinary action is needed to set examples and warn contrepreneurs that they may be dealt with in a heavy-handed fashion. The British Columbia Securities Commission, for instance, should never have lifted in May 1988 an indefinite trading ban against notorious drug trafficker, William "Fats" Robertson. It should never, in January that same year, have allowed Charles Stuart, subject of a lifetime trading ban in British Columbia, to act as an agent for a mysterious offshore company which was buying a large chunk of Technigen Corp. stock. The provincial New Democrats made a fuss over the issues involved, with information they had been fed by Adrian du Plessis and others. But no politician or party in Canada, or elsewhere, understands how dangerous the situation really is.

Some regulators in Ontario are somewhat better, mostly because of their past dealings with the contrepreneurs. In June 1988, the Ontario Securities Commission refused to lift its trading ban against a company formerly linked to Irving Kott, Tricor Holdings, now run by his son. Tricor had not revealed who the beneficial owner or owners were behind the offshore companies which controlled a large block of its stock. The Ontario commission said that trading was a privilege not a right and that it had a right to know who was behind the stock holding.

Similarly, the financial system itself has started to take some action. In 1988 the Bank of Montreal issued a new policy that it will no longer lend money if the loan is secured by any Vancouver stock. If other banks or brokers follow this lead, changes will come about swiftly and illegal activities may stop altogether.

This book is a bid for sweeping changes here at home and abroad. As one of the seven signatories to the money laundering communiqué this year, Canada must take the problem seriously. The world should consider forming a united front against crime to forge international cooperation agreements, extradition treaties, and joint police task forces. Here in Canada, our government should set an example, and send a message to the crooks, by establishing a Royal Commission to probe the links between organized crime, money laundering, and our stock-market frauds. In the absence of such sweeping measures, the contrepreneurs will continue to commute freely in a defenseless world. Theirs is an evil empire which must be destroyed.

Index